America's State Governments

This timely and important new work takes a critical look at government in the American states and illustrates the disconnect between state government institutions and their constituents. The text illuminates three basic political problems of state governments: weak constitutional and institutional foundations; a lack of civic engagement; and long histories of unchecked public corruption. In addition, the book explains why some states did and others did not respond promptly to the COVID-19 pandemic and examines America's long-standing problem of police and prosecutorial misconduct—providing a context for understanding the demonstrations and protests that rocked American cities in the summer of 2020 For students and citizens of state politics, the book concludes with a proposal aimed at civic literacy and action.

Jennifer Bachner is Director of the Program in Data Analytics and Policy at Johns Hopkins University.

Benjamin Ginsberg is the David Bernstein Professor of Political Science and Chair of the Center for Advanced Governmental Studies at Johns Hopkins University.

Praise for *America's State Governments*

"States play enormously important roles in the American federal system. But this fascinating account shows how short they fall in delivering equal access to democratic participation, effective policy in the public interest, or even basic justice, for both political and structural reasons. Entertainingly written and full of new data and eye-opening examples, this book shows how low citizen interest and knowledge, declining media coverage, institutional weakness, and insufficient ethics protections result in interest group dominance, unrepresentative policies, and sometimes outright corruption. A must-read for anyone interested in the state (no pun intended) of American governance."

–Andrea Louise Campbell,
Massachusetts Institute of Technology

"The major strength of this textbook is that it offers the freshest take on state politics in literally decades."

–Douglas Harris,
Loyola University Maryland

"Engaging and analytically challenging."

–Ian J. Drake,
Montclair State University

"Rather than focus on comparing states with one another—the dominant approach in state politics research and texts—this book emphasizes their overall role in the federal system and their commonalities. This is an interesting and compelling approach."

–Michael Berkman,
Pennsylvania State University

America's State Governments
A Critical Look at Disconnected Democracies

Jennifer Bachner and Benjamin Ginsberg

NEW YORK AND LONDON

First published 2021
by Routledge
52 Vanderbilt Avenue, New York, NY 10017

and by Routledge
2 Park Square, Milton Park, Abingdon, Oxon, OX14 4RN

Routledge is an imprint of the Taylor & Francis Group, an informa business

© 2021 Taylor & Francis

The right of Jennifer Bachner and Benjamin Ginsberg to be identified as authors of this work has been asserted by them in accordance with sections 77 and 78 of the Copyright, Designs and Patents Act 1988.

All rights reserved. No part of this book may be reprinted or reproduced or utilised in any form or by any electronic, mechanical, or other means, now known or hereafter invented, including photocopying and recording, or in any information storage or retrieval system, without permission in writing from the publishers.

Trademark notice: Product or corporate names may be trademarks or registered trademarks and are used only for identification and explanation without intent to infringe.

Library of Congress Cataloging-in-Publication Data
Names: Bachner, Jennifer, 1983- author. | Ginsberg, Benjamin, author.
Title: America's state governments : a critical look at disconnected democracies / Jennifer Bachner and Benjamin Ginsberg.
Description: New York, NY : Routledge, 2020. | Includes bibliographical references and index. | Summary: "This text critically analyzes government and governance in the American states. For students and citizens of state politics, the book concludes with a proposal aimed at civic literacy and action"– Provided by publisher.
Identifiers: LCCN 2020007491 (print) | LCCN 2020007492 (ebook) | ISBN 9780367468477 (paperback) | ISBN 9780367468484 (hardback) | ISBN 9781003031499 (ebook)
Subjects: LCSH: State governments–United States.
Classification: LCC JK2408 .B24 2020 (print) | LCC JK2408 (ebook) | DDC 320.473–dc23
LC record available at https://lccn.loc.gov/2020007491
LC ebook record available at https://lccn.loc.gov/2020007492

ISBN: 978-0-367-46848-4 (hbk)
ISBN: 978-0-367-46847-7 (pbk)
ISBN: 978-1-003-03149-9 (ebk)

Typeset in Sabon
by Swales & Willis, Exeter, Devon, UK

To Daniel and Sandy

Contents

List of Figures viii
List of Tables ix
Acknowledgments x
Prologue xi

1 Introduction: Disconnected Democracies 1

2 State Constitutions 10

3 The States in the Federal System 34

4 State Governors 59

5 State Legislatures and Representative Government 82

6 State Justice Systems 100

7 Corruption in State and Municipal Government 128

8 Conclusion: What is to be Done? 155

Index 171

Figures

2.1 Paths to State Constitutional Change	12
4.1 Estimated Improvement in Rankings from Executive Unity	67
4.2 Estimated Improvement in Rankings from Governors' Tenure Potential	68
4.3 Estimated Interactive Effects of Executive Power and Civic Engagement	70
4.4 Distribution of "Separately Elected" (SEP) Executives across the U.S	74
5.1 Growth in State Spending over Time	84
5.2 Percentage Responding "Don't Know"	85
5.3 Historical Coverage of State Politics	86
5.4 Modern Front-Page Coverage of State Politics	87
5.5 Lobbying in New York State	89
5.6 Spending on Lobbying in California, 2002–2017	90
5.7 Distribution of Scores of State Ethics Laws	92
5.8 Lobbying, Citizen Engagement and Legislative Outputs	94
5.9 Effect of Party Strength on Bills Enacted	95
7.1 Public Corruption Convictions, PIN vs. EOUSA	135
7.2 New York Times Coverage of Political Corruption, 1850–2019	140
7.3 Corruption and Special Purpose Districts	151
8.1 High School Civic Education Requirements	159

Tables

1.1	Survey Responses about State Governments and Elections	5
2.1	Constitutional Amendments and Revisions in the 50 States	16
4.1	Independently Elected State Officials	61
4.2	"Separately Elected" State Executive Categories	62
4.3	State Executive Powers	65
4.4	Marginal Effects of Political Participation on Policy Outcomes	71
4.5	Gubernatorial Powers by State	77
4.6	Regression Results (without Political Participation Interaction)	79
4.7	Regression Results (with Political Participation Interaction)	81
5.1	Number of Registered Lobbyists in the U.S. States, 2017	88
5.2	Influences on Legislative Outputs	96
5.3	Influences on Policy Outcomes	97
7.1	Common Forms of Public Corruption	129
7.2	Federal Corruption Convictions by State (PIN), 2007–2017	132
7.3	Federal, State and Local Government Corruption (TRAC), 1986–2018	136
7.4	State Corruption Ranking (TRAC), 2012–2017	137
7.5	Public Corruption in Illinois by the Numbers, 2015	149
8.1	Percentage Responding "Don't Know" to Survey Questions about Their State	156
8.2	Civic Education and Knowledge: Survey Results	162
8.3	The Effect of Coursework in American Government/Civics on Voting	163
8.4	The Interactive Effect of Coursework and Parental Politicization on Voting	165
8.5	Civic Education Requirements in the U.S.	169

Acknowledgments

The authors are grateful to a number of individuals who provided advice and guidance as we wrote this book. These include: Edwin Bender, National Institute on Money and Politics; Ian Drake, Montclair State University; Kathryn Hill, Johns Hopkins University; Susan Long, Transactional Records Access Clearinghouse (TRAC); Jeffrey Milyo, University of Missouri; Ken Masugi, Claremont Washington Program; Pete Quist, National Institute on Money in Politics; Dorothea Wolfson, Johns Hopkins University; and Yunshan Ye, Johns Hopkins Libraries. At Routledge, we wish to thank everyone who assisted in the production of this book, particularly our editor, Jennifer Knerr.

Prologue

America's state governments are important. They provide the essential health, public safety, educational, transportation and other services upon which Americans depend every day. In times of crisis, there is a perception that Americans look to the federal government for help. But, the states, and especially their governors and executive departments, are the actual "first responders" when Americans are threatened by natural or man-made disasters. Every year, the states deal with floods, hurricanes, fires, shootings and public health problems. In the realm of public health, for example, the states have been fighting a little-noticed war against the spread of such diseases as drug resistant tuberculosis. Likewise, states have taken a leading role in combating opioid abuse and overdoses through a variety of policy initiatives. Under the United States Constitution, the federal government is a government of limited and enumerated powers. The states, however, as we shall see below, have a plenary "police power," which gives them the right and duty to take necessary steps to protect the public health and safety. Under their police powers, the states can order quarantines, require vaccinations and, if necessary, order public gatherings and businesses closed.[1]

The 2020 corona virus crisis underscores the importance of the states. In March 2020, cases of COVID-19, which had already caused thousands of deaths in Asia and Europe, began to appear in the U.S. as well. In the first weeks, the federal government was slow to craft a response. Several state governors, however, moved quickly to deal with what they knew would be the public health emergency soon facing their states. As COVID-19 struck, former governor George Pataki of New York observed, "Right now the governors are in the forefront and appropriately so."[2]

Early in March some states began to implement policies of "social distancing," discouraging large gatherings in order to slow the spread of the virus. Initially, state governments limited themselves to making nonbinding recommendations to their citizens but soon saw that more stringent measures would be needed. Ohio Governor Mike DeWine postponed Ohio's scheduled primary elections, a step copied by Georgia, Kentucky, Louisiana and Alabama. Governor Kate Brown of Oregon, a state that now votes entirely by mail, urged a general shift to mail-in balloting in view of the possibility that voters waiting in line to cast their ballots might spread the disease.

On Sunday, March 15, Governor DeWine, became the first state executive to order all restaurants and bars in the state closed. The next day, the governors of Connecticut, New Jersey and New York ordered the closing of all restaurants, bars, gyms, movie theaters and casinos in their states to slow the virus's spread. At the same time, DeWine and Governor Larry Hogan of Maryland ordered extended school closings—a decision soon copied by most other states. These state measures sparked a cycle of massive business closings and employee layoffs, but the governors deemed these to be unavoidable in light of the public health emergency.

By the end of March, the federal government finally began to ramp up its own response to the crisis by sealing the nation's borders to most travelers, expanding access to corona virus testing, distributing medical supplies and making additional hospital facilities and equipment available. The federal government also pumped trillions of dollars into the economy in an attempt to ease the economic disruptions and job losses caused by efforts to slow transmission of the virus. But, even as the federal government began to respond, state governments remained on the front lines of the battle against the pandemic, enforcing social distancing and, in the case of New York, even deploying the national guard to quarantine a large section of the city of New Rochelle where a severe viral outbreak had manifested itself.

As the crisis continued, governors began to meet with one another to share ideas and strategies. On March 18, the nonpartisan National Governors Association, chaired by Maryland's Governor Hogan, organized a "governors only" conference call to discuss best practices for confronting the pandemic. Other governors began calling one another to share ideas and experiences. Governor Jay Pritzker of Illinois, for example, reported that he had called two colleagues, Governor Gretchen Whitmer of Michigan to discuss school closings and Governor Jay Inslee of Washington to take advantage of Inslee's experience with virus outbreaks in nursing homes. On March 19, all the governors met with President Trump to offer suggestions regarding the federal response to the epidemic based upon their own first-hand experience.

Significantly, the states that took the fastest and most stringent actions, including Ohio, New York and Maryland, were generally also states whose governors exercise the most legal and constitutional power. As we will discuss in Chapter 4, the 50 states vary enormously in the powers granted to the governor by their constitutions. Governor DeWine of Ohio, Governor Andrew Cuomo of New York and Governor Hogan of Maryland exercise a great deal of constitutional authority and are accustomed to using it. Many other state governors have little constitutional authority and cannot act very quickly or decisively. This makes an enormous difference in the day-to-day quality of state government. In Chapter 4 we will see that good government requires a strong governor, and the COVID-19 crisis only reinforces our point.

In a new survey we conducted (the details of which are presented in Chapter 2), we found that 69 percent of Americans believe that their state government does a better job of serving its citizens than the federal government. During the COVID-19 crisis, it seems this confidence was well-placed. While the media has increasingly shifted its focus to national politics over the past decade, with local and state news coverage nearly erased, Americans continue to look to their proximate elected officials for leadership. As the *New York Times* explained amid the crisis,

> [F]or now, the country is turning to governors, some of them little-known nationally, for reassurance and leadership in a fashion that sharply breaks with the Washington-centric lens through which government has been viewed in a period of national and celebrity-oriented politics.[3]

In March 2020, America's state governments faced a stress test of their capacity to serve their citizens, and many exemplified the power of these often-overlooked bodies to govern effectively during a once-in-a-century challenge. Let us try to understand some of the factors affecting state governments' ability to govern in normal times as well as times of crisis.

Jennifer Bachner
Benjamin Ginsberg

Notes

1 David B. Rivkin and Charles Stimson, "A Constitutional Guide to Emergency Powers," *The Wall Street Journal*, March 20, 2020, p. A17.
2 As quoted in Jonathan Martin and Alexander Burns, "In a Crisis, Governors Flexed Their Executive Muscles as the White House Balked," *The New York Times*, March 18, 2020, A11.
3 Martin and Burns, 2020.

1 Introduction
Disconnected Democracies

The United States Constitution creates a federal system that leaves a great deal of power in the hands of the individual states. Each year, the states collectively adopt nearly 20,000 new laws, an average of 400 per state, while the U.S. Congress in recent years has, on average, enacted hardly more than 150 new statutes. The states are especially important in the realms of law enforcement education, healthcare, environmental policy and transportation. In all these areas, to be sure, the states share power with the federal government but possess considerable discretionary authority.

The most fundamental power exercised by the states is that of coercion—the power to develop and enforce criminal codes, administer health and safety rules, and regulate the family via marriage and divorce laws. The states also have the power to regulate individuals' livelihoods: physicians, attorneys, plumbers, hair dressers and those wishing to practice a host of other occupations, must obtain licenses from their state. Even more fundamental, the states have the power to define private property: private property exists because state laws against trespass and theft define who is and who is not entitled to use a piece of property. Ownership of a car, for example, is not worth much unless the state is willing to enforce the owner's right to possession by making it a crime for anyone else to drive the car without the owner's permission. Similarly, "ownership" of a house or piece of land means that the state will enforce the owner's possession by prohibiting others from occupying the property without the consent of its owner. At the same time, under its power of eminent domain, the state may seize private property for anything it deems to be a public purpose. If the state, however, does seize such property, it is required by its own constitution and the federal constitution to compensate the owners for their loss. The decision to take the property, though, is well within the states' recognized powers.

When it comes to matters of public health, as we saw during the 2020 coronavirus crisis, the states have very substantial power. This was recognized as long ago as 1824 in the U.S. Supreme Court case of *Gibbons v. Ogden* where the Court declared that the states certainly had the power to enact quarantine laws and "health laws of every description."[1] To protect the public's health in the face of an epidemic, states can ban public gatherings, order curfews, restrict travel, close businesses and even close churches and, as we saw in 2020, arrest ministers for violating closure orders. States cannot act in an arbitrary manner or invent a health crisis where none exists, but so long as they are responding reasonably to a recognized threat to the public's health, the states' powers are enormous—generally exceeding those of the federal government.

A state's authority to regulate these fundamental matters, commonly referred to as the police power, encompasses its power to regulate the health, safety, welfare and morals of its citizens. Policing is what states do —they coerce individuals in the name of the community in order to maintain public order. When an individual is issued a traffic ticket, or taken into custody for most other crimes, the state is exercising its police power, often through the agency of a county or city police officer. Counties and cities are effectively agencies of their states. State legislatures created local governments and state constitutions and laws define the powers of these governments. The status of counties and cities relative to their states should not be confused with the status of the states relative to the federal government. The 50 states, for their part, are much more than agencies of the federal government. Their existence is recognized and their powers implied under the U.S. Constitution. While a state can abolish any of its counties, the federal government cannot abolish a state.

The governments of the 50 states are structurally similar to the federal government. Each state possesses a written constitution and three branches of government. In every state but Nebraska (whose legislature is unicameral), the legislative branch is divided into two houses. Yet, beneath this familiar appearance, are a number of unpleasant realities that can undermine the quality of many American state governments, most importantly weakening the ties or connections that should exist between a government's actions and its citizen's interests and desires. Some, albeit not all the states, could be characterized as "disconnected democracies." Their institutions are democratic in form but lack firm connections with the citizens they should serve. In particular, many state governments face three basic political problems. These are weak constitutional and institutional foundations; a lack of civic engagement; and long histories of public corruption unchecked by adequate ethics and conflict of interest rules. Let us consider each of these matters in turn.

Institutional and Constitutional Structure

The Constitution of the United States is a brief document setting forward a number of basic legal and institutional principles to guide future law makers. While the U.S. Constitution can be amended, most of its basic principles have remained intact since its adoption in 1789. State constitutions, on the other hand, are lengthy and malleable documents. They are frequently amended and are filled with picayune details. New York's constitution, for example, specifies the widths of the state's ski trails.[2] Alabama's constitution regulates trash collection fees.[3] These constitutions do not offer adequate guidance for state legislators on large questions while serving as straightjackets on small matters that could better be decided in the legislative process.

The institutional structures established by many state constitutions are also problematic. One difficulty is the office of state governor. Like the president of the United States, the governor is a chief executive. The president, however, is a unitary executive. At the federal convention, some of the delegates favored the creation of a two- or three-person executive or even an executive council to direct the affairs of the nation's executive branch. Most delegates, however, thought that a plural executive would be too unwieldy to properly manage the government or energetically and effectively pursue the nation's interests. Among the states, however, all but a handful elect plural executives. In many states, governors share power with an independently elected attorney general, state treasurer, secretary of state, state auditor, secretary of agriculture and several other executive officials. This plural executive model means that executive power is fragmented in most states and the ability of the governor to manage the executive branch and use its power to pursue public interests is constrained.

Another problematic state institution is the justice system. The constitutions of many states allow, or sometimes stipulate, the election of major trial court and appellate judges. At the federal level, of course, judges are nominated by the president, confirmed by the Senate and appointed for life. The framers of the national constitution were strongly opposed to the popular election of judges, believing that elected judges would allow popularity to interfere with the impartial administration of justice. A number of studies seem to indicate that the federal constitution's framers were correct to be concerned. Elected state judges seem to be responsive to "get tough" demands from voters and mete out harsher sentences than appointed judges.[4] In recent years, heavy campaign spending in judicial elections by interest groups with a stake in the outcome has raised concerns that justice is for sale in some states. State and county prosecutors are also subject to election (federal prosecutors are appointed) and may too easily be swayed by electoral considerations when making prosecutorial decisions.

Civic Engagement

Some citizens take great pride in their states. According to one survey, 77 percent of Alaska's residents, 70 percent of Utah's citizens and 68 percent of all Texans viewed their state as the best possible place to live. Alas, in the same survey, large majorities of the residents of Rhode

Island, Illinois, Louisiana, New Jersey and several other states said they would prefer to live elsewhere.[5] Indeed, according to 2017 data compiled by a national moving company, United Van Lines, tens of thousands of people followed their inclinations and voted with their feet, fleeing Illinois and New Jersey, in particular.[6]

Whether or not they take pride in their states, most citizens know very little about their states' governments and political processes. In October of 2018, we conducted a nationally representative survey to test citizens' levels of basic knowledge about their own state's government, history and political processes.[7] The survey of 1500 respondents was conducted via the internet using Qualtrics. We found that the American public is strikingly uninformed about basic facts.

Table 1.1 presents the responses to some of our survey questions about state governments, elections and policy jurisdictions. We discuss additional findings from the survey in Chapters 5 and 8, such as respondents' familiarity with the most important issues discussed in their state's legislature and the policy areas in which states spend the most money. Table 1.1 shows, for example, that large majorities don't know who represents them in their state's legislature. Only 38 percent responded that their state has a constitution when, in fact, every state has one. With respect to whether voting absentee is an option in their state, 4 percent responded "no" and 27 percent didn't know the answer, yet every state has some form of absentee voting. Just 17 percent of respondents indicated that their state has special districts, but again, all states have them.

We also found that many respondents are confused about which areas of policy are largely controlled by state governments. While education policy is primarily determined by states, 37 percent of respondents either think the federal government is mostly in charge or responded "don't know." Likewise, 36 percent of respondents failed to recognize that the states are mostly in charge of law enforcement.

Contributing to citizens' lack of information and involvement is Americans' geographic mobility. About 40 percent of all Americans do not currently live in the state in which they were born. This means that the state about which they might have learned something in elementary school civics is no longer their state of residence. But, even more important in explaining why most citizens know so little about their states is the sharp decline in recent decades in media coverage of state and local politics. Because of budget cuts, according to the Pew Research Center, between 2003 and 2014, the number of newspaper reporters assigned to cover state capitols declined by 35 percent.[8] At the same time, more than half the reporters who cover state news do so only on a part time basis and, as for television news, only 14 percent of local TV stations assign a full-time or even part-time reporter to their state's capitol. The result is that state news receives little media coverage. No wonder citizens know so little about their state's government. The

Table 1.1 Survey Responses about State Governments and Elections

In your state ...?

	Yes/answered	No	Don't know
Who is the governor?	67%	-	33%
Who is your state senator?	19%	-	81%
Who is your state representative?	28%	-	72%
Is there a state constitution?	38%	26%	36%
Is the attorney general elected?	21%	64%	15%
Are ballot initiatives allowed?	41%	6%	53%
Can citizens register and vote on the same day?	25%	40%	35%
Is voting absentee an option?	67%	4%	27%
Can members of the legislature hold other jobs?	35%	21%	44%
Are there special purpose districts?	17%	11%	72%

Who is mostly in charge of ...?

	Federal Government	State Governments	Don't know
Law enforcement	12%	64%	24%
Zoning laws	7%	62%	30%
Education	15%	63%	22%

Responses are from a nationally representative survey of 1500 U.S. residents. Row percentages may not sum to 100 because of rounding.

decline of state news coverage has also contributed to corruption and mismanagement as crooked officials see that their actions are unlikely to receive media scrutiny.[9]

Also reflecting this lack of civic knowledge is a low level of citizen involvement in state and local politics. Voter turnout in American national elections is among the lowest in the Western world—about 60 percent in presidential years and 40 percent in off-year elections. In some states, as many as 20 percent of those who vote for national candidates do not cast votes for state legislative candidates and other candidates for state office on the same ballot. This is a phenomenon called "roll-off," and generally reflects lack of information and name recognition. Many voters are insufficiently familiar with state politics to cast a vote for state-level officials even if they are already at their polling places choosing national leaders. Consistent with this idea, voter turnout in special state legislative elections called to fill prematurely vacant seats, averages about 24 percent of eligible voters.[10] With no other offices at stake, few voters have the interest or knowledge sufficient to bring them to the polls to choose state legislators. Exacerbating the problem of political interest and knowledge is the declining level of party competition in many states. In recent years, America has divided into red states and blue states and this division is especially marked in state-level election outcomes. After the 2018 elections, one party controlled both houses of the state legislature in 48 of the nation's states. Only in Minnesota were the two houses controlled by different parties. Nebraska, of course, has a unicameral legislature.

Low levels of citizen knowledge and involvement in state politics have a number of repercussions. Among the most important of these is a weakening of state legislatures and an increase in their permeability to interest groups. Legislative assemblies depend for their power on the support of significant groups in society. The power of the U.S. Congress, for example, was greatest in the 19th century when it was closely tied to emergent political and social forces. Later, as the presidency became the institution to which new groups looked to achieve their political aspirations, Congress's power waned.[11] By the same token, if important social forces and interests believe that a state legislature actively represents their views and aspirations, they are likely to give it their support. In the 1850s, both Northerners and Southerners looked to their state legislatures, more than the U.S. government, to protect what they saw as sectional interests and the power of those legislatures grew accordingly. If, on the other hand, a legislature lacks a strong constituency, it becomes vulnerable to encroachments by other institutions. The fact that Americans have little knowledge of or interest in their state legislatures means, for example, that hardly anyone is concerned or even aware when Congress expands its power over traditionally state matters such as education and law enforcement, as it has done in recent years.

At the same time, the absence of popular interest in or knowledge of state legislative affairs, coupled with only spotty media coverage, means that the way is open for special interests to dominate legislative politics. Without popular interest or media coverage many states are a perfect environment—veritable Petrie dishes—for interest group politics. In recent years, lobby groups have flocked to the state capitols seeing a permissive environment in which to promote their clients' interests.[12]

Corruption

This brings us to the third problem confronting many states, the matter of endemic corruption. Many states have weak lobbying and conflict of interest rules and few rules governing campaign contributions. For example, none of New Mexico's part-time legislators are required to register as lobbyists even if they work on behalf of their full-time employer's interests from the floor of the legislature.[13] In many other states, ethics rules allow representatives to promote legislation that serves their own financial interests.[14] In other states, lobbyists can work as "citizen volunteers," complete with identification badges and parking spaces in the executive branch agencies that regulate their employers' activities.[15] Even where conflict of interest and lobbying disclosure rules seem adequate, enforcement is lax and watchdog agencies generally underfunded and understaffed.[16]

Several, albeit not all, states also have long histories of out and out theft by public officials. Common forms of public corruption include bribery, kickbacks, embezzlement and misuse of public funds. In both public and private affairs, some corruption is inevitable. Corruption may be kept in check but never eliminated altogether.[17] A number of states, however, seem to have had little success in keeping public corruption even minimally in check. Illinois, Louisiana, New York and several others have significant histories of corruption dating back for a century or more.

Take Illinois, for example. During the course of the state's history, six Illinois governors have been indicted on corruption charges. A seventh, Joel Matteson (governor from 1853–1857) was not indicted even though $200,000 in stolen state funds were found in shoe boxes in the governor's residence. Matteson claimed to have no knowledge of the funds and promised to return the money to the state. Lennington Small, Illinois's governor during the 1920s, was charged with embezzling over $1 million in state funds. Small was acquitted by a jury, but some suspicions were raised when four of the jurors subsequently received state jobs.[18] In 1973, former Illinois Governor Otto Kerner was convicted of bribery, conspiracy and income tax evasion while serving as governor. That same year, Governor Dan Walker was convicted of engaging in a fraudulent loan scheme. During the 1990s, Governor George Ryan was convicted of racketeering. And, of course, in 2008, Governor Rod Blagojevich was charged and subsequently convicted of conspiring to auction off the Senate seat vacated by former President Barack Obama.

Corrupt Illinois governors represent only the tip of the state's shady iceberg. Since World War II, over 1500 state and municipal official in Illinois have gone to jail for acts of official corruption. This number includes 36 members of the Chicago city council since 1972. To put this number into some perspective, only about 200 individuals have served on the 50-person city council since that date, giving the council an 18 percent corruption rate.[19] Of course, many Chicagoans would argue that this seemingly astonishing number understates the actual level of corruption among Chicago's aldermen. The others, according to many locals, simply haven't been caught.

States with long histories of public corruption often find it difficult to rein in governmental theft. Politicians elected or appointed to office in a corrupt environment—especially those whose election or appointment was tainted by corrupt practices—are more likely to perpetuate than to endeavor to bring an end to the practices that brought them to power.[20] Suppose that Illinois Governor Blagojevich had succeeded in selling former President Obama's Senate seat? Would the purchaser have been inclined to join the battle against corruption in the state? It seems rather unlikely.

State corruption is not only morally wrong but it exacts an enormous pecuniary cost. One study found that during a ten-year period, spending on such matters as government contracts, wages and debt service in America's ten most corrupt states (as measured by numbers of federal indictments and other indicators) was an average of $1300 per capita more than similar spending in the other states. $1300 per capita suggests that just the marginal cost of corruption in these states amounted to tens of billions of dollars that might have been spent on useful state services or retained by taxpayers. No wonder that most residents of states like Illinois and Louisiana that rank high in levels of corruption would like to move elsewhere.

Reconnecting States and Citizens

Taken together, these core problems of state government—weak constitutional and institutional foundations, lack of civic engagement, and histories of corruption—affect all the states, albeit some more than others. These political and institutional maladies undermine the ties that should exist between the states' governments and their citizens' interests. In the chapters to come, we will look carefully at the place of the states in the federal system, at the major institutions of state government and at popular participation in the political lives of the 50 states. We will identify problems and conclude by asking what can be done to reconnect state governments with their citizens.

Notes

1 22 U.S. 1 (1824).
2 Emily Zackin, *Looking for Rights in All the Wrong Places* (Princeton, NJ: Princeton University Press, 2013), p. 18.
3 Pamela M. Prah, "Alabama's Past, Future on Ballot," Aug. 13, 2012. www.pewstates.org.

4 Kate Berry, "How Judicial Elections Impact Criminal Cases," Brennan Center for Justice, Dec. 2015. www.brennancenter.org/publication/how-judicial-elections-impact-criminal-cases.
5 USA Today, "Which U.S. States Have the Most Pride?" Apr. 25, 2014. www.usatoday.com/story/news/nation-now/2014/04/25/state-pride-gallup-montana-alaska/8140879/.
6 Karsten Strauss, "The U.S. States People Are Fleeing (And the Ones They Are Moving To)," *Forbes*, Jan. 10, 2018. www.forbes.com/sites/karstenstrauss/2018/01/10/the-u-s-states-people-are-fleeing-and-the-ones-they-are-moving-to/#6934532f26c3.
7 Respondents were nationally representative based on race, gender, education and region.
8 Jodi Enda, Katerina Matsa and Jan Boyles, "America's Shifting Statehouse Press," Pew Research Center, Jul. 10, 2014. www.journalism.org/2014/07/10/americas-shifting-statehouse-press/.
9 Kriston Capps, "The Hidden Costs of Losing Their City's Newspaper," *Citylab*, May 30, 2018. www.citylab.com/solutions/2018/05/citylab-daily-the-hidden-costs-of-losing-your-citys-newspaper/561536/.
10 Ballotopedia, "State Legislative Special Elections, 2018," https://ballotpedia.org/State_legislative_special_elections,_2018#Historical_data.
11 Samuel Huntington, "Congressional Responses to the Twentieth Century," in David Truman, ed., *The Congress and America's Future* (New York: Spectrum, 1965), pp. 5–31.
12 Liz White and Ben Wieder, "Amid Federal Gridlock, Lobbying Rises in the States; Special Interests Outnumber State Lawmakers 6–1," *Center for Public Integrity*, Feb. 11, 2016. www.publicintegrity.org/2016/02/11/19279/amid-federal-gridlock-lobbying-rises-states.
13 Hicholas Kusnetz, "Conflicts of Interest Run Rampant in State Legislatures," Center for Public Integrity, May, 2014. www.publicintegrity.org/2013/03/18/12313/conflicts-interest-run-rampant-state-legislatures.
14 Decca Muldowney, "The Malleable Conflicts of Interest in State Legislature Rules," *Pacific Standard*, Jun. 7, 2018. https://psmag.com/news/conflicts-of-interest-in-state-legislatures.
15 Brad McElhinny, "Lobby Rules May Not Apply to Volunteer Bray Cary Either," *WV Metro News*, Dec. 14, 2017. http://wvmetronews.com/2017/12/14/lobbying-rules-may-not-apply-to-volunteer-bray-cary-either/.
16 Nicholas Kusnetz, "Only Three States Score Higher than D+ in a Center for Public Integrity Investigation," www.publicintegrity.org/2015/11/09/18693/only-three-states-score-higher-d-state-integrity-investigation-11-flunk.
17 Frank Anachiarco and James B. Jacobs, *The Pursuit of Absolute Integrity* (Chicago, IL: University of Chicago Press), 1998.
18 Claire Suddath, "A Brief History of Illinois Corruption," *Time*, Dec. 11, 2008. http://content.time.com/time/nation/article/0,8599,1865681,00.html.
19 Dick Simpson, Thomas Gradel, Marco Rossi and Katherine Taylor, "Continuing Corruption in Illinois," May 15, 2018. http://dig.abclocal.go.com/wls/documents/051518-Corruption-Illinois.pdf.
20 Shane Tritsch, "Why is Illinois So Corrupt?" *Chicago Magazine*, Dec. 2010. www.chicagomag.com/Chicago-Magazine/December-2010/Why-Is-Illinois-So-Corrupt-Local-Government-Experts-Explain/.

2 State Constitutions

Our survey revealed that most Americans are not aware that their state has a constitution. But, not only does every state have its own constitution, some are actually older than the federal constitution. The Constitution of Massachusetts was adopted in 1780, seven years before the federal convention met to write the United States Constitution. In some instances, indeed, the state constitutions have served as models for the federal document. Before women were enfranchised by the 19th Amendment to the federal constitution, ratified in 1920, they had already won the right to vote under the constitutions of 27 states. Similarly, the constitutions of several states had already provided for direct popular election of members of the upper houses of their state legislatures before the federal constitution's 17th Amendment, ratified in 1913, provided for direct popular election of United States senators.

The federal constitution is a document that defines the scope of governmental power, guarantees the rights and liberties of citizens and establishes the basic institutional framework through which governmental power is to be exercised. During the founding era, the federal government was understood to be a government of defined and limited power. Article I, Section 8 and other portions of the federal constitution enumerate the main powers of the federal government. Many of the federal constitution's framers were reluctant to add what eventually became the Bill of Rights, viewing their goal as creating, not limiting, governmental power. State governments, on the other hand, were understood to exercise plenary legislative powers, that is, the power to make laws regarding all matters neither ceded to the federal government nor prohibited by the U.S. Constitution. In an often-quoted opinion, the Kansas Supreme Court declared, "When the constitutionality of a statute is involved, the question presented is, therefore, not whether the act is authorized by the constitution, but whether it is prohibited thereby."[1] As a result, the authors of state constitutions have generally seen little need to grant powers to the states. Instead, their focus has been on limiting the powers of the state legislatures, or directing their use.[2]

The constitutions of the 50 states, as we observed in the Introduction, have the same general structure as the federal constitution. Each state constitution creates a government consisting of three branches and separated powers. Each state constitution provides for elections and popular representation. All the state constitutions guarantee civil liberties and a variety of civil rights. Indeed, as we shall see below, most guarantee many more rights than are explicitly addressed in the federal constitution. One obvious difference between the state and federal constitutions is that the state documents contain provisions regarding counties, cities and other units of local government that are seen as subordinate to the states. Hence, state constitutions address the powers and structure of various sorts of local governments in considerable detail.

Putting aside local government provisions, the state constitutions have a superficial resemblance to the federal constitution. They differ, however, from their federal counterpart in a number of respects that, taken as a whole, can detract from the ability of the states to govern effectively. In particular, many of the state constitutions are too malleable; they are filled with policy provisions and many substantive rights, and they restrict legislative power in the fiscal realm. The cumulative result of these problems has been to reduce the capacity of state legislatures to legislate effectively.

Malleability

As befits a document asserting basic principles, the federal constitution is not easy to change. Amending the U.S. Constitution requires a two-thirds vote in the Congress followed by ratification by three-fourths of the states, or passage of the proposed amendment by a national convention followed by ratification by three-fourths of the states. Since it was drafted in 1787, the federal constitution has been amended only 27 times, with only 17 of these amendments added since the Bill of Rights was adopted in 1791. Of course, the meaning of the federal constitution has been altered over the course of more than two centuries by judicial interpretation. Even this has produced some controversy as originalist and textualist jurists like the late Justice Antonin Scalia have argued that judges should confine themselves to deciding cases on the basis of the original and plain meaning of the Constitution's text.[3]

State constitutions are, by contrast, easier to change and are much more frequently revised and amended. The terms "revision" and "amendment" are sometimes used interchangeably, though amendment refers to the addition or subtraction of constitutional language while revision refers to the idea of substantial change up to and including the replacement of one constitution by another. Revision is generally associated with state constitutional conventions, while amendments are the product of state legislatures and popular initiative. Some state constitutions make this distinction while others are vague.

The federal constitution's framers thought malleability was fraught with risk and were especially wary of political processes that involved popular mobilization. In *Federalist 62* James Madison defended the idea of staggered terms in the proposed Senate by asserting that this would guard against the danger of "mutability in the public councils," and too great a frequency of change in the laws.[4] At the state level, by contrast, since the 18th century, the ideal of popular sovereignty seemed to require processes that allowed citizens a major role in shaping their states' constitutions. And, to this day, state constitutions are subject to change through processes that include popular initiative or, more commonly, popular ratification.

State constitutions can be changed in any of six ways (see Figure 2.1). These are legislative proposal, direct legislative action, popular initiative, state constitutional convention, constitutional commission and judicial action. The most common, accounting for 90 percent of state constitutional amendments, is a legislative proposal followed by popular ratification. In every state except Delaware, the legislature (usually by either a two-thirds or three-fifths vote of each house) may propose a constitutional amendment which is then placed on the next general election ballot for popular ratification. In 12 states, a proposed constitutional amendment must be passed by two successive sessions of the

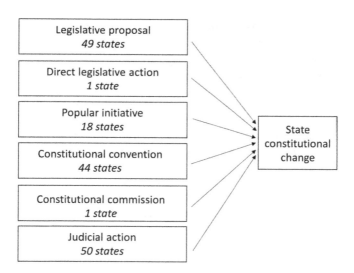

Figure 2.1 Paths to State Constitutional Change.
This figure shows the four ways state constitutions can be changed.

legislature. In all but one state, approval by a majority of voters in either a general or special election is sufficient to then add the amendment to the state's constitution. New Hampshire requires approval by two-thirds of the state's voters. Generally, amendments are limited to a single purpose. A variety of causes cannot be bundled into one proposal. To allow interested parties to make their cases to the public and give voters time to consider the proposed constitutional amendment, states generally require at least a three-month interval between the proposal and a ratification vote.

In Delaware, state law allows a second mode of constitutional amendment. This is direct action by the state legislature. The Delaware constitution may be amended by a two-thirds vote of two consecutive legislatures. Popular ratification is not needed.

A third route of state constitutional change is the popular initiative. In 18 states, a proposed constitutional amendment may be placed on a general or special election ballot if its supporters can collect the signatures of a certain percentage of the state's voters. This percentage ranges from three in Massachusetts to 15 in Arizona with some geographic distribution of signatures usually required. Nineteenth century Populists and Progressives viewed the initiative as a means of circumventing the state legislatures and it has served that function. In recent decades, for example, popular initiatives brought about two major changes in state government—tax limitations such as California's Proposition 13 and the imposition of legislative term limits in several states—that, for better or worse, would certainly not have been approved by any state legislature. Most states do not specify or limit the subject matter of a popular initiative, though some state constitutions do restrict the uses of the initiative. Massachusetts, for example, prohibits the use of the initiative for matters concerning religion, judicial tenure, judicial decisions, abolition of courts, local matters, appropriations and protected rights.[5]

Sometimes the supporters of an initiative employ volunteers to collect signatures while, more often, paid signature gatherers working for firms specializing in grass-roots political activity are retained for the purpose. Some states prohibit the use of paid signature gatherers or require some form of disclosure if they are used. If the necessary signatures are obtained, the measure is placed on the general election ballot for ratification. Usually a popular majority is sufficient to ratify the proposed amendment. In Massachusetts and Mississippi, constitutional proposals that obtain the requisite number of petition signatures are sent to the state legislatures rather than the citizenry for ratification. This procedure is called indirect ratification. Popular constitutional initiative should not be confused with popular legislative initiative. In 23 states, proposed pieces of legislation may be placed on the general election ballot to be approved or not by a popular vote. If approved, such a proposal becomes an ordinary statute, not a constitutional provision.

State constitutions may also be changed by constitutional conventions or through the recommendations of constitutional commissions. In 44 states there are laws that govern how a constitutional convention may be called, and more than 200 such conventions have met during the course of American political history. The most recent state constitutional convention met to consider Rhode Island's constitution in 1986. State constitutional conventions should not be confused with a national constitutional convention, sometimes called a convention of the states, to consider changing the federal constitution. No national convention has been held since the federal constitution was drafted in 1787, despite periodic calls for revision of the U.S. Constitution.

Under varying rules conventions may be called by state legislatures or through a ballot initiative or some combination of the two to examine the state's constitution and recommend changes up to and including the writing of a new state constitution. In 14 states, voters are asked at regular intervals, typically every 20 years, whether a constitutional convention should be called. More often than not, voters reject calls for a convention, responding to campaigns by organized interests afraid that a convention might upset established political arrangements. In 2017 New York voters, rejected the constitutionally mandated call for a convention after a campaign by a diverse coalition of liberal and conservative groups ranging from organized labor through business interests that did not want to risk losing their current political advantages. Public employees' unions, for instance, feared losing constitutionalized collective bargaining rights in a convention. New York has not convened a constitutional convention since the 1930s, despite the question being asked on the ballot every 20 years.

Conventions may be called for limited or unlimited purposes. When the state legislature initiates a call for a convention it often specifies the issues the convention may consider and bars it from taking up other questions. In states that allow a convention to be summoned by popular initiative, the convention generally exercises plenary constitutional power. Generally, proposals drafted by such a convention must then be submitted to the state's voters for ratification in a general or special election, though in Delaware the state legislature can ratify constitutional proposals approved by a convention without any need for popular ratification.

A constitutional commission, for its part, is a body created by a state legislature to examine the state's existing constitution and to recommend changes. Such recommendations may be sent to the state legislature which may, at its discretion, place the recommendations on the general election ballot as proposed constitutional amendments. In Florida, however, commission recommendations can be adopted directly by the electorate. The Florida constitution calls for two commissions that convene automatically every ten years. The first of these, the "Constitutional Revision Commission," consists of 37 members, 15 appointed by the governor, nine by the Speaker of the House, nine by the president of the Senate and three by the chief justice of the Florida Supreme Court. The Constitutional Revision Commission is empowered to consider the entire state constitution. A second commission, "The Taxation and Budget Reform Commission," is a 29-member body that only reviews fiscal and budgetary matters. The Florida commission system is responsible for a good deal of constitutional change in the state.[6]

Finally, state constitutions may be changed by actions of the courts. Both state and federal courts may find that provisions of a state's constitution violate the federal constitution or even other portions of the state constitution. In 2019, for example, the Superior Court of North Carolina invalidated two amendments to the state's constitution that had been adopted the previous year. The Court said that the state's legislature had been the product of racial gerrymandering and so could not pass laws that would amend the state's constitution.

As should be evident from this brief description, amending a state's constitution is no trivial matter. Yet, each year, a number of amendments are proposed and ratified. Over time, most states' constitutions have been amended many times and many state constitutions have been completely revised several times. As Table 2.1 indicates, the Alabama constitution has, as of 2019, been amended 909 times, while Louisianans have lived under no fewer than 11 different constitutions since the state was admitted to the Union in 1812. Collectively, the states have amended their constitutions more than 6000 times and continue to add amendments every year.

Constitutional malleability may have both advantages and disadvantages. The 1776 Virginia Declaration of rights, authored by George Mason, declared that "no free government, or the blessings of liberty, can be preserved to any people but ... by a frequent recurrence to fundamental principles."[7] Thomas Jefferson thought state constitutions should be revised once every generation. Jefferson wrote that citizens should have the chance to take account of new political insights and experiences and to make a democratic response to the political, social and economic changes confronting them by altering the fundamental purposes of their states' governments. Citizens might wish to create new institutions, and new governmental processes to accomplish new purposes.[8] For better or worse, this Jeffersonian idea seems reflected by the post-Reconstruction constitutions written by the Southern states to reassert white rule, and the 1870 Illinois "Granger Constitution," which sought to confront the problem of monopoly and, to that end, created new governmental agencies enabling the state to set railroad rates and generally regulate business activities within its borders.[9]

Another example is the 1972 Montana "environmental" constitution whose preamble declares,

Table 2.1 Constitutional Amendments and Revisions in the 50 States

State	Number of Constitutions	Year Current Constitution Adopted	Number of Times Amended	Notes
Alabama	6	1901	909	
Alaska	1	1956	28	
Arizona	1	1912	156	
Arkansas	5	1874	100	
California	2	1879	514	*at least 514*
Colorado	1	1876	163	
Connecticut	2	1965	32	
Delaware	4	1897	100	*at least 100*
Florida	6	1968	140	
Georgia	9	1983	87	
Hawaii	1	1959	269	
Idaho	1	1890	140	
Illinois	4	1970	14	
Indiana	2	1851	24	*since 1970*
Iowa	3	1857	48	
Kansas	1	1861	97	
Kentucky	4	1891	42	
Louisiana	11	1975	195	
Maine	1	1820	173	
Maryland	4	1867	233	
Massachusetts	1	1780	119	
Michigan	3	1963	34	
Minnesota	1	1857	120	
Mississippi	4	1890	50	*at least 50 since 1968*
Missouri	4	1945	117	
Montana	2	1973	30	
Nebraska	2	1875	234	
Nevada	1	1864	103	*at least 103*
New Hampshire	3	1783	146	
New Jersey	3	1948	54	
New Mexico	1	1912	68	
New York	4	1895	202	*at least 202*
North Carolina	4	1971	42	
North Dakota	1	1889	166	
Ohio	2	1851	169	
Oklahoma	1	1907	28	*since 2006*

(*Continued*)

Table 2.1 (Cont.)

Oregon	1	1859	253	
Pennsylvania	5	1968	45	
Rhode Island	6	1986	4	*since 2006*
South Carolina	6	1896	15	*hundreds before 2006*
South Dakota	1	1989	6	*since 2006*
Tennessee	3	1870	7	*since 2006*
Texas	4	1876	498	
Utah	1	1896	17	*since 2006*
Vermont	1	1793	51	
Virginia	6	1971	12	*since 2006*
Washington	2	1889	108	
West Virginia	2	1872	20	
Wisconsin	2	1848	101	
Wyoming	1	1889	7	*since 2006*

The data in this table come from Ballotpedia (https://ballotpedia.org/Number_of_state_constitutional_amendments_in_each_state).
The data include amendments for which there are available records.

> We the people of Montana grateful to God for the quiet beauty of our state, the grandeur of our mountains, the vastness of our rolling plains, and desiring to improve the quality of life, equality of opportunity and to secure the blessings of liberty for this and future generations do ordain and establish this constitution.

Subsequent articles of the Montana constitution created various environmental rights which have been enforced by the state's courts.

A large percentage, though, of the state constitutional revisions and amendments adopted over the decades do not involve changes to the states' basic political orientations or governmental frameworks. Instead, they simply reflect efforts by one or another interest group to require the state legislature to engage or not engage in some very specific course of action. California's constitution at one time mandated the number of rounds and length of each round in boxing matches held in the state, while Alabama's constitution still specifies trash collection rates in one county. The malleability of state constitutions has led to many being filled with very specific policy matters that might seem more appropriate for ordinary legislation. Once a constitution is filled with details, moreover, it is likely to become even more subject to further amendment and revision as each detail invites the attention of one or another interest group. As Chief Justice John Marshall observed in *McCulloch v. Maryland*, in order for a constitution to "endure for ages to come," it could not "partake of the prolixity" of a legal code, "but would rather have to confine itself to making great outlines."[10] Most contemporary state constitutions are certainly characterized by such "prolixity."

Of course, for those hoping to launch some new program, persuading the state legislature to enact a bill might seem easier than amending the state's constitution. After all, hundreds of laws are enacted every year in each state. Garnering the approval of a relative handful of state legislators might seem a far less daunting project than, say, collecting the tens of thousands of petition signatures needed to achieve a place on the ballot, and then winning the support of a majority of the state's voters— the most common route to constitutional change. And, recall, that a state legislature has plenary power. It may make laws on any topic whatsoever, unless barred by the federal constitution or the state's own constitution. Why not seek legislative rather than constitutional relief for a problem?

The reason is that amending a state constitution is not so difficult as to discourage groups or even individuals from attempting to add their preferences to a state's basic document where, once inserted, they might be quite resistant to efforts by opposing forces to dislodge them, and might, as constitutional provisions, have a continuing impact on law making and court decisions in the state. Such provisions function, in the words of California's Supreme Court, "as laws the state legislature cannot repeal or amend."[11]

Donald Lutz has written that constitutions should neither be too easy nor too hard to change. A process of revision and amendment that is too easy eliminates the distinction between constitutional matters and normal legislation while one that is too hard makes it impossible to rectify mistakes and interferes with the idea of popular sovereignty that is at the heart of democratic government.[12] Are state constitutions too easy or too difficult to change? The answer is *both*. It is much easier than might be appropriate to change matters of basic design by sometimes poorly considered constitutional amendment. At the same time, it is more difficult than might be desirable to remove constitutionalized policies, constitutional provisions that often require a distribution of state funds on behalf of some fortunate interest group, once such policies become part of a state's basic document.

As to the problem of too easily changing a constitution's basic design, during the 1970s a number of states, most notably California and Massachusetts, adopted constitutional amendments limiting legislative powers of taxation and effectively transferring a large portion of their states' tax burdens from homeowners to other citizens. During the 1980s constitutional initiatives in several states produced various limits on spending that constrained the ability of their state legislatures to achieve goals that many citizens supported. And, during the 1990s 20 states adopted constitutional amendments that set several different sorts of limits on state legislative terms. Taken together, these three waves of constitutional reform weakened state legislatures at a time when demands on state governments, including those imposed by federal mandates, were increasing. It was, from our perspective, too easy in a number of states, to undermine the basic institution of representative government via constitutional amendment.

On the other side of the coin, once constitutionalized, distributive policies favoring one or another interest group are more immune to change than they might have been as mere statutes. Thus, Alabama's venerable constitutional provisions providing public subsidies for the cotton, grain and catfish industries are far less vulnerable to change than they might have been as ordinary provisions in the state code. Is there any reason why the economic interests of catfish farmers deserve greater protection than those of any other industry? It seems unlikely. Thus, the malleability of state constitutions makes constitutional change both too easy and too difficult. Even if unintentional, this seems an impressive if misguided bit of constitutional legerdemain.

Before we leave the matter entirely, let us consider another aspect of the problem of constitutionalizing ordinary policies at the state level.

Constitutionalizing Policy and Thwarting Representative Government

At the federal level, constitutional provisions are generally different from congressionally enacted statutes. The federal constitution is, for the most part, a statement of basic principles of governance and politics, while congressionally enacted statutes focus on particular policy goals or problems. Statutes must comport with the Constitution. Any that contradict constitutional principles can be struck down as "unconstitutional" by the courts.

State constitutions do establish frameworks for state government. None, however, stop there. According to one analysis, about 40 percent of the provisions in the state constitutions are "policy-oriented."[13] That is, rather than strengthen the framework of government, they seek to accomplish sometimes very narrow policy goals through constitutional rather than legislative means. This constitutionalization of policy is one reason that state constitutions are so long. The U.S. Constitution contains only about 4500 words, or 7591 words if all 27 amendments are included. The state constitutions average about 26,000 words. The longest is Alabama's which, as of 2019, includes some 909 amendments and consists of over 360,000 words.

Length, alone, does not mean that the state constitutions are defective. Length resulting from a clutter of individual policy provisions, though, is problematic. Beginning in the 19th century, a variety of interest groups within the states discovered the political value of constitutionalizing their policy preferences. Incorporating a preference in the state constitution might be somewhat more difficult than securing the enactment of legislation on the same topic, once constitutionalized a policy preference was less amenable to change and trumped legislation on the same issue.[14] Thus, delegates to a number of 19th century state constitutional conventions in the Western states, claiming that state legislatures were unequal to the task, favored what they called "constitutional legislation" to accomplish such goals as restraining the power of railroad corporations and limiting state government debt.[15] Thus, a number of states adopted constitutional provisions regulating railroad rates and creating new state agencies empowered to regulate corporations in the state. This began the process of transforming state constitutions into "long legislative codes."[16] This process continued during the Progressive era when lack of confidence in state legislatures led to the adoption of many state constitutional provisions limiting state legislative authority and requiring greater transparency in legislative proceedings.

Of course, Progressives sought to restrain and circumvent state legislatures because they believed many legislators were beholden to business and other interest groups—which many were. Those self-same pressure groups, however, also saw the benefits of constitutionalizing their own interests and so began to use the amendment process to use state constitutions for their own purposes. Thus, California constitutions over the past century have contained provisions providing benefits for the state's financial institutions, lawyers, the alcoholic beverage industry, construction contractors, utility companies, the fishing industry, farmers, realtors, the transportation industry and native American interests, among others.[17] In Florida, gambling interests were able to amend the state's constitution to allow slot machines in Miami-Dade and Broward counties while the new medical marijuana industry campaigned successfully for a constitutional amendment permitting the production and possession of marijuana in the state, ostensibly only for medical purposes. The Louisiana constitution, as we saw, establishes a special fund to subsidize the state's farming and fishing industries. The Missouri constitution encourages the state's medical institutions to engage in stem cell research.

Not to be outdone, contemporary public interest groups have also worked to constitutionalize their policy preferences. Recently, as part of a nation-wide campaign to secure state constitutional protections for farm and game animals, groups advocating for animal rights were able to add an amendment to the Florida constitution, specifying the ways in which the state's hog farmers were to care for pregnant sows. New porcine rights included comfortable enclosures and freedom from unreasonable tethering. Agricultural and hunting interests have countered these efforts in several states by adding "right to farm" and "right to hunt" amendments to state constitutions to limit the ability of animal rights groups to impose new constitutional limits on these endeavors.

People of good will may, of course, differ on any of these particular policies. Farmers may see pigs mainly in pecuniary terms while other Americans may, if they wish, concern themselves with porcine comfort and welfare. The question, though, is where these interests should seek protection. Some see it as a tribute to American democracy that in a number of states ordinary voters have an opportunity to change their states' basic governing document. Douglas Reed, for example, writes, "state constitutions give great credence and power to democratic majorities."[18] Yet, does this opportunity for popular involvement in constitutional revision actually advance democratic values?

The winners of a battle to bring about the enactment of a statute by the state legislature are by no means certain to have an undue advantage if, at some future date, some opposing group, seeks to replace it with its own policies. This pattern describes the familiar give and take of legislative struggle. Today's victories are impermanent and may give way to defeat tomorrow if the popular and legislative moods shift. Once a policy interest is incorporated into a state's constitution, however, it becomes difficult to dislodge and can have a broad effect upon the powers of the state legislature for years to come. This is, of course, the reason that interests work to constitutionalize their preferences. Through constitutionalization, the scales are tipped against future generations of citizens who might favor some other set of ideas and interests. In this way, the constitutionalization of discrete policy preferences creates civic inequality more than it promotes democracy. Some citizens benefit from enshrined programs while others would face quite an uphill fight to change matters. Beneath its democratic facade, when one group of citizens constitutionalizes its preferences, the result is to curb the political opportunities available to future generations. This problem is exacerbated when new rights, rather than simple policies, are constitutionalized.

Constitutional Rights

America's federal constitution, as has often been observed, contains few substantive rights. The Bill of Rights is mainly a list of limitations on government power while even the rights described in the Bill, such as the right to trial by jury or to confront witnesses are rights that citizens possess in their relations with the government. These are essentially procedural rights. The federal constitution, unlike European constitutions, offers citizens no guarantees of protection from nongovernmental dangers such as poverty, hunger, lack of education and lack of healthcare.[19] Many of the state constitutions, on the other hand, spell out positive rights in such realms as education, welfare, health, and the environment. Such rights can be found throughout state constitutions, not merely in a constitution's formal declaration of rights.

Federal constitutional rights apply mainly against action by the government which, since the Supreme Court's gradual application of the Bill of Rights to the states, includes state and local governments. Thus, neither the federal nor the state government may abridge free speech, a freedom of the press or the freedom to worship. State constitutional rights, for their part, can restrain private as well as governmental action and can offer a promise that the state will act to secure some public good like education or healthcare for its citizens. This promise may be very specific, requiring the state government to undertake some course of action or at least sufficiently specific to provide a cause of action in the state's courts where litigants can argue that the state has failed to live up to its constitutional obligations to provide its citizens with such rights as education and proper healthcare. State constitutional rights are enforced, defined and sometimes expanded by state courts. Generally speaking, a state court decision based on a right in the state's constitution will not be reviewed by the U.S. Supreme Court.

Education is the oldest of the positive rights to be found in state constitutions. Even before the enactment of the federal constitution, several state constitutions contained education clauses. The Pennsylvania Constitution of 1776, for example, required each county to establish schools and to provide, "such salaries to the masters paid for by the public, as may enable them to instruct youth at a low price."[20] Similarly, the Georgia Constitution of 1777 and the Vermont Constitution of 1786 required counties to create and maintain public school. In the early 19th century, a number of other state constitutions declared that education was essential to the preservation of a free government and asserted that equality of educational opportunities was an important goal. Kentucky's early 19th century constitution stipulated that common schools should be free and open to all children while Connecticut's 1818 constitution provided that school funds should be used for the equal benefit of all the people of the state.[21] By the 1880s, most state constitutions assigned to the legislature the responsibility for establishing and maintaining schools. Some state constitutions spelled out the administrative structure of the state's school system while others left it to the legislature to implement the constitution's mandates.

In the aftermath of the U.S. Supreme Court's *Brown v. Board of Education* decision, several state constitutions were amended to prohibit racial segregation in the public schools. Subsequently, education reformers launched a number of successful campaigns to amend state constitutions to mandate funding equity in the state's school districts and to address issues of educational quality. In 1998 and 2002 for example, after vigorous campaigns by teachers' groups and others, Florida adopted a number of constitutional amendments declaring education to be a fundamental value and requiring the state to provide an education for its children that was uniform, efficient, safe, secure and of high quality.[22] In effect, the constitution of Florida and of most other states, as well, made education a right and provided some general criteria to assess whether or not the state was living up to it responsibilities.

Advocates soon found that a right accompanied by some general guideposts offered opportunities for litigation aimed at persuading courts to fill in the details and, perhaps, expand certain rights. This is precisely what has taken place since the 1980s as state judges, asked to interpret their own states' constitutions, have gradually expanded educational rights and required states to provide more and more funding to satisfy what judges saw as constitutional guarantees. Every state has seen challenges to its educational financing arrangements, charging violations of state constitutional guarantees of equity, adequacy and educational quality.[23]

The main issue addressed by state courts in the 1970s and early 1980s was the question of disparities in educational spending. Traditionally, education was funded by local property taxes which produced substantial disparities in levels of spending between schools situated in wealthier and poorer areas. In 1973, the U.S. Supreme Court had declared in the case of *San Antonio Independent School District v. Rodriguez* that Texas's reliance upon local property taxes to fund the state's education system did not violate the U.S. Constitution's equal protection clause.[24] The Court found that education was neither explicitly nor explicitly guaranteed by the federal constitution.

Stymied in the federal courts, advocates sought to take advantage of existing education rights in the state constitutions, where possible campaigning to add additional rights and to ask state courts to enforce these rights. This turned out to be a successful strategy. In fact, in a series of cases decided during the 1980s and 1990s, the Texas Supreme Court found that the same school-financing system upheld by the U.S. Supreme Court in *Rodriguez* violated the Texas constitution.[25] But, even earlier, litigants hoped to use state courts to compel states to increase and equalize educational spending across school districts. And, in the 1970s, state courts started to hold that under their states' constitutions education was a fundamental interest so that claims of educational inequality deserved the highest level of judicial scrutiny.[26]

In 1977, for example, the Connecticut Supreme Court declared in the case of *Horton v. Meskill* that education was a basic right in Connecticut, that students were entitled to equal enjoyment of the right to education, and that reliance only on local property taxes to fund school systems was unconstitutional.[27] The state was required to provide support to poorer districts that would equalize spending across districts. Subsequently, the Connecticut Supreme Court ordered the state to increase educational spending to comply with the equalization mandate. In a similar vein, Wyoming's Supreme Court held in 1980 that the state's educational district-based funding system violated the Wyoming constitution's requirement of educational equity for all the state's schoolchildren. The Court ruled that education was a fundamental right under the state's constitution and that equality of financing was needed to ensure "equality of quality."[28]

The New Jersey Supreme Court reached a similar conclusion in a series of cases stretching from the 1970s to the 1990s. In 1997, the Court declared,

> The finiteness of judicial power, however, does not diminish the judicial obligation to vindicate constitutional rights. Plaintiffs seek affirmation of their constitutional right to an opportunity that will enable them to achieve a thorough and efficient education, that is a level of education which will allow them to assume a place in society as competitive and effective workers and contributors ... Accordingly, the interim remedy that we mandate to effectuate that right is the improvement of regular education through increased funding.[29]

Between 1989 and the present, education advocates have taken a step beyond educational equality and have sought to persuade state courts that their constitutions required the states to increase their overall levels of educational spending to reflect such constitutional language as "efficient," and "high quality." On the whole, this effort has also been successful with a number of state courts finding constitutional violations and ordering remedies. In 2003, for example, New York's highest court, the Court of Appeals, ruled that the state had failed in its constitutional obligation to provide a sound basic education to New York City's schoolchildren. The Court required the state to implement major funding increases to comply with its constitutional obligations.[30] The state failed to meet a Court-imposed deadline for appropriating additional funds and, in 2004 the Court appointed three referees to develop a funding plan. The referees recommended that the legislature be required be required to provide New York City schools with an additional $5.6 billion in annual operating aid and $9.2 billion over five years for school renovation and construction in order to provide students with their constitutional right to a sound basic education. The state legislature partially complied with this recommendation, funding the $9.2 billion in capital costs but declining to further subsidize the schools' operating budgets. After further litigation, the Court of Appeals accepted this compromise.[31]

One moral of this story is that over the past several decades advocates were able to use the process of state constitutional revision to develop new state educational rights, and then turn to the state courts to more fully specify and expand these rights and, in some cases, to order significant remedies if these rights were being violated. Since education is certainly important, these might seem to be positive developments.

We might, however, consider this history from a slightly different perspective. By developing broad state constitutional rights to education and encouraging the state courts to further expand and enforce these rights, education advocates have removed substantial control over roughly 25 percent of most states' budgets from the legislature and transferred it to the judiciary.[32] In a number of states, in addition to New York, court decisions, based on constitutional claims, have reshaped educational policy and finance.[33] Two major New Jersey court decisions, for example, *Robinson v. Cahill* and *Abbot v. Burke*, interpreted the state constitutional requirement of a "thorough and efficient" system of education to order the state legislature to change the way in which education was funded in the state.[34] In a similar vein, the Texas Supreme Court relied on the Texas state constitution's "efficiency" clause to restructure school spending in that state.[35] In 2012, Washington's state Supreme Court ruled that the legislature was violating the state's constitution by not providing enough funding for public schools. In 2015, the Court began fining the state $100,000 per day for being in contempt. Most of this money went to the state's school system and by June 2018, billions had been redirected to the schools.[36]

When a court orders a state legislature to spend more money on education, it is also ordering the same legislature to spend less on other programs, raise taxes, or both. Taxes and spending are by American tradition and constitutional writ, matters to be decided by the legislative branch of government, presumably representing the views of the state's citizens. When the rights found in a state's constitution are increased and their scope broadened by the courts, the result could hardly be seen as democratic.

Of course, many state judges are elected, but this should not be seen as making the judiciary a democratic or representative institution. The president of the United States is elected but the presidency is by no means a democratic institution. One person cannot represent all the people of the United States. Moreover, a mode of selection should not be confused with a mode of decision making. Presidents make many of their decisions behind closed doors and often fail to provide full explanations for their actions. Similarly, a judge or even a panel of judges cannot claim to properly represent the millions of residents of New York or California or Texas. Judges, to be sure, provide written explanations for their decisions but, unlike legislators, are not required to bargain and compromise with the many parties who may be affected by a matter. Decisions made by judges do not bear the same democratic stamp as legislative choices and it appears inappropriate in a democracy to afford judges' opinions more weight on matters of policy than the views of the legislature. In American constitutional theory, legislators make the law while judges consider the application of the law to particular individuals.

The problems created by the incorporation of substantive rights into state constitutions and their enforcement by the courts is aggravated by the fact that education is not the only substantive right currently found in state constitutions. A number of state constitutions include a variety of provisions that are sometimes termed "workers' rights" relating to such matters as workers' hours and working conditions, and employer liability for injury. These provisions, however, amount to a set of regulations, accompanied by sanctions, governing the conduct of private employers rather than guarantees that the state will provide some public good for all or a designated potion of the state's citizens. For the most part, indeed, unlike education, the costs of workers' rights are borne by employers and other private entities rather than state governments.

A number of state constitutions also include rights that, like education, potentially require substantial state expenditures for the acquisition of public goods. New York's constitution, for instance, includes a right to public assistance for the poor. The constitution states, "The aid, support and care of the needy are public concerns and shall be provided by the state."[37] In a similar vein, Alabama's constitution requires "adequate maintenance of the poor." Colorado's constitution pledges, "an old age pension to all residents 60 years of age or older." The North Carolina constitution declares that, "Beneficent provision for the poor, the unfortunate and the orphan is one of the first duties of a civilized and a Christian state. Therefore, the General Assembly shall provide for and define the duties of a board of public welfare."[38]

The constitutions of three states give public employees collective bargaining rights, while public employee pension rights are protected by the constitutions of seven states including New York, Michigan and Illinois.[39] Illinois' constitution declares that the accrued and future retirement benefits of public employees are constitutionally protected, effectively prohibiting the legislature from making any changes for current employees.[40] Unfunded but constitutionally mandated pension liabilities have led the state not only to borrow beyond its means but even to borrow to pay the carry costs on its debt.

Many state constitutions also contain provisions relating to healthcare. Such provisions can be found in the constitutions of Alaska, Hawaii, Michigan, North Carolina, New York and Wyoming. Alaska's constitution declares that, "the legislature shall provide for the promotion and protection of public health," while Wyoming's constitution states, "as the health and morality of the people are essential to their well being ... it shall be the duty of the legislature to protect and promote these vital interests."[41] Some state constitutions specifically require the legislature to provide healthcare for the poor and for the insane. These constitutional provisions could potentially be used as the bases for litigation sponsored by advocacy groups to compel states to increase health spending. It is not difficult to imagine an effort to constitutionalize additional healthcare rights accompanied by a strategy of litigation aimed at judicial enforcement of these rights.

One area in which activist groups are following precisely this script is the realm of environmental rights. About half the state constitutions refer to environmental protection or quality and several declare that a clean and healthful environment is a right. Several states, including Montana, as we saw above, have incorporated specific legislative mandates into their constitutions. The New Mexico constitution, for example, states, "The legislature shall provide for control of pollution and control of despoilment of the air, water and other natural resources of this state."[42] New Jersey's constitution is even more specific. A 1996 amendment requires the state to clean hazardous waste sites and underground storage tanks and sets aside 4 percent of the revenue from the state's corporate tax to pay for the effort. In several states, including California, the constitution creates new governmental agencies to implement constitutionally mandated environmental policy. The California constitution, for instance, creates a Fish and Game Commission to protect wildlife in the state.[43]

The growth of environmental constitutionalism resulted from a concerted effort by environmental groups, which often were already organized at the state level, to insert environmental guarantees into state constitutions. Environmental organizations sent experts to testify before state constitutional conventions, sometimes drafting suggested constitutional amendments for the conventions to consider.[44] Environmentalists also lobbied state legislatures and launched initiative campaigns to introduce new environmental provisions into state constitutions. Zackin reports that between 1963 and 1978 environmental provisions were incorporated into fourteen state constitutions.[45]

Environmental activists undertook these efforts precisely because they believed that by so doing they would transfer the power to make decisions from the state legislatures where they were often unsuccessful to the courts where they believed their chances for success were better. Zackin observes that most proponents of environmental rights thought constitutional provisions asserting such rights would be helpful primarily as the bases for litigation.[46] In the legislative arena, environmentalists competed with many well heeled corporate interests and the need to constantly remind the public of environmental risks. Before state appellate courts, though, well trained and experienced public interest lawyers could make their cases to judges more likely to understand and be swayed by scientific evidence. In this way, the environmental movement hoped to make great strides without having to constantly make its case to the state legislatures.[47]

Thus far, this tactic has been most effective in Montana where the state's Supreme Court held in the 1999 case of *Montana Environmental Information Center (MEIC) v. Department of Environmental Quality* that the Montana constitution's environmental provisions created judicially enforceable rights. The case involved a gold mining company that planned to discharge ground water into the Blackfoot River. The Court held that the statute, which would have permitted this discharge, violated Montanan's right to a clean and beautiful environment guaranteed by the state's constitution.[48] The fact that a constitutional right was involved, said the Court, meant that the statute in question should receive the highest level of judicial scrutiny. MEIC involved the constitutionality of a statute. Two years later, the Montana Supreme Court applied the same standard when blocking a private action by a land developer.[49] Many other state constitutions now contain environmental rights similar to those found in Montana and it seems likely that sooner or later these will be held to be judicially enforceable.[50]

Like education, environmental quality is undeniably important. Once enshrined in a state constitution as a substantive right, however, environmental quality is a claim on state resources that transfers decision making power over taxes and spending from the state legislature to the courts. And we should not forget that the potential costs of enforcing substantive rights is difficult to predict. The procedural rights guaranteed by the federal constitution, such as trial by jury, while critically important, do not place much of a burden on the public treasury. Providing a judicially mandated "high quality environment" or a "sound education" if construed broadly, would not leave the state legislatures with much money for other worthy purposes.

Restrictions on State Legislative Power

Adding new rights to state constitutions already constrains the taxing and spending powers of state legislatures. Money spent on schools or the environment is not available to be spent on other purposes. Most states, however, also place direct restrictions on legislative taxing and spending powers. The federal constitution mainly empowers Congress to raise and spend money for public purposes and to borrow money "on the credit of the United States." As to restrictions, the federal constitution stipulates only that revenue bills must originate in the House of Representatives and that money may be drawn from the Treasury, "but in consequence of appropriations made by law."

State constitutions, by contrast, are filled with restraints on spending, borrowing and taxation. Many of these provisions have their origins in the aftermath of the nation-wide economic collapse of 1837 when nine states defaulted on their debts.[51] Every state at that time adopted some form of debt restriction, as did states that subsequently entered the Union. Three general types of fiscal restraints can be found in state constitutions. These are debt limits, tax and expenditure limits (commonly known as TELs) and balanced budget requirements. Most state constitutions contain debt provisions either prohibiting the state from issuing state-guaranteed general obligation bonds or requiring voter approval or legislative super majorities for the issuance of such bonds. TEL provisions, found in a number of state budgets, restrict taxation and expenditure levels in the state by requiring that tax or spending levels or both be tied to population growth, inflation or other factors. Balanced budget requirements demand that any spending increases be offset by tax increases. State constitutions also contain a variety of earmarks such as those requiring the revenues from particular taxes to be spent on specified educational or environmental or other programs.

Such constitutional restrictions seem prudent. However, they encourage what Eileen Norcross calls, "fiscal evasions," through which many state governments endeavor to reduce the impact of the fiscal constraints they find in their constitutions.[52] In the course of circumventing constitutional requirements, sometimes to fund newly constitutionalized rights, states often hide the full costs of public spending. States have become extremely creative in their use of fiscal evasions. They use revenue bonds, lease-financing arrangements, subject-to-appropriation debt and a variety of other techniques such that, according to one estimate, nearly three-quarters of all state debt is not classified as debt and not subject to state constitutional debt limits.[53] Since these evasive forms of debt are not guaranteed by the full faith and credit of the state, governments must pay a somewhat higher rate of interest to lenders than would otherwise be the case. In many states, moreover, government efforts to evade debt limitations have given rise to a host of various types of unelected and unaccountable public authorities that currently control a large portion of the nation's infrastructure. This is one reason that responsibility for America's crumbling infrastructure is often difficult to determine.

This situation has come about because constitutionally prescribed debt limits generally do not affect non-guaranteed debt used to finance capital projects including toll roads, toll bridges and housing developments that will, in principle, produce revenue that will eventually retire the bonds.[54] These bonds are issued by off-budget entities (OBEs) and, today, constitute the bulk of state debt in some states. To cite one example, more than 90 percent of New York's approximately $50 billion in debt consists of bonds issued by OBEs. States are "morally" but not legally required to guarantee such debt in the event of a default by the issuing authority. The costs of projects financed by OBEs do not appear in the state budget and can often be difficult even for budget experts to quantify. New York Comptroller Thomas DiNapoli complained that, "The state's real fiscal picture is impossible to pin down," because of the long-standing use of budget gimmickry.[55] Moving expenditures "off-budget" through the creation of OBEs—and there are now nearly 40,000 OBEs of various sorts across the nation—hides their cost and allows legislatures to satisfy electoral and constitutional demands for spending while imposing payment obligations on future generations.

Debt financing, sometimes through OBEs can also help states circumvent balanced budget requirements. For example, in 2011 New Hampshire balanced the state's budget, as was constitutionally required, by issuing $6 billion in bonds including bonds backed by anticipated tuition revenues from the University of New Hampshire to cover an anticipated budget shortfall. For its part, Illinois relies heavily on off-the-books borrowing to cover its current expenditures as well as interest on its long-term obligations. Like a feckless homeowner before the 2008 mortgage crisis, the states borrow money to pay the carrying costs of previous loans.

James Buchanan observed that law makers always have an incentive to create what he called "fiscal illusions."[56] The illusions are designed to convince citizens in their capacity as voters that they are receiving benefits while simultaneously persuading them in their capacity as taxpayers that spending for these benefits is less costly than it actually is. Through deficit spending, moreover, costs can be passed on to future generations of taxpayers while the benefits can be enjoyed today. The states' fiscal illusions are sustained by complex budgeting schemes, the use of off-the-books borrowing and so forth. The illusion prevents citizens and even law makers from understanding the implications of their actions and prevents rational policy choices. Buchanan argues that the creation of fiscal illusions is an inherent problem in democratic politics and perhaps he is right. State constitutions, however, tend to aggravate this problem. Because of their malleability, state constitutions include an ever-growing number of broad rights, such as "educational quality," and the right to a "high quality environment." State courts, for their part, have generally been happy to offer expansive interpretations of these rights. At the same time, state constitutions contain strict fiscal limitations designed to prevent legislatures, from borrowing excessively and engaging in deficit spending. The clash of expansive rights and strict limits exacerbates the problem identified by Buchanan. Legislators are given even more reason to create fiscal illusions—a fog, Norcross aptly calls it—that make it difficult, if not impossible, to understand a state's actual economic health.[57]

The combination of constitutionalized expenditures, budgetary limitations and fiscal chicanery is one factor contributing to a state fiscal crisis affecting a number of states that are kept financially afloat only by enormous federal transfers. The 2009 American Recovery and Investment Act (ARRA) of 2009 allocated $144 billion to bail out state and local governments, with a disproportionate amount going to states like Illinois and California where off-budget deficit spending had grown beyond any sustainable limit. What has been called a "silent bailout" continues today in the form of federal transfers of nearly $500 billion a year to fund Medicaid and other programs where the federal contribution exceeds the state's expenditure. On average, the states rely on federal transfer payments for more than 30 percent of their general revenue, with some receiving transfers amounting to more than 40 percent of their total revenues.

Evaluating Constitutional Rights and Restrictions

A constitution should be evaluated as a whole rather than piece by piece. A constitutional provision that seems reasonable when viewed in the abstract may be found to weaken the constitutional framework as a whole. Some have argued that the 17th Amendment to the federal constitution has this character.[58] In the case of state constitutions, the malleability that seems to be a democratic feature can also be used to shelter policies from democratic processes.

At the same time, constitutionalized rights, each of which seems desirable, transfer power from the state legislatures to the courts—a shift in power hardly consistent with democratic values. Finally, constitutionalized rights, coupled with strict fiscal limits, encourage budgetary evasions and the creation of a fog in which neither voters nor legislators can actually understand a state's fiscal status. Are these problems soluble? We will leave that for our final chapter.

Notes

1 State ex. Rel. Schneider v. Kennedy, 587 P2d 844, 850 (Kan. 1978). See, G. Alan Tarr, *Understanding State Constitutions* (Princeton, NJ: Princeton University Press, 1998), p. 7.
2 Tarr, *Understanding State Constitutions*, p. 16.
3 Ralph Rossum, *Antonin Scalia's Jurisprudence: Text and Tradition* (Lexington, KS: University Press of Kansas, 2006).
4 *The Federalist*, No.62. www.constitution.org/fed/federa62.htm.
5 Gerald Benjamin, "Constitutional Amendment and Revision," in G. Alan Tarr and Robert F. Williams, eds., *State Constitutions for the Twenty-first Century, Vol. 3* (Albany, NY: State University of New York Press, 2006), p. 188.
6 Benjamin, p. 191.
7 Virginia Declaration of Rights, Section 15.
8 G. Alan Tarr, "Introduction," in Tarr and Williams, eds., *State Constitutions for the Twenty-first Century*, p. 3.

9 Tarr, *State Constitutions*, p. 3.
10 17 U.S. 316 (1819).
11 Rice v. Howard, 136 Cal. 432 (1902).
12 Donald Lutz, "Constitutional Politics in the States," in Tarr, ed., *Understanding State Constitutions*, pp. 26–27.
13 Christopher W. Hammons, "State Constitutional Reform: Is it Necessary?" *Albany Law Review* 64 (2001): 1327, 1338.
14 Robert F. Williams, *The Law of American State Constitutions* (New York: Oxford University press, 2009), Ch.1.
15 Christian G. Fritz, "The American Constitutional Tradition Revisited: Preliminary Observations on State Constitution-Making in the 19th Century West," *Rutgers Law Journal* 25 (1994): 945, 964–971.
16 Stephen S. Griffin, *American Constitutionalism: From Theory to Politics* (Princeton, NJ: Princeton University Press, 1998), pp. 33–42.
17 David Lawrence, *California: The Politics of Diversity* (Boston, MA: Cengage Publishing, 2007), p. 43.
18 Douglas S. Reed, "Popular Constitutionalism: Toward a Theory of State Constitutional Meanings," *Rutgers Law Journal* 30 (1999): 871.
19 Emily Zackin, *Looking for Rights in All the Wrong Places* (Princeton, NJ: Princeton University Press, 2013).
20 Paul Tractenberg, "Education," in Tarr and Williams, eds., *State Constitutions*, p. 243.
21 Connecticut Constitution of 1818, Article VIII, Section 2, quoted in Tractenberg, p. 244.
22 Tractenberg, p. 248.
23 Tractenberg, p. 241.
24 411 U.S. 1 (1973).
25 Jeffrey S. Sutton, *51 Imperfect Solutions: States and the Making of American Constitutional Law* (New York: W.W. Norton, 2018), p. 31.
26 Christopher Roellke, Preston Green and Erica H. Zielewski, "School Finance Litigation: The Promises and Limitations of the Third Wave," *Peabody Journal of Education* 79, no. 2 (2004): 104–133.
27 172 Conn 615 (1977).
28 *Washakie County School District No. One v. Herschler,* 1980 WY 5, 606 P.2d 310, 5145.
29 Abbott v. Burke, 693 A.2d 417 (N.J. 1997).
30 *Campaign for Fiscal Equity v. State of New York,* 719 N.Y.S. 2d 475 (2003).
31 Teachers' College, Columbia University, "The Campaign for Fiscal Equality Lawsuit Was the Bes Hope for City Schools. It Failed." 2009. www.tc.columbia.edu/articles/2009/january/the-campaign-for-fiscal-equity-lawsuit-was-the-best-hope-for/.
32 David M. Primo, "State Constitutions and Fiscal Policy," Mercatus Center, 2016. www.mercatus.org/publication/state-constitutions-and-fiscal-policy.
33 Primo, p. 9.
34 *Robinson v. Cahill,* 62 N.J. 473 (1973). *Abbott v. Burke,* 100 N.J. 269 (1985).
35 Lawrence O. Picus and Linda Hertert, "Three Strikes and You're Out: Texas School Finance after Edgewood III," *Journal of Education Finance* 18, no.4 (1993), pp. 366–389.
36 Moriah Balingit, "Student's Attorneys Argue for Constitutional Right to Literacy," *The Washington Post,* Aug. 14, 2018, p. 1.

37 Helen Hershkoff, "Welfare Devolution and State Constitutions," *Fordham Law Review* 67 (1999): 1403.
38 Discussed in Williams, "Rights," in Tarr and Williams, eds., *State Constitutions*, pp. 25–26.
39 Primo, p. 12.
40 Liz Farmer, "How Are Pensions Protected State-by-state?" *Governing Magazine*, Jan. 28, 2014. www.governing.com/finance101/gov-pension-protections-state-by-state.html.
41 Kathleen Swendiman, "Health Care: Constitutional Rights and Legislative Powers," Congressional Research Service, Jul. 9, 2012. www.everycrsreport.com/reports/R40846.html.
42 Zackin, p. 150.
43 Barton H. Thompson, Jr., "The Environment and Natural Resources," in Tarr and Williams, eds., *State Constitutions*, p. 313.
44 Zackin, p. 149.
45 Zackin, p. 151.
46 Zaxkin, p. 173.
47 Zackin, p. 173.
48 988 P.2d 1236 (Mont. 1999).
49 *Cape-France Enterprises* v. *Estate of Peed*, 29 P.3rd 1011 (Mont. 2001).
50 Bryan P. Wilson, "State Constitutional Environmental Rights and Judicial Activism: Is the Big Sky Falling?" *Emory Law Journal* 53 (2004): 627.
51 G. Alan Tarr, "State Constitutional Politics: An Historical Perspective," in G. Alan Tarr, ed., *Constitutional Politics in the States* (Westport, CT: Greenwood Press, 1996), p. 13.
52 Eileen Norcross, "Fiscal Evasion in State Budgeting," Mercatus Center, July, 2010. www.mercatus.org/publication/fiscal-evasion-state-budgeting.
53 Richard Briffault, "The Disfavored Constitution: State Fiscal Limits and State Constitutional Law," *Rutgers Law Journal* 34 (2003): 907.
54 Primo, p. 15.
55 Nicholas Confessore, "Grab Bag of Gimmickry Hides State Deficit," *The New York Times*, Apr. 6, 2010. https://cityroom.blogs.nytimes.com/2010/04/06/albany-accounting-hides-deficit-size-comptroller-says/.
56 See James M. Buchanan, *Public Finance in the Democratic Process: Fiscal Institutions and Individual Choice* (Chapel Hill, NC: University of North Carolina Press, 1967).
57 Norcross, p. 4.
58 Ralph Rossum, *Federalism, the Supreme Court and the 17th Amendment: The Irony of Constitutional Democracy* (Washington, DC: Lexington Books, 2001).

3 The States in the Federal System

Federalism refers to a division of powers and functions between a national government and partially autonomous regional governments within the nation's borders. Federal systems are fairly common and, in addition to the United States, include such nations as Switzerland, Canada and Germany. Federalism was a central element of America's Constitution of 1787 which assigned specific powers to the national government and left others to the states.

Both levels of American government continue to be important and in terms of the laws and practices that have the most immediate impact upon Americans' lives, the states remain sovereign, or at least semi-sovereign. Over the course of American history, however, the balance of power between the federal government and the governments of the states has gradually shifted toward the national government. During the 19th century, the states were considerably more important than the central government. During the 20th century, the power of the national government increased, and in the 21st century the states are engaged in a fitful rear guard action against the inexorable encroachment of federal power.

Once quasi-sovereign entities, the states are gradually becoming administrative appendages of the federal government, albeit retaining some capacity to harass and harry the Feds, as in the current imbroglio over the refusal by "sanctuary states," including California, Washington, Vermont and Illinois, to cooperate with federal immigration authorities. We should note that within California some cities and counties have defied the state's resistance to federal policy. Bakersfield, for example, declared itself a "law and order" city, and not a sanctuary.[1] A small number of states have sporadically engaged in what some have labeled "uncooperative federalism," refusing to assist Congress in implementing federal programs to which they objected.[2] During the Trump years, states governed by Democrats sought to oppose federal policies in such realms as taxation, healthcare, drug policy and health policy, in addition to immigration. Uncooperative federalism had mixed results, partly because most states during this period were under Republican control.

During the 2020 coronavirus pandemic, a nearly forgotten issue of state versus federal power came to the fore. Beginning in March, 2020, a number of states sought to restrict entry by travelers from other states, especially those coming from New York, Louisiana, New Jersey and other areas especially hard hit by the virus. Generally, travelers entering the state were required to quarantine themselves for 14 days and law enforcement officers were instructed to enforce the quarantine. Some states applied these restrictions to their own citizens returning home as well as to others seeking to enter the state, but other states focused on cars with out-of-state license plates. Rhode Island, for example, ordered all out-of-state travelers to be stopped at the border and sent into quarantine if they intended to remain in the state.

These state policies represent a direct challenge to the power of the national government and probably violate the U.S. Constitution. The "privileges and immunities" clause of the U.S. Constitution (Article IV, Section 2, Clause 1) prohibits any state from treating citizens of other states in a discriminatory manner. The U.S. Supreme Court has held that this language implies that no state can bar interstate travel. In the case of *Paul v. Virginia* the Court said that the federal constitution gave, "the citizens of each state ... the right of free ingress into other states, and egress from them."[3] No doubt, this issue will be aired and litigated in the coming years.

The Growth of Federal Power

Federal power has tended to grow most rapidly during time of economic and military emergency—the Great Depression, World War II, the Korean War, the 2008 economic crisis and so forth.[4] The 9-11 terror attacks led to the creation of a new Homeland Security agency and a host of new federal regulations aimed at thwarting terrorism through government surveillance of nearly all American communications, and financial regulations aimed at preventing terrorists from using the U.S. financial system.

But, even though accelerated by national crisis, the gradual shift in power to the federal government that began in the early decades of the 20th century is coincident with and part and parcel of the rise of the presidency. The framers of the Constitution hoped that the presidency would be an "energetic" office with the capacity to make and enforce decisions and that executive energy would suffuse through the entire national government. Despite a slow start, the framers were eventually proven correct. Since the Progressive era and New Deal, presidents have been able to strengthen institutions they controlled, namely, those of the executive branch of the national government, while subordinating Congress and gradually leading the national government's eclipse of the states. Many commentators correctly describe contemporary American politics as an era of presidentialism without taking note of the fact that presidential dominance of the national government also tends to undermine federalism.

The eclipse of the states is lamented by some who echo the Antifederalist view articulated during the founding era to the effect that state and local governments are closer and more sympathetic to the people than the national government.[5] Others who lament the declining power of the states cite James Madison's assertion that state governments can provide an important check on federal power.[6] While there is some merit to each of these perspectives, generally speaking, as we will see in Chapter 5, the governments of at least some states seem closer to powerful interest groups than to their citizens. The federal government, moreover, has done more to protect citizens from oppressive actions by the states than the states have done to protect citizens from the federal government. One might imagine circumstances under which the states could be a useful check on the federal government but at the present time their capacity to rein in the federal government's actions is minimal.

To begin at the beginning, many of the Constitution's framers, particularly Alexander Hamilton, had hoped to create something close to a unitary national government and to severely circumscribe the power of the individual states. The fact that the framers established a federal system in which the states retained significant powers reflected the political realities of the founding period. Each of the original 13 states possessed its own military force consisting of a citizen militia, and a well-established set of governmental institutions staffed by legislators, judges and executive officials who often had no desire to see their power and autonomy submerged in a new national regime. New York's Governor Clinton, for example, opposed the idea of a stronger national government mainly because he enjoyed his position as the chief executive of what amounted to an important independent nation. The states, moreover, possessed distinct economic interests which their representatives at the constitutional convention were reluctant to entrust fully to a national government. The Southern states were determined to protect their plantation economies and the institution of slavery upon which these were based. Smaller states like New Jersey and Delaware feared that their commercial interests would not be adequately protected within a larger nation.

At the same time, many citizens identified with their own states. The people of North America were not Americans. Instead, they already had several generations to become Virginians, New Yorkers, Pennsylvanians and so on. Well-established popular identification with the 13 states compelled even the most nationalistic of the framers to accept the idea that state governments would continue as important entities. In a sense, the framers confronted the same realities faced today by advocates of a stronger European Union (EU). The nations of Europe have historically distinct identities, well-entrenched governments and many loyal citizens. Uniting these nations is no easy matter and, like America's founders, the architects of the EU have generally found it necessary to erect the new regime upon federal foundations. Even this, as shown by America's secession crisis of 1860 and the United Kingdom's more recent efforts to leave the EU, cannot always solve the problem of disparate interests and identifications.

Despite the fact that 13 of America's 50 states existed before the creation of the United States of America, the federal constitution, unlike the treaties establishing the EU, should not be understood as a compact among the states. The Constitution's Preamble deliberately begins with the phrase, "We the People," not "we the states." The Constitution's structure, moreover, was designed to incorporate the state and national governments into a common governmental framework, not to keep them separate and distinct from one another. In particular, the state and federal governments were to function synchronously as elements in the Constitution's complex system of checks and balances. As James Madison put it in *Federalist 51*:

> In the compound republic of America, the power surrendered by the people is first divided between two distinct governments, and then the portion to each subdivided among distinct and separate departments. Hence a double security arises to the rights of the people. The different departments will control each other, at the same time that each will be controlled by itself.[7]

Federal checks on the states would consistent of four elements. First, Article I, Section 10 of the Constitution prohibited the states, from among other things, confiscating property by debasing the currency, from engaging in piracy, and from depriving citizens of due process. Article III of the Constitution established the principle of federal judicial supremacy, which has allowed the federal courts to regularly strike down state and local actions. The Constitution's supremacy clause would mean that federal law would supersede state laws with which it might conflict. Moreover, the very existence of a national government would compel the citizens and officials of each state to contend with voices and interests beyond their own borders. This, said James Madison in *Federalist 51*, would improve the quality of public decision making by "enlarging the sphere" of political discussion.

The states, for their part would possess several ways to check the actions of the federal government. The state legislatures would appoint members of the federal Senate as well as appoint the presidential electors who would choose the president. As Madison put it, "Each of the principle branches of the federal government will owe its existence more or less to the favor of the state governments."[8] According to the

10th Amendment, the states would continue to possess all powers not delegated to Congress. And, in an emergency, the states might even band together to form a political and even military opposition to a tyrannical federal government.[9]

The Brief Rise and Long Fall of the National Government's Power

During the earliest years of the Republic, several factors combined to enhance the stature of the new federal government. The first of these was the deportment of President George Washington. Washington understood that his conduct in office would influence the way in which Americans viewed not only the presidency, but the new nation as well. He made a point of touring the country, making public appearances and always comporting himself with great dignity so as to build respect for his office.[10]

Virtually everything Washington did set a precedent.[11] Washington's proclamation of American neutrality in the 1793 war between Britain and France, followed by the signing of "Jay's treaty" in 1794, normalizing trade relations with Britain, established the principle of presidential primacy in the realm of foreign relations. It was Washington, moreover, who insisted that the president be addressed as "Mr. President," a respectful and dignified form of address, but not suggestive of the exaggerated courtesies favored by monarchies. Washington sent regular messages to Congress, and made a regular appearance and speech—the forerunner of today's State of the Union address. Washington took firm control over major government appointments, including, in 1795, making the first recess appointment. Washington also made it a practice to call meetings of the secretaries of the new government's departments, laying the foundations for the president's cabinet. Washington invented the principle of "executive privilege" when he refused to give the House documents it requested regarding a diplomatic matter. Subsequent presidents expanded the idea that presidents were not obligated to give Congress records of their deliberations. The Supreme Court ultimately recognized the doctrine in the 1974 case of *U.S. v. Nixon* when presidents were held to possess executive privilege though, in the matter at hand, Nixon was ordered to give Congress the "Watergate tapes" that recorded meetings in the oval office.[12] And, by refusing to run for a third term, Washington created the two-term tradition, broken only by Franklin D. Roosevelt, and codified in 1951 by the Constitution's 22nd Amendment.

A second important factor contributing to the standing of the national government was the fact that many members of the initial group of high-ranking national officials were what historians Stanley Elkins and Eric McKitrick called, "young men of the revolution."[13] That is, those politicians who sought national, rather than state or local office tended to be veterans of the Revolutionary War or members of the Continental Congress who had come to possess a national perspective and a firm commitment to the cause of national unity. One of the most important of these individuals was Chief Justice John Marshall who led the High Court from 1801 to 1835. Marshall had been an officer in the revolutionary army, serving with George Washington during the winter at Valley Forge. Marshall (along with James Madison) served in the 1788 Virginia convention called to ratify the proposed new constitution. Later, Marshall was one of the commissioners sent to France to represent the United States in naval negotiations. Marshall became popular throughout America for firmly refusing French Foreign Minister Talleyrand's demand for a bribe in what came to be known as the XYZ Affair. Marshall was elected to Congress and subsequently appointed secretary of state.

Thus, when President John Adams appointed Marshall as chief justice in 1801, Marshall had already committed his life to the cause of the national government. As chief justice, Marshall wrote a number of key decisions affirming federal judicial supremacy and strengthening the power of the national government. These, of course, included *McCulloch v. Maryland* (1819) which declared that the Constitution's "necessary and proper" clause gave Congress the power to take actions "implied" by even if not explicitly delegated in Article I, Section 8; *Cohens v. Virginia* (1821) which affirmed the supremacy of federal law over state law; and *Gibbons v. Ogden* (1824) which offered a broad definition of commerce between the states and affirmed that federal law superseded state law in this realm. Today, the Constitution's commerce clause, broadly interpreted by the courts, is among the most important underpinnings of federal power.

A third factor that enhanced the stature of the new federal government was the War of 1812. In terms of its military objectives, the war was a disaster. The "war hawk" faction of Southerners and Westerners in Congress, led by House Speaker Henry Clay, believed that America could expand its domain by conquering Canada. The invasion of Canada, though, was a total failure and a British punitive expedition landed on America's coast and burned the nation's new capital, Washington, D.C. During the war, popular support for the barely two-decade-old nation waned as a British blockade sharply reduced American trade and depressed the economy. The New England states, which had opposed the war from the beginning, even threatened to secede from the Union to form their own confederation.

During the winter of 1815, however, events in Louisiana electrified the nation. Frontier general Andrew Jackson smashed a British army attempting to seize New Orleans. The Battle of New Orleans was fought after the U.S. had already agreed to a peace treaty with England but news of the end of the war had not reached far-off Louisiana in time to stop the engagement.[14] After two years of bad news and popular malaise, Jackson's victory produced celebrations throughout the nation. Jackson, who came to be known as "Old Hickory," had made himself America's greatest hero, a living legend and a future president. Even more important, pride in Jackson's victory lit the spark of what was to become pride in America. Though the war had failed to achieve its aims, it had begun the slow process of transforming citizens' attachments to their states into a sense of American nationalism.

The States' Rights Coalition

In 1828, Andrew Jackson was elected America's seventh president. Jackson was a proponent of presidential power and national power vis à vis the states. Among Jackson's most important actions as president was his determination to oppose South Carolina's claim that states possessed the power to nullify the application of federal laws within their own territory. What came to be known as the *Nullification Crisis* began with opposition throughout the South to high tariffs on European manufactured goods. During this period of American history, the tariff was a central political issue, pitting the North whose industries sought protective tariffs, against the South which, as an importer of manufactured goods and a low-cost producer of agricultural exports, favored free trade. In 1828, John C. Calhoun who had been John Quincy Adams's vice president and subsequently became Jackson's vice president, anonymously drafted an "Exposition and Protest." In this document, Calhoun put forward South Carolina's claim that it had the right to prevent the federal government from undertaking any actions within the state's own territory that were deemed by the state legislature to run counter to the state's interests. Calhoun was following firmly in the footsteps of Thomas Jefferson and James Madison who had secretly drafted what came to be called the Kentucky and Virginia Resolutions of 1798 and 1799. In response to the federal Alien and Sedition Acts, Jefferson and Madison had asserted that the states had the right, individually and collectively, to declare unconstitutional federal laws null and void.[15]

The nullification issue remained hypothetical until 1832 when Jackson signed tariff legislation deemed injurious by South Carolinians. By this time, Jackson had broken with Calhoun and denied him another vice-presidential nomination. The South Carolina legislature appointed Calhoun to the U.S. Senate where he now openly advocated the doctrine of nullification. At Calhoun's urging, a state convention was called in South Carolina that declared the new tariff as well as prior tariffs to be null and void within South Carolina. President Jackson responded to the South Carolinians by securing the enactment of a "Force Bill," authorizing him to use troops to enforce the tariff.[16] Jackson declared himself to be ready to lead an army to South Carolina if it should become necessary but a compromise ended the crisis. Jackson signed a new tariff bill lowering rates to appease the South Carolinians and rescinded the Force Bill. South Carolina rescinded its nullification ordinance but not before making a symbolic point by nullifying the about-to-be repealed Force Bill. Jackson had been willing to compromise but had shown his determination to preserve the Union by military force if necessary.

Jackson was a strong proponent of national power. Ironically, however, after Jackson left office the political party that he and his followers had built, now calling itself the Democrats, weakened the national government. The Democratic party had been constructed as a congeries of state party organizations. Within each state, a clique of party notables reigned supreme, controlling political nominations, patronage positions and, when the birth of the Whig party in the 1830s reignited inter-party competition, state party notables directed the armies of party workers charged with mobilizing voters. Each state's paramount party leaders often had themselves appointed to the U.S. Senate by the state legislatures they controlled.

After the departure of their supreme leader, Old Hickory, these state party notables saw no reason to defer to the wishes of meddlesome outsiders, such as presidents, when it came to managing the affairs of their own states. From their posts in the U.S. Senate, state party leaders became a log-rolling coalition for state power or states' rights coalition, confining the federal government to a narrow range of activities and limiting its revenues to customs duties and the proceeds from public land sales. Each clique of state party leaders controlled its own state and was united with other state party leaders in agreeing that the federal government should refrain from bothering them and should leave most matters of governance in the hands of the states. The leaders of the Southern states were especially vehement members of this states' rights coalition, seeing in the sovereignty of the states the best security against outside efforts to interfere with slavery. The regime produced by the states' rights coalition is often called one of "dual federalism," implying a division of functions between the federal and state governments. The division, though, was unequal. From the 1830s to the 1930s, excepting the brief interlude of the Civil War, Americans were governed primarily by their states with the federal government playing a distinctly secondary role.

The Civil War and Reconstruction

During the Civil War, in which the Southern states mobilized their militia forces to support secession from the Union, President Abraham

Lincoln expanded the role of the presidency and power of the national government more generally. With the fall of Fort Sumter and the outbreak of the Civil War, President Lincoln issued a series of executive orders for which he had no clear legal basis. Without even calling Congress into session, Lincoln combined the Northern state militias into a 90-day national volunteer force, called for 40,000 new volunteers, enlarged the regular army and navy, diverted $2 million in unspent appropriations to military needs, instituted censorship of the U.S. mails, ordered a blockade of the Southern ports, suspended the writ of habeas corpus in the border states and ordered the arrest by military police of individuals whom he deemed to be guilty of engaging in or "contemplating" treasonous actions.

The departure of virtually all the Southern Democrats from both the House and Senate meant that the coalition for state power that normally kept the federal government a small and toothless institution had, at least temporarily, disappeared. Lincoln used the absence of the normally solid bloc of states' rights Southern Democrats, along with claims of wartime emergency to substantially increase the size and reach of the federal government particularly in the realm of finance.

Before the war, Congress had sharply limited the federal government's resources to safeguard the primacy of the states. The war, however, created a justification for an enormous expansion of the federal government's financial base. Accordingly, Lincoln called Congress into special session in 1861 and pointed to the need for an escalation in revenues to support the war effort. One result was the enactment of the 1861 Revenue Act which established America's first federal income tax. Subsequently, Lincoln and Treasury Secretary Salmon Chase persuaded Congress to authorize the issuance of $50 million in Treasury notes, redeemable in gold or silver specie, to meet military payrolls.

With financial needs increasing, Lincoln and Chase turned to Congress again, proposing an expedient suggested to Lincoln by an Illinois entrepreneur. The president asked Congress to authorize the Treasury to authorize the issuance of $150 million in paper currency, not redeemable in specie, to meet military expenses. These notes were authorized by the 1862 Legal Tender Act which created America's first national paper currency, declared to be "lawful money and a payment of all debts public and private."[17] The notes were nicknamed "greenbacks" because they were printed on both sides in green ink. During the course of the war, Congress authorized the issuance of nearly $450 million in paper currency by the Treasury and by the newly created national banks. The greenbacks gave the national government direct control over the money supply and a flexible capacity to fund its operations. As you might have guessed, the Civil War greenbacks were the direct forebears of the paper dollars in your wallet today.

Finally, needing still more money for the war, Lincoln and Chase turned to an Ohio banker, Jay Cooke, and asked him to place $500 million in government bonds that could not be sold to domestic banks or foreign investors. Cooke developed a plan to market these securities to ordinary citizens who had never before purchased government bonds. He thought he could appeal to the patriotism of ordinary Americans, and he believed that widespread ownership of government bonds would give ordinary Americans a greater concern for their nation's welfare.[18] Cooke established a network of 2500 sales agents throughout the North and used the press to promote the idea that purchasing government securities was both a patriotic duty and a wise investment. In every community, Republican party organizations worked hand in hand with Cooke's sales agents, providing what historian Eric McKitrick calls the "continual affirmation of purpose" needed to sustain popular support and the regime's finances through four long years of war.[19] Cooke's idea was used again during World Wars I and II and Cooke's bonds are the forebears of today's U.S. savings bonds.

Thus, not only did Lincoln enhance presidential power to fight the war, he also expanded the power of the national government. Some of Lincoln's wartime measures ended with the Confederate surrender but some, like the greenbacks, remained in place. And all, including the federal income tax and "federalization" of the state militias, constituted precedents for the future.

During the period of "Reconstruction" in the aftermath of the war, Congress responded to turmoil in the South and Southern efforts to restore white rule in the region by proposing three important constitutional amendments—the 13th Amendment (ratified in 1865), abolishing slavery, the 14th Amendment (ratified in 1868) which prohibited the sates from depriving citizens of rights to which they were entitled by the federal constitution and the 15th Amendment (ratified in 1870), prohibiting the states from depriving citizens of voting rights on the basis of race. Each of these amendments included an enforcement clause, giving the federal government the power to act against state efforts to abridge the rights guaranteed by these amendments. Enforcement, particularly of the 14th and 15th Amendments, would eventually become a major vehicle for the expansion of federal power.

During the 1870s, the North grew tired of the turmoil and bloodshed associated with Reconstruction. After 1876, Reconstruction was brought to a close and important elements of the prewar regime were rebuilt. Blacks were disfranchised throughout the South and white rule restored. As white Democrats regained their places in the House and Senate, the prewar coalition for state power reasserted itself, with senators, in particular, determined to reassert their own places as leaders of quasi-autonomous states. For a time, this coalition exercised considerable power, protecting the South's emergent system of racial segregation and, in alliance with pro-business forces, using states' rights as a rubric for blocking proposed federal legislation that intruded upon property rights. The alliance of states' rights and property rights forces in the Congress also sought, through the vigorous practice of senatorial courtesy, to ensure that appointees to the federal bench would be solicitous of both private property and the sovereignty of the states.[20] The Supreme Court decision that epitomizes this alliance is the 1918 case of *Hammer v. Dagenhart* in which the Court struck down a statute prohibiting the interstate shipment of goods manufactured with the use of child labor. The statute did not outlaw the production of such goods within states and only prohibited their interstate shipment seemingly in keeping with congressional power under Article 1, Section 8, to regulate commerce between the states. The Court, however, declared that the intent had been to outlaw the use of child labor and that the statutory language had been a ruse.[21]

Progressivism

During the late 19th and early 20th centuries, Progressivism undermined this alliance of states' rights and property rights forces and paved the way for an expansion of national power. Progressivism was a political movement that took hold in the U.S. at the turn of the century, linking important elements of the business community with upper-middle-class, old-stock Americans who opposed continued immigration and were angered by the political corruption that seemed to be commonplace in America at that time. Progressives believed that the national government could be a powerful instrument for the betterment of society and were willing to give their political backing to politicians who shared their views. Progressives also championed political reform. In particular, Progressives attributed many of the ills of the political process to the political party "machines" that dominated politics in a number of states and major metropolitan areas. From the Progressive perspective the party machines fostered corruption and, perhaps even worse, contributed to the political power of the immigrant groups who were among the machines' chief clients.

Accordingly, Progressive reformers campaigned vigorously against machine politics and during the late 19th and early 20th centuries were able to introduce reforms at both the state and national levels designed to weaken the power of the political parties and loose their hold on the political process. Among the two most important of these Progressive reforms were civil service, introduced at the federal level by the 1887 Pendleton Act, followed by numerous state and local acts, and the requirement of primary elections for the nomination of candidates for every office below the presidency. Presidential primaries were introduced by some states in the early 20th century but did not become dominant until the 1970s. These party reforms weakened political party organizations and, in turn, encouraged members of Congress to throw off party discipline in the House and Senate. The collapse of party discipline was emblemized by the 1910 "revolt" against House Speaker Joe Cannon which stripped the leader of many of his powers and allowed members greater freedom of action when it came to voting. This decline in party discipline reduced the power of congressional leaders and gave the presidency a more central role in American political life. In this new political order, the ability of the states' rights coalition to exercise power through Congress was reduced.

At the same time, the support of property rights forces for state ascendency also waned. Some of America's most important corporate chieftains including J.P. Morgan and John D. Rockefeller agreed with Progressives that federal power could be useful. These business leaders began to see uniform federal regulation as preferable to a host of disparate state rules and saw in federal regulation a mechanism for controlling national markets and limiting market access by new firms.[22] Under the banner of Progressivism, this alliance of major business leaders and middle-class reformers supported the creation of a more energetic national government led by the president rather than Congress, and new federal bureaucracies that would expand the reach of national administrative power.

As the leaders of the executive branch and of the national government, if given a chance, presidents will usually work to bolster the power of both by undertaking or supporting actions that will enhance the administrative, extractive and enforcement or coercive powers of the national government. That is, presidents will tend to support actions that strengthen the institutions of the executive branch, solidify the tax base needed to support these institutions, and bolster the police and military forces controlled by the executive.[23] Congress had held the power of the presidency in check for most of the 19th century, but during the Progressive era, the power of the presidency was unleashed.

Presidents Theodore Roosevelt, William Howard Taft and Woodrow Wilson helped bring about a major expansion of the federal government, including a host of new federal regulations, the creation of the Department of Commerce and Labor, new powers for the Interstate Commerce Commission, creation of the Federal Reserve and Federal Trade Commission, and a constitutional amendment (the 16th) authorizing a national income tax. Even the unassuming Warren Harding worked to enhance presidential control of the federal government's budget by supporting the creation of a Bureau of the Budget (today's White House Office of Management and Budget) in 1921. During this same period, adoption of the 17th Amendment reduced the power of the state governments by requiring direct popular election of senators, rather than permitting them to be appointed by the state legislatures.

All in all, during the Progressive era the United States began to build a more powerful federal government. Strengthened presidents and the heads of new federal agencies worked to expand the power of the national government they led. At the same time, the nation's most dynamic political groups and forces started to look to the national government for programs and policies to serve their interests.

The ascendance of political forces and politicians and with a more national outlook during the Progressive era and, subsequently, the New Deal period, also paved the way for the Supreme Court's rediscovery of the 14th Amendment. The Supreme Court may lag behind, but it seldom stands for long against the prevailing political forces of the day, especially when these control the White House. As ratified in 1868, Section 1 of the 14th Amendment, as noted above, prohibited the states from depriving their citizens of rights to which they were entitled under the federal constitution. For the next several decades, however, the 14th Amendment was all but ignored by the courts. During the Progressive era, and increasingly in the 1930s, the Supreme Court began to rule that the 14th Amendment implied that provisions of the Bill of Rights applied to the states as well as the federal government. This idea was called "incorporation," and eventually all ten amendments constituting the federal constitution's Bill of Rights were incorporated and thus applied to actions by the states. This incorporation of the Bill of Rights represented an enormous limitation upon the traditional police power of the states and an expansion of the power of the federal courts to overturn state court decisions and state laws. Later, of course, the 14th Amendment became the constitutional basis for federal civil rights laws which, again, expanded the power of the national government.

The New Deal

The growth of federal power accelerated during the New Deal. Against the backdrop of the nation's greatest economic crisis, and with the support of overwhelming Democratic majorities in the Congress, President Franklin D. Roosevelt presided over an enormous expansion of the role of the federal government. The Progressive presidents had already begun to expand the administrative capabilities of the federal government and FDR more than followed suit. During his first 100 days in office, sometimes called the "First New Deal," Roosevelt and his advisers introduced some 14 new programs, each administered by a new government agency. These included creation of the Federal Deposit Insurance Corporation, the Securities and Exchange Commission, the Agricultural Adjustment Administration and the Civilian Conservation Corps. Between 1935 and 1938, sometimes called the "Second New Deal," Roosevelt presided over the passage of still more legislation including the Social Security Act and the National Labor Relations Act.

To administer these and hundreds of other pieces of legislation required the creation of a score of new agencies and the recruitment of hundreds of thousands of additional federal workers.

Constitutionally speaking, the growth of federal power depended upon the Supreme Court's willingness to broaden the scope of congressional power under the Constitution's commerce clause. In the states' rights era, the Court had interpreted the commerce clause narrowly, sharply restricting federal power. After Roosevelt threatened to increase the Court's size and appointed new justices, three major decisions of the New Deal court overturned earlier decisions like *Hammer v. Dagenhart* and gave an expansive interpretation to Congress's power to regulate commerce between the states. In *NLRB v. Jones & Laughlin Steel Corp* (1937), the Court declared that the constitutional power to regulate commerce was the power to enact, "all appropriate legislation" needed to promote commerce and ensure its safety.[24] In *U.S. v. Darby* (1941), the Court expressly overruled *Hammer v. Dagenhart* and said that the power to regulate commerce included the power to regulate production. In this case the Court famously brushed aside the 10th Amendment which reserves to the states all power not explicitly delegated to the federal government as a meaningless "truism."[25] In *Wickard v. Filburn* (1942), the Court declared that virtually any activity related to commerce, however indirectly, could be regulated by Congress.[26] With these three decisions, the commerce power became a bulwark of federal power, justifying federal legislation in realms ranging from manufacturing to discrimination in public accommodations, to even the cultivation of marijuana.

The growth of the federal government increased still again during World War II, when numerous new agencies were created to support the war effort in every area from the mobilization of troops, to the production of supplies and munitions, to maintaining civilian morale. The war added to the government's administrative capacity—which it did not surrender in the post-war era. Today, the executive branch, overseen by the president, consists of 15 government departments as well as some 70 independent agencies and a host of boards, commissions and quasi-public entities. Each of these departments and agencies consists, in turn, of a host of offices, bureaus, services, agencies, authorities, commissions and other subdivisions—more than 500 in the government departments, alone. The oldest department is the Department of State, created in 1789 and the newest is Homeland Security created in the wake of the 9-11 terrorist attacks. Many of these bureaucratic entities possess the power to make rules directly affecting citizens. Others agencies, such as the Department of Defense (DoD), do not have such authority but even agencies without formal rule-making power develop policies and manage programs that can have a substantial impact on every citizen. DoD, for example, manages the nation's military efforts and its success and failures have what might be called existential implications for Americans.

Each of the 15 government departments is led by a secretary, who is a member of the president's cabinet. Reporting to the secretary is a deputy secretary, while individual offices and activities are led by undersecretaries and assistant secretaries. The major independent agencies, such as the Social Security Administration, are usually headed by a senior official whose title might be commissioner, administrator or director and who is, in turn supported by deputies and assistant deputies. Government departments range in size from tiny Department of Education which employs only about 4200 individuals to the massive Department of Defense, which oversees some 700,000 civilian employees and 1.3 million military personnel. DoD is also responsible for maintaining the military readiness of 1.1 million reserve and National Guard troops. The independent agencies also vary in size. The Social Security Administration employs about 60,000 individuals while some of the smaller agencies are staffed by only a few dozen individuals.

In addition to these formal agencies of the federal government, America's federal bureaucracy includes a number of entities whose precise legal status is ambiguous. These are the so-called "quasis." The quasis are hybrid organizations that exercise public power under congressional charters while remaining at least partially in private hands. These include such government sponsored enterprises (GSE) as the Corporation for Public Broadcasting, the Legal Services Corporation and the National Passenger Railroad Corporation. One important form of quasi is the Federally Funded Research and Development Center (FFRDC), a type of private entity organized at the government's initiative to provide contract services to the government. The oldest and best known FFRDC is the Rand Corporation, created in 1948 to undertake research for the U.S. military.

Thus, since the New Deal, the administrative capability of the federal government has increased dramatically. In 1930, the federal government employed slightly more than 900,000 workers, many working for the postal service. Today, if we include the legions of contract workers who sit alongside federal workers in most offices, the number of federal civilian employees may be close to 10 million. The federal agencies and their millions of employees allow the federal government to collect information, to develop plans and to manage programs throughout the nation.

During his administration, President Roosevelt also increased the extractive or revenue producing capacity of the federal government. The Constitution's 16th Amendment, allowing the levying of an income tax, was ratified in 1913. Prior to the New Deal, however, a high tax threshold and numerous exemptions meant that only about 3 percent of

American adults were subject to the tax. These individuals were expected to file a tax return on which they reported their previous year's income and to make whatever payment might be required. The system was one that depended upon more-or-less voluntary compliance by a small number of well-to-do individuals. This, coupled with low rates, meant that income taxation was not, at first, a major source of federal revenue.

During the 1930s, the Roosevelt administration raised rates and closed a number of loopholes but did not fundamentally change the reach of the federal income tax.[27] By 1940, however, the government faced sharply increased costs for military preparedness and possible mobilization for war. President Roosevelt and the Congress reached a consensus on the need for higher tax rates and the development of a tax system that would expand the number of individuals subject to income taxation.[28] Hence, the 1940 Revenue Act lowered the income threshold for taxation, adding nearly two million new taxpayers and the 1941 Revenue Act lowered the threshold again, adding another two million taxpayers so that about five million Americans would now be subject to income taxation.[29]

The 1942 Revenue Act, adopted in the wake of the Pearl Harbor attack, was a turning point in the history of American income taxation. The Act raised rates, cut exemptions and lowered the threshold of income subject to taxation so that some 40 million Americans would now be required to pay income taxes.[30] Treasury Secretary Henry Morgenthau and his economic advisors strongly advocated the adoption of a permanent system of payroll withholding, already being used for Social Security taxes and, briefly, in the 1942 "Victory Tax," which would increase the efficiency of collection and sharply reduce noncompliance. Payroll withholding would produce a steady rather than episodic flow of income into the government's coffers and would provide data from employers, via the soon to be ubiquitous third-party information return, to compare with taxpayers' own accounts of their incomes. These data would allow the Internal Revenue Service (IRS) to easily determine whether taxpayers' filings were truthful and accurate. The idea of payroll withholding was presented by Treasury as a device designed to help taxpayers by allowing them to meet their obligations, as Assistant Treasury Secretary Randolph Paul told Congress, "with a maximum of convenience and a minimum of hardship."[31] Treasury's main goal, of course, was to increase taxpayer compliance and generate more revenue. Payroll withholding was the central feature of the 1943 Revenue Act which raised rates, yet again, and mandated "collection at the source."

The result of the gradual increase in tax rates mandated every year between 1940 and the end of the war, accompanied by payroll withholding, was conversion of the income tax from a minor tax levied on wealthy Americans into a major tax levied on all Americans—from a class tax to a mass tax. Before 1940, the federal income tax had barely produced $1 billion per year, but by 1945, the income tax was generating $40 billion per year in revenue. During the course of the war, federal income tax receipts were $164 billion, more than half the cost of the conflict.[32] Tax rates declined after the war but never returned to their prewar levels. Today, the federal government's vast bureaucratic apparatus is funded by a system of taxation, centered around the income tax, that generates nearly $3.5 trillion in revenue each year. This amount dwarfs the revenue of any state (California is highest at about $160 billion) and is more than three times the revenue of all the states added together.

Subordination of the States

Since the 1930s, the federal government's enormous flow of cash has played an important role in its subordination of the states. Many New Deal era programs took the form of what are known as grants-in-aid to the states. A grant-in-aid is federal funding given to the states for a particular purpose. Each state may choose to accept or decline the grant and whatever conditions might be attached to it. In the 1920s the Supreme Court had declared that such grants raised no constitutional questions since the states were free to accept or reject them.[33] Such grants were also supported by the emergent *conservative coalition* of Southern Democrats and Republicans who, like the earlier states' rights/ property rights coalition, remained resistant to the further growth of federal power. Southerners were anxious to protect the region's system of segregation while some Republicans, mainly those representing small business, opposed increased taxes and new federal authority over the economy. By 1935, federal grants to the states, including emergency relief funds, amounted to more than $2 billion per year. Today, that amount has grown to more than $600 billion per year—about a third of the states' budgets—and covers programs in health, education, employment, housing, food and nutrition, social services and a host of other areas. The regime of grants-in-aid in which states could exercise considerable discretion in the use of federal funding came to be called *cooperative federalism* and seemed to pose no threat to the autonomy of state governments. It turned out, however, that the states had been lured by the carrot of federal grants and would now face the stick of federal mandates.

Gradually, during the 1960s, even as some new federal programs like Medicaid continued to rely on the states for implementation, state discretion over the use of federal funding came under attack and cooperative federalism gave way to what is variously called *regulated* or *coercive* federalism. In this period, the Civil Rights Movement weakened the conservative coalition while the Southern states' defense of segregation tarnished the image of state government. During the Kennedy and

Johnson administrations, liberal members of Congress and federal officials became convinced that the states could not be trusted to implement national purposes.[34] In the Economic Opportunity Act, a central component of Lyndon Johnson's War on Poverty, for example, federal funds went directly to cities, counties and local groups, bypassing state governments, altogether.[35] Over the ensuing years, state discretion was often limited by legislation that attached requirements and conditions to federal grants-in-aid. For example, the 1973 Rehabilitation Act required state governments to make public transit accessible to disabled persons as a condition of continued receipt of federal funds for public transit. The 2010 Affordable Care Act (ACA) required the states to expand Medicaid coverage as a condition for the continued receipt of Medicaid funds. The Supreme Court ultimately struck down this particular requirement. However, numerous federal grant programs impose mandates on the states and with few exceptions, the states accept federal regulation in order to continue receiving the funds that so vital to their daily operations.

Coercive Capacities

A third key dimension of governmental power is coercion. In the 19th century the federal government had little coercive capability. All internal policing was handled by the states with virtually no federal law enforcement presence in the nation. Virtually all criminal cases were handled by state courts. Indeed, there was virtually no federal criminal law to enforce. The first significant federal police force was the Prohibition Enforcement Agency established in 1919 to enforce the National Prohibition Act. Later, President Roosevelt created the Federal Bureau of Investigation (FBI) which quickly became America's first national police force and the spearhead of a substantial national police apparatus. At the same time, with the brief exception of the Civil War period, the nation's military forces were mainly composed of state militias. Recall that James Madison thought that in an emergency the states could mobilize their militias to stop a tyrannical federal government.

Today, the federal government's coercive capabilities have increased substantially. The U.S. Constitution mentioned only three criminal offenses—counterfeiting, piracy and treason—leaving all the others to the states to define and punish. Today, there are more than 4000 federal criminal statutes enacted by Congress to deal with such matters as environmental protection, securities regulation, corporate governance, product and workplace safety, terrorism and a myriad of other matters. In addition, more than 10,000 federal regulations promulgated by administrative agencies carry criminal or civil penalties.[36] In many cases, federal criminal law overlaps or duplicates state law but, generally speaking, federal law preempts state law and, if they choose to claim it, federal law enforcement personnel will have jurisdiction over an investigation where either federal or state law might apply.

To maintain the federal government's ability to enforce federal criminal law more than 120,000 agents work for 22 law enforcement agencies including the FBI, the Department of Homeland Security and the Drug Enforcement Administration. This number, though growing quickly, still equals less than 20 percent of the number of state and local police officers. Most state and local officers, however, are engaged in patrolling or investigating mundane local crimes. Federal law enforcement agencies were created or expanded to deal with major problems that crossed state borders, including narcotics, organized crime and terrorism. Tens of thousands of additional federal agents are employed by agencies that have no obvious law enforcement responsibilities. These agents are tasked with enforcing rules and regulations promulgated by their agencies.

Today, virtually every federal agency—even the most seemingly mundane—employs its own armed agents. Thousands of armed agents are currently employed by bureaucracies such as the Bureau of Land Management, the Fish and Wildlife Service, the Environmental Protection Agency, the Labor Department, the Department of Education and the National Oceanic and Atmospheric Administration (NOAA) Fisheries Office of Law Enforcement.[37] These are agencies not usually seen as having involvement in criminal matters but, increasingly, these regulatory and service agencies are mandated to enforce the growing number of federal criminal statutes and employ armed agents to do so.

NOAA agents, for example, have been involved in a number of recent controversies. In 2012 the agency was widely criticized for ordering 46,000 rounds of jacketed hollow-point bullets, a form of ammunition designed to cause maximum damage to the internal organs and tissue of human targets. The press wondered why weather forecasters would need this type of ammunition, generally banned under international law. A NOAA spokesperson clarified the matter, explaining that the ammunition was not intended for weather forecasters but was, instead, being issued to agents of its Fisheries Office.[38]

The NOAA Fisheries Office also made headlines in 2008 when a group of NOAA agents, armed with assault rifles, raided a Miami business suspected of having violated a NOAA regulation pertaining to trading in coral. It turned out that the coral had been properly obtained but the business owner had failed to complete some of the necessary forms. She was fined and sentenced to one year's probation.[39] Quite possibly the assault rifles had not been needed to deal with this bookkeeping dispute.

In still another case involving NOAA, Nancy Black, a well-known marine biologist and operator of whale-watching boats, saw her home and office raided by NOAA agents—also brandishing assault rifles. Black was charged with offenses relating to the allegation that one of her boat captains had whistled at a humpback whale that approached his boat. Such whistling, if proven, could constitute illegal harassment of a whale, a serious offense under NOAA regulations implementing the federal Marine Mammal Protection Act of 1972. The government lacked evidence to prove illegal whistling but claimed that Black had altered a video of the event, itself a violation.

Federal law is enforced by federal courts. Federal courts hear barely 3 percent of the number of cases heard by state courts, though about 80 percent of state and local cases involve misdemeanors. Federal cases tend to be more important and, moreover, if the federal government has any interest in a matter it is likely to be investigated by federal law enforcement and heard in a federal court. Over the past several decades, the federal courts have given a very broad definition to what constitutes a federal question under Article III of the Constitution. Federal courts have stripped the states of much of their sovereign immunity and 11th Amendment protection against law suits. Federal courts, moreover, have expanded the role of the 1871 Civil Rights Act, codified as 42 U.S.C. 1983. Section 1983 lay dormant for a number of decades but was rediscovered by the federal courts during the civil rights era and is, today, the most important single vehicle for federal court constitutional rulings against state governments and their officials.[40] Section 1983 allows individuals to sue state or local governments when an official acting "under color of law" deprives them of rights created by the Constitution or federal statutes.

Section 1983 provides a federal cause of action for individuals who have been victims of discrimination by state and local officials because of their race, gender, sexual orientation and several other factors. Generally speaking, when a statute creates a federal cause of action, federal court jurisdiction preempts whatever jurisdiction a state court might have had. In 1976, Congress facilitated 1983 litigation through the adoption of the Civil Rights Attorney's Fees Awards Act. This piece of legislation awards attorneys' fees to victorious parties, encouraging lawyers to take cases for impecunious plaintiffs. In recent years more than 35,000 civil rights suits have been filed each year against state and local officials in federal courts, not counting prisoner rights suits which are also filed under Section 1983.[41]

During the 1980s several Supreme Court decisions seemed to suggest that the Supreme Court was not entirely unsympathetic to the idea of federalism. But these decisions depended upon the presence of Chief Justice Rehnquist and Justice Sandra Day O'Connor. O'Connor was especially significant because she was the only justice in decades to have served in a state legislature. Presidents generally appoint justices who attended elite national universities, served on the federal bench and almost invariably have a national outlook. Over time, moreover, the Supreme Court generally follows the lead of the president. And, the president leads the *national* government.

Law enforcement is one element of the federal government's coercive capability. The other is military force. Over the past century, the states have been almost completely disarmed while the federal government has acquired a near monopoly of military force in America. Colonial militiamen made up the bulk of Washington's Continental Army. Short tours of duty reduced their military effectiveness but when they returned home, they held their communities to the patriot cause and deprived the British of locally produced food and supplies.

Once independent, the United States continued to rely primarily on state militiamen backed by a tiny regular army garrisoning frontier regions. The federal Militia Acts of 1792 and 1795 provided for the enrollment of able-bodied, free white men between ages 18 and 45 in the state militias and authorized the president to call the militias to national service for a period not to exceed three months. Most officers were appointed by the state governors. Virtually all the American soldiers who fought in the War of 1812 were state militiamen. The majority served for six months or less and their performance was spotty. In some instances, rival units refused to cooperate with one another and battles were lost because militiamen decided to return home in mid campaign. After the 1812 War, the organized state militias were supplanted by local volunteer units that drilled on weekends.[42] Some of these units, still led by officers appointed by the state governors, were used to quell civil disturbances and saw action against Native Americans. During the Civil War, the Union army consisted of a mix of state militia forces and, for the first time, conscripts drafted directly into the military service of the United States. After the war, the draft was ended and the state militias again became the backbone of America's military. In the 1870s, the state militia forces were reorganized and renamed the National Guard. At the outbreak of the Spanish American war in 1898, the Volunteer Act diluted the identities of the state guard units by requiring them to enroll troops from outside their states and gave the president rather than the governors the power to appoint all general officers and their staffs.

The 1903 Dick Act subordinated the Guard to the regular army, declaring the National Guard to be a United States force rather than a congeries of state units. State governors might continue to use Guard troops to deal with emergencies but, presidential orders superseded gubernatorial orders and, if the president summoned a guard unit for federal service, it lost its identity as a state force and was integrated into the regular army. During World War I, the army chief of staff, General Peyton March, issued General Order 73 which prohibited members of the Guard from even attaching any state insignia to their uniforms. The 1952 Armed Forces Reserve Act integrated Guard units into the military reserves, making the National Guard little more than a component of the national reserve forces. Each state had once possessed its own army. This is no longer the case. The states have been disarmed and the federal government holds a monopoly on military force.

The importance of coercive capability is not that the federal and state governments are likely to go war with one another as they did in 1860. The issue is, rather, which level of government has an unquestioned ability to prevail in political confrontations where violence is threatened. Thus, the police and military forces of the federal government were available to come to the assistance of the civil rights movement when peaceful protestors came under attack by local police as well as by armed thugs in the Southern states. Once national guardsmen were placed under federal command, and federal troops and the FBI were sent into action, there was no doubt of the outcome. There was no question of armed state resistance. Governor George Wallace of Alabama threatened to "stand in the schoolhouse door" to block integration of the University of Alabama but retreated quickly in the face of federal troops. The civil rights laws enacted by the federal government during this period superseded state laws in such realms as employment, housing public accommodations, education and voting rights. The enforcement of these laws in a hostile environment depended both upon federal judicial supremacy backed by the overwhelming law enforcement and military presence of the federal government.

The Nation and the States

Between the 1830s and the early years of the 20th century, America was dominated by a states' rights coalition, working through Congress, that held the power of the national government in check. Beginning in the Progressive era and continuing into the New Deal, as we saw, new political forces supported the construction of a more powerful and activist federal government led by the executive rather than Congress. The states are not irrelevant. In areas ranging from animal control to zoning, state and local governments are at the forefront. But where the federal government chooses to exercise its power, federal institutions, federal law, federal courts and federal law enforcement are America's dominant institutions of government.

As to checks and balances, the federal government can clearly check the states and does so every day with its mandates and judicial power. The states can do very little to check the actions of the federal government. Is this a bad thing? During the course of American history, the federal government has forced the states to end slavery, to end segregation and expanded the protections of the Constitution's Bill of Rights to the citizens of all the states. What positive checks have the states offered since the 1798–1799 Kentucky and Virginia Resolutions? Very few. So, perhaps we should not lament the eclipse of the states.

Over the past few years, of course, much has been made of the refusal of several municipalities and such states as California to enforce federal immigration laws. California proudly declared itself to be a "sanctuary state" that would not help federal authorities arrest and deport undocumented immigrants. Some have compared this refusal to that of the Northern states that refused to enforce the Fugitive Slave Law in the 1850s. This is all well and good, but in the 1850s, the federal government lacked the institutional capacity to enforce the law on its own and depended upon state cooperation. Today, the federal government controls its own massive law enforcement apparatus and a state's failure to cooperate is little more than a nuisance to Washington officials.

The public health crisis of 2020 thrust the states back into the forefront of governance. Their plenary police powers gave the states, especially those with vigorous governors, an early and important role in responding to the crisis. We should, however, take note of the fact that the states ultimately had to depend upon the resources of the federal government to acquire and deploy medical equipment and, when it came to bolstering the nation's economy during the pandemic, it was the federal government that developed and funded an enormous relief package. For all their police power, the governors directed much of their energy to entreating the federal government to provide them with more supplies and resources.

Notes

1 Michael Greenberg, "California: The State of Resistance," *The New York Review*, Jan. 17, 2019, p. 50.
2 Heather K. Gerken and Joshua Revesz, "Progressive Federalism: A User's Guide," *Democracy* 44 (Spring, 2017). https://democracyjournal.org/magazine/44/progressive-federalism-a-users-guide/.
3 75 U.S. 168 (1869).
4 Robert Higgs, *Crisis and Leviathan: Critical Episodes in the Growth of American Government* (New York: Oxford University Press, 1987).
5 Herbert Storing, *What the Anti-Federalists Were For: The Political Thought of the Opponents of the Constitution* (Chicago, IL: University of Chicago Press, 1981), ch.3.
6 Ralph A. Rossum, *Federalism, the Supreme Court and the Seventeenth Amendment: The Irony of Constitutional Democracy* (Boston, MA: Lexington Books, 2001).
7 Edward Mead Earl, ed., *The Federalist, No. 51* (New York: Modern Library, 1953), p. 339.
8 *The Federalist, No. 45*, p. 301.
9 *The Federalist, No.46*, pp. 309–311.
10 Jeffrey Tulis, *The Rhetorical Presidency* (Princeton, NJ: Princeton University Press, 1987), p. 69.

11 Fred Greenstein, *Inventing the Job of President: Leadership Style from George Washington to Andrew Jackson* (Princeton, NJ: Princeton University Press, 2009).
12 418 U.S. 663 (1974).
13 Stanley Elkins and Eric McKitrick, "The Founding Fathers: Young Men of the Revolution," *Political Science Quarterly* 76, no. 2 (June, 1961): 181–216.
14 Donald Hickey, *The War of 1812: A Forgotten Conflict*, rev. ed. (Champaign, IL: University of Illinois Press, 2012).
15 Jonathan Elliott, ed., *The Virginia and Kentucky Resolutions of 1798 and '99 With Jefferson's Original Draught Thereof* (London: Forgotten Books, 2017).
16 William Ellis, *The Union at Risk: Jacksonian Democracy, States' Rights and Nullification Crisis* (New York: Oxford University Press, 1989).
17 Margaret Myers, *A Financial History of the United States* (New York: Columbia University Press, 1970), p. 155.
18 Ellis Paxson Oberholtzer, *Jay Cooke: Financier of the Civil War* (Philadelphia, PA: Jacobs, 1907).
19 Eric L. McKitrick, "Party Politics and the Union and Confederate War Efforts," in William N. Chambers and Walter Dean Burnham, eds., *The American Party Systems: Stages of Political Development*, 2nd ed. (New York: Oxford University Press, 1975), p. 147.
20 For examples see, Rayman L. Solomon, "The Politics of Appointment and the Federal Courts' Role in Regulating America: U.S. Courts of Appeals Judgeships from T.R. to F.D.R.," *American Bar Foundation Research Journal* 9, no. 2 (Spring, 1984): 285–343.
21 247 U.S. 251 (1918).
22 Gabriel Kolko, *The Triumph of Conservatism: A Reinterpretation of American History, 1900–1916* (New York: The Free Press, 1963).
23 Benjamin Ginsberg, *Presidential Government* (New Haven, CT: Yale University Press, 2016), ch.2.
24 301 U.S. 1 (1937).
25 312 U.S. 100 (1941).
26 317 U.S. 111 (1942).
27 W. Elliot Brownlee, *Federal Taxation in America: A Short History*, 2nd ed. (New York: Cambridge University Press, 2004), p. 87.
28 Brownlee, pp. 108–109.
29 Steven A. Bank et al., *War and Taxes* (Washington, DC: Urban Institute Press, 2008), pp. 90–92.
30 Bank et al., p. 98.
31 Bank et al., p. 100.
32 Bank et al., p. 95.
33 Cynthia Cates Colella, "The United States Supreme Court and Intergovernmental Relations," in Robert Jay Dilger, ed., *American Intergovernmental Relations Today* (Englewood Cliffs, NJ: Prentice-Hall, 1986), p. 47.
34 Teerry Sanford, *Storm Over the States* (New York: McGraw-Hill, 1967).
35 Daniel Patrick Moynihan, *Maximum Feasible Misunderstanding* (New York: Free Press, 1970).
36 Paul Larkin and John-Michael Seibler, "Taking Stock of Federal Regulatory Crimes," *The Heritage Foundation*, Oct. 3, 2017. www.heritage.org/government-regulation/report/taking-stock-federal-regulatory-crimes.
37 Brian A. Reeves, "Federal Law Enforcement Officers, 2008," U.S. Department of Justice, Bureau of Justice Statistics, Office of Justice Programs, June, 2012.

58   *The States in the Federal System*

38 Robert Johnson, "This Is Why NOAA Supposedly Ordered 46,000 Rounds of Ammunition," *Business Insider*, Aug. 14, 2012. www.businessinsider.com/this-is-why-the-noaa-supposedly-ordered-46000-rounds-of-ammunition-2012-8.
39 Louise Radnofsky, Gary Fields and John R. Emshwiller, "Federal Police Ranks Swell to Enforce a Widening Array of Criminal Laws," *Wall Street Journal*, Dec. 17, 2011, p. 1.
40 Erwin Chemerinsky, *Federal Jurisdiction*, 7th ed. (New York: Wolters Kluwer, 2016), p. 512.
41 Chermerinsky, p. 512.
42 John K. Mahon, *History of the Militia and the National Guard* (New York: Macmillan, 1983), p. 84.

4 State Governors

Most, if not all, the framers of the U.S. Constitution thought that a strong executive was a necessary component of effective governance. As Alexander Hamilton observed in *Federalist 70*, "A feeble executive implies a feeble execution of the government. A feeble execution is but another phrase for a bad execution; and a government ill-executed, whatever it may be in theory, must be in practice a bad government."

Hamilton particularly viewed a unitary executive, that is an executive branch led by one person, as essential to imparting "energy" to a government and very deliberately incorporated this idea in the federal constitution even though, or perhaps because, several state governments at that time were led by plural executives or executive councils. Alexander Hamilton wrote in *Federalist 70* that a plural executive tended to "conceal faults and destroy responsibility," and to "tincture the exercise of the executive authority with a spirit of habitual feebleness and dilatoriness." Hamilton also argued that an effective executive required reasonably long tenure in office with the possibility of reappointment and "competent" authority such as veto, appointment and budgetary powers.

Accordingly, the framers placed the national government's executive power in the hands of an independently elected and unitary presidency. Presidents do not share power with other executive branch officials—they are the undisputed leaders of the executive branch. Other executive branch officials are appointed and are subject to dismissal by the president, albeit with senatorial approval in the case of major appointments. Presidents also exercise significant budgetary and other powers of governance.

Many Americans think of state governors as chief executives similar in powers and functions to presidents, albeit serving at the state level. Governors, however, are quite different from presidents. Governors have many of the responsibilities of the president but most have far less power. As to responsibility, governors work with leaders of the legislature to promote a policy agenda. Like presidents, governors prepare a budget and, like presidents, governors usually find themselves in battles with the legislature over spending and taxes. Most governors, with the consent of the legislature, appoint the leaders of major state agencies. Governors oversee the operations of the executive branch in realms ranging from healthcare and road maintenance to public safety and emergency responses to natural and manmade disasters. Governors are always held responsible for the state's fiscal health and prosperity. Governors are also expected to further their states' economic development by encouraging investment and seeking to promote the sale of the state's farm products and manufactured goods around the world.

In times of crisis, such as natural disasters or public health emergencies, governors can issue executive orders and wield the states' police powers. Despite these quasi-presidential responsibilities, governors have nowhere near the executive power of the president. To begin with, the constitutions of virtually all 50 states place governors at a legal disadvantage vis à vis state legislatures. Under the federal constitution, both Congress and the president are said to exercise implied as well as specifically enumerated powers. State constitutions, on the other hand, enumerate the powers of the executive but not those of the legislature. Courts have taken this to mean that state legislatures exercise plenary powers—limited only by specific constitutional prohibitions—while governors can exercise only those powers specifically granted to them under the state constitution.[1] As a result, in legal struggles between the governor and the legislature, it is the latter that is more likely to prevail.

Moreover, the constitutions of most states severely constrain gubernatorial powers. Many state governors possess only limited budgetary appointment and veto powers and are only elected for brief terms with no possibility of reelection. The most important constraint on gubernatorial power, though, is one that sharply distinguishes governors from presidents. Unlike presidents of the United States, most state governors share some or all their executive power with other members of a plural executive. In 44 states, the executive power is jointly exercised by several individually elected officials who may include the attorney general, state treasurer, the state auditor and the secretary of state, among other officials. In 18 of these states, even the lieutenant governor is elected separately from the governor, while in two other states the elected speaker of the state senate also serves as the lieutenant governor (see Table 4.1). All told, more than 300 separately elected officials hold major executive offices in the 50 states.[2]

Pitfalls of the Plural Executive

In states with plural executives, multiple officials serve as independent actors with no direct power to supervise one another's actions. In many states, each member of a plural executive has his or her own interest group supporters and, often, a political party affiliation different from that of the governor. Each may view the others, including the governor,

Table 4.1 Independently Elected State Officials

Position	Number of States
Governor	50
Lieutenant governor	18*
Attorney general	44
Treasurer	39
Secretary of state	37
Auditor	24
Board of Education	14
Agriculture secretary	13
Comptroller	10
Insurance commissioner	12
Public utilities commissioners	6
Land commissioner	5
Labor commissioner	4
Election administrators	4
Consumer affairs director	3
Adjutant general	1
Natural resources director	1
Commerce secretary	1

* In two additional states, Tennessee and West Virginia, the elected speaker of the Senate is also lieutenant governor. Five states have no lieutenant governor.

Source: Book of the States 2016, Table 4.10.

as political and perhaps future electoral rivals. Competition between governors and other elected executive officials can be fierce. In Montana, Missouri and Nebraska in recent years, governors have been reluctant to leave the state's borders lest the lieutenant governor take advantage of the governor's absence to undermine gubernatorial programs while serving as acting governor.[3] In Nebraska, for example, the governor's out-of-state trip allowed the lieutenant governor to cast a tie-breaking vote in the state legislature, leading to the passage of a bill that the governor had opposed. Before the governor could return, the lieutenant governor then signed the bill into law.[4]

Indeed, elected executive branch officials sometimes litigate against one another as in California where the state comptroller and attorney general recently took positions in court adverse to those of the governor.[5] Each independently elected state officer controls a portion of the executive power and must negotiate with the others when some coordinated effort is needed. Table 4.2 reorganizes the information reported by Table 4.1 on a state by state basis to show the five levels of "separately elected" (SEP) state executives as defined by Ferguson. In only six states is the governor (or

Table 4.2 "Separately Elected" State Executive Categories

SEP Level	Definition	Number of States
1	Governor along with 7+ critical policy officials elected	5
2	Governor with less than seven policy officials elected (at least 2 critical)	10
3	Governor/lieutenant governor team with some critical and some process officials elected	18
4	Governor/ lieutenant governor team with some process officials elected	11
5	Governor or governor/lieutenant governor team elected	6

These definitions come from Ferguson (2018).

Note: There were ten states assigned a half level (e.g. 2.5) that we rounded up to the nearest whole level for clarity. Process officials include the attorney general, secretary of state, treasurer and auditor.

governor along with a lieutenant gubernatorial running mate) the only elected executive official (SEP level 5). In 15 states (SEP levels 1 and 2), on the opposite end of the spectrum, the governor and at least two critical policy officials are independently elected.[6]

Plural executives can pose a number of problems. For example, in 2008, the state of California faced a massive budget deficit of approximately $40 billion annually. This deficit was partly the result of tax limitations imposed by ballot initiatives passed in previous years. To deal with the deficit, then Republican Governor Arnold Schwarzenegger developed a number of emergency measures aimed at reducing state spending by several billion dollars per year. These included a plan to reduce the salaries of most state employees until a new state budget was passed by the legislature and, additionally, to furlough hundreds of thousands of state workers several days each month.

Governor Schwarzenegger's plans were vehemently opposed by independently elected California State Controller John Chiang, a Democrat, who refused to implement the governor's directives. Chiang asserted that, not only were the governor's plans unwise, they intruded upon the controller's constitutional independence to administer the payment of state monies. According to Chiang, the California constitution gave his office, as well as those of other elected executive officials, such as the treasurer and lieutenant governor, independent power within the executive branch.[7] Eventually, California's courts ruled in favor of the governor, but not before Schwarzenegger had sued the controller twice and defended himself in a third action in which Chiang joined a state employee union suit against the governor. The governor's efforts to resolve the budget crisis could not be implemented for more than a year while these cases worked their way through the courts.

In a similar vein, in 2017 Kentucky's Republican Governor Matt Bevin issued executive orders restructuring the state's various education-related boards. Bevin's orders were opposed by Democratic Attorney General Andy Beshear, an independently elected executive official who, as it turned out, planned to run for governor in the near future. Beshear issued an ultimatum to the governor, threatening legal action if the orders were not rescinded within seven days. The governor and attorney general reached a compromise before the deadline was reached.[8] In 2019, Beshear ran for governor and unseated Bevin.

During the same year, Maine's governor and attorney general became locked in a struggle when Democratic Attorney General Janet Mills, an official chosen by the state legislature, refused to allow her office to represent Republican Governor Paul LePage in several controversial cases involving refugee admissions and Medicaid eligibility. The attorney general, who disagreed with LePage's positions, declared that she would neither represent the governor nor provide funds from her office to allow the governor to seek outside counsel. The governor sued the attorney general declaring that,

> all state agencies and the executive branch are at risk of not being able to carry out their constitutional and statutorily-mandated functions if the attorney general declines to represent them, while at the same time remaining in control and possession of the entire appropriation for state legal representation.[9]

Not only did LePage lose his case but, to add insult to injury, Mills ran against and defeated LePage in the 2018 gubernatorial race.

The consequences of multiple independently elected executives can seep down through state government to produce conflicts or incompatible policies among state agencies accountable to different elected officials. Take a Virginia case identified by legal scholar, Justin Weinstein-Tull. Two federal statutes offered federal funds to states to create an organization to protect the rights of individuals with disabilities or mental illness. Virginia created a state agency called the Virginia Office for Protection and Advocacy (VOPA). VOPA soon came into conflict with the state director of mental health hospitals over the alleged mistreatment of patients at those hospitals run by the state. The issues at stake could not be resolved administratively since the two agencies reported to different configurations of elected officials. The result was years of litigation before a decision by the U.S. Supreme Court in favor of VOPA resolving the issues in question. Eventually, the two agencies were consolidated.[10]

Independent Executive Agencies

In addition to independently chosen executive branch officials, state constitutions may also establish or allow the statutory creation of independent executive agencies over which the governor exercises little or no authority. In Virginia, according to the state website, six independent agencies do not report through any of the three branches of state government. The responsibilities of Virginia's independent agencies include: protecting the interest of consumers by regulating various businesses; operating the state lottery; administering the Virginia Workers' Compensation Act and the Crime Victims Compensation Program; administering the state-wide public employee retirement system; offering tax advantaged college savings programs; and helping with disability-related problems like abuse, neglect and discrimination. Similarly, in Texas, legislation allows certain financial regulatory agencies to become "self-directed semi-independent" (SDSI) entities outside gubernatorial control. Such entities, which include the state's banking department, real estate commission, consumer credit commission and a number of others, fund their own operations through fees they are allowed to charge for their services.

Gubernatorial power is also circumscribed by the fact that in every state a measure of executive power is surrendered to municipal governments which remain, nevertheless, subject to state supervision, and to a host of special districts over which governors exercise virtually no authority.

Thousands of special districts in every state—Illinois alone boasts more than 8000—are responsible for a host of executive functions ranging from sanitation and mosquito abatement through land development, education and the maintenance of roads, bridges and tunnels. These districts generally have elected governing boards, levy taxes and issue bonds and effectively function as states within the state. Most citizens are only vaguely aware of the operations of special districts whose governing board elections and bond issue referenda are barely publicized and attract only about 10 percent of those eligible to vote. We will have more to say about special districts in Chapter 7 where we discuss the problem of corruption in state governments.

The Elements of Gubernatorial Power

As we noted above, students of governors' institutional power generally point to several factors as affecting the power of the office. In addition to unity, these include the governor's eligibility for reelection and the governor's appointment, budgetary and veto powers. To examine the effects of these powers on policy outcomes, we employed Ferguson's 2018 coding scheme. The coding is based upon data collected by the Council of State Governments and, as noted above, uses a modified version of the scoring system originally developed by Joseph Schlesinger and updated by Thad Beyle and, subsequently, by Margaret Ferguson, to assess governors' institutional power along what can be seen as Hamiltonian dimensions. For our analysis, we defined each power as a binary variable with every state executive coded as either strong (1) or weak (0) with respect to each of these five powers (see Table 4.3). A full list of the states' executive

Table 4.3 State Executive Powers

Gubernatorial Power	Strong (1)	Weak (0)
Executive Unity	Governor/lieutenant governor team elected alone or with some process officials (n=17)	Governor elected along with critical policy officials (n=33)
Tenure Potential	Governor elected for a four-year term with unlimited reelection potential (n=12)	Two-year term, reelection capped at one or two terms, or combination of these factors (n=38)
Appointment Power	Governor either appoints or shares appointment power (n=21)	Someone else appoints (n=29)
Budget Power	Governor has full responsibility over budget (n=27)	Governor shares responsibility (n=23)
Veto Power	Governor has item veto power with either majority or supermajority needed to override (n=11)	Governor has more limited veto powers (n=39)

Note: For each power, states are coded as either strong (1) or weak (0). This is a modified version of the scoring system developed by Ferguson (2018, Table 8.4).

powers codes appears in the chapter's Appendix. These elements of gubernatorial power seem directly consistent with Alexander Hamilton's assessment of the requirements for an effective executive cited above.

Do the Institutional Powers of the Governor Matter?

The question before us is what difference these differences in power make. The framers of America's Constitution thought that executive power was an essential ingredient of good government. The dependent variables in our analysis are therefore state rankings in four critical areas of public policy in which state governments exert substantial influence: (1) public safety, (2) healthcare, (3) education and (4) the environment. These rankings are taken from several reputable organizations that specialize in evaluating state-level policy outcomes, including U.S. News and World Report and The Commonwealth Fund.[11] For each policy area, we examine several different measures. For example, in the area of healthcare, we examine the influence of gubernatorial power on affordability, prevention, hospital use, public health and health disparity. For each measure, the states are ranked from 1–50, where a lower numerical ranking means the state is performing better.

The analysis examines whether executive unity and the other measures of gubernatorial power are, as Alexander Hamilton might have predicted, associated with beneficial outcomes as indicated by states' rankings in the several policy domains.

The regression models used in the analysis also include a set of relevant controls. We include two measures of partisanship: (1) a state's democratic advantage (in terms of citizens' party affiliation) and (2) the governor's party identification.[12] By controlling for both citizen and gubernatorial partisanship, we ensure that the estimated relationship between institutional powers and policy outcomes is not driven by alignment with a particular party. The models also control for a state's economic environment, using states' unemployment rates and size of the population, using both the absolute number of residents and population density.[13]

Effects of Executive Unity

Figure 4.1 displays the estimated effects of executive unity on a state's ranking across the four policy areas under analysis. All of the estimates reveal a positive effect, and most are statistically significant. For example, in the area of healthcare, the results show that states with strong governors are associated with a 13 place improvement in their affordability ranking. Strong governors are also associated with a 12 place improvement in states' preventive health programs ranking and a 4 place improvement in their public health ("healthy lives") ranking.

Similar results are evident in elementary and secondary education; states with unified executives are associated with a 10 place increase in ranking. We also uncover positive, significant results in the areas of financial safety, emergency preparedness, climate change efforts and public transportation. The complete regression results appear in the Appendix. Taken together, the models provide strong evidence of a positive link between unified state executives and desirable outcomes across a broad range of policy areas. In this respect, strong governors definitely appear to produce more beneficial policy outcomes.

Effects of Tenure Potential

While executive unity exerts the most consistent influence, the results also demonstrate that a governor's tenure potential is positively associated with good public policy results (see Figure 4.2). These effects are strongest in the areas of healthcare and safety. We find that states whose governors have four-year terms and no term limits average a 17 place improved ranking in public health and a 14 place improved ranking in the reduction of health disparities between poor and well-to-do residents.[14] In the area of safety, tenure potential is associated with a 14 place improvement in road safety ranking and 16 place improvement in financial safety ranking. These findings are consistent with the scholarship on gubernatorial term limits, which suggests that reelection provides governors with both the experience and accountability that

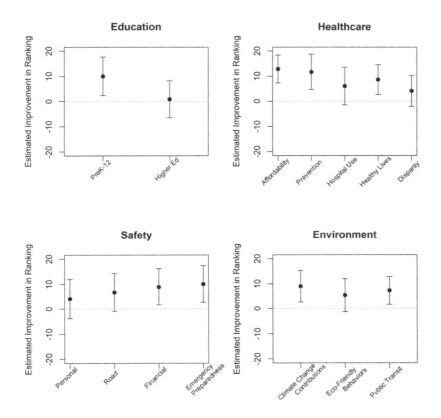

Figure 4.1 Estimated Improvement in Rankings from Executive Unity.

Note: These graphs present the estimated effect of having a unified state executive on a state's ranking across policy areas. Each estimate is presented with its 90 percent confidence interval.

bolster policy outcomes.[15] Reelected governors, and those who have the potential to be reelected, develop competence in governing their state and are motivated to produce results for which their constituents will reward them at the polls.

Take, for example, former Tennessee governor (now senator), Lamar Alexander. Alexander was elected governor in 1978. Tennessee had long limited its governors to one term but amended its constitution during Alexander's first term, allowing him to serve two consecutive terms in office. Tennessee's executive is unified with only the governor independently elected. The speaker of the state Senate holds the title of lieutenant governor but has no executive power. The title means merely that

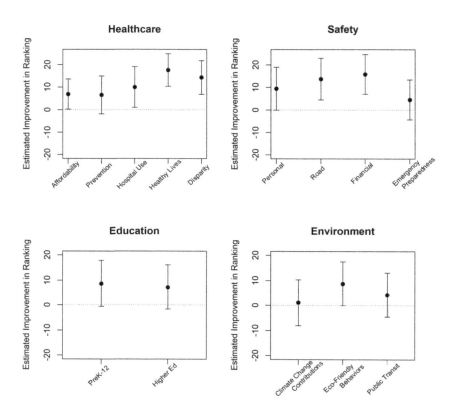

Figure 4.2 Estimated Improvement in Rankings from Governors' Tenure Potential.

Note: These graphs present the estimated effect of a governor's tenure potential power on a state's ranking across policy areas. Each estimate is presented with its 90 percent confidence interval.

he or she would succeed the governor in the event of gubernatorial death or disability. Leveraging his unified powers and eight consecutive years in office, Alexander was able to achieve a number of policy successes that required several years of planning, coordination and execution. For instance, for more than five years Alexander cultivated Japanese business executives resulting in the construction of a $500 million Nissan plant in Smyrna, Tennessee, then the largest ever single investment in the state's history. In a similar vein, in 1983, after several years of planning, Alexander launched, and for the next two years worked to implement, a "Better Schools" program, which increased math, science and computer education for the state's public school students. This program helped to bring about a slow but steady improvement in Tennessee's student scores on national tests.[16] Advocates of short gubernatorial terms and term limits assert that these contribute to a more democratic electoral process but, even if they do, as the Tennessee example suggests, gubernatorial term limits can come at the expense of policies likely to promote the wellbeing of a state's citizens.

Political Participation and Executive Power

Though gubernatorial power appears to be beneficial, we also find that higher levels of civic engagement can, at least to some extent, compensate for weak governors. Active and engaged citizens may compel various executive officials to cooperate with one another and, perhaps, to work with the state legislature to achieve desirable policy outcomes. We shall investigate this latter idea in the next chapter. For now, however, we examine the interaction between executive unity and one measure of political participation, namely a state's voter turnout in the 2018 election.[17] Prior research demonstrates that participation in midterm election captures citizens' interest in salient policy issues.[18] There might be reason to believe that in states where citizens are more deeply interested in critical policy issues, they may be able to compensate for weak governors. Perhaps, engaged citizenries may motivate state governments to achieve good policy outcomes even when the governor is institutionally hindered.

The results bear out this theory in several specific policy areas, though not in others. In the area of education, for instance, we find a significant interactive effect between gubernatorial strength and participation with respect to higher education. In states with weak governors, an increase in political participation (from the 25th to 75th percentile of midterm voter turnout) is associated with a 10 place improved ranking (see Table 4.4). In states with strong governors, this change in turnout is associated with a negligible effect on a state's higher education ranking. This interactive effect, however, is absent in the area of elementary and secondary education (where gubernatorial strength matters a lot but civic engagement does not moderate its influence). We also observe a significant interactive effect in the areas of public health, financial safety and eco-friendly behavior.

Figure 4.3 plots the predicted ranking as voter turnout increases in all four of these policy areas for both weak-governor state and strong-governor states. In all four cases, there is a strong, statistically significant effect of political participation on state ranking when the governor is weak, and an insignificant effect when the governor is strong. The full regression results are presented in the Appendix.

70 *State Governors*

Surveys consistently show that many Americans are skeptical that their participation in elections matters. A 2018 Pew Research Center poll found that 44 percent of those who did not participate in the midterm election made that choice because they did not believe their vote would make a difference. Our findings, however, suggest that political participation at the state level can matter a great deal. There are 33 states with plural executives. Our results suggest that voter engagement in these states could be transformative in the areas of education, health, safety and the environment. When governors lack the

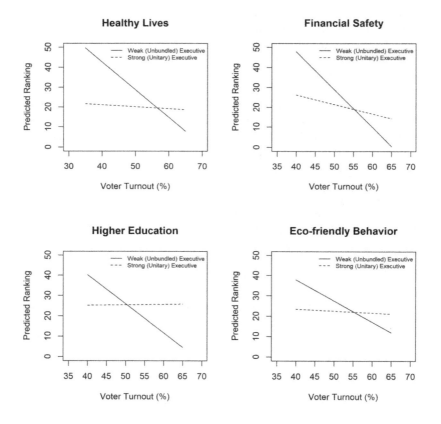

Figure 4.3 Estimated Interactive Effects of Executive Power and Civic Engagement.

Note: These graphs present the estimated interactive effect of executive unity and political participation on a state's ranking in four policy areas. The full regression results on which these estimates are based can be found in the Appendix.

Table 4.4 Marginal Effects of Political Participation on Policy Outcomes

Policy Area	States with Weak (Plural) Executives	States with Strong (Unified) Executives
	Effect of increasing turnout 25th percentile → 75th percentile	
Public Health	10.3 place better ranking*	0.7 place better ranking
Financial Safety	13.7 place better ranking*	3.5 place better ranking
Higher Education	10.2 place better ranking*	0.2 place worse ranking
Eco-friendly	7.4 place better ranking*	0.5 place better ranking

Note: This table presents first differences calculated using the results presented in the Appendix. Turnout at the 25th percentile is 47.2 percent and turnout at the 75th percentile is 54.5 percent.
* Statistically significant at the 5 percent level.

institutional capacity to deliver high-quality public services, voters can exert at least some compensatory influence.

The History of Gubernatorial Power

Since strong gubernatorial institutions seem beneficial, why do most states have weak gubernatorial institutions? The answer is America's history. Their revolutionary experience had left Americans with a deep distrust of executive power. Accordingly, the constitutions of the nine states that adopted new basic documents in the immediate aftermath of America's break with Great Britain provided for strong legislatures and weak governors. The new constitutions of eight of these states stipulated that the governor would be chosen by the state legislature, and in seven states the governor would serve only a one-year term. Every new state constitution provided for an executive council, usually chosen by the legislature, with the authority to block the governor's actions. Most constitutions gave the legislature, not the governor, the authority to appoint subordinate officials of the executive branch.[19]

Within a few years, examples of ineffective governance at the state level as well as the national level under the Articles of Confederation helped to convince the framers of the Constitution that a strong executive was needed to impart "energy" to the new regime. Alexander Hamilton was critical of the indecisiveness of the states' executive councils and pointed to them as institutions to be avoided in the construction of the national executive.[20] For his part, James Madison declared,

Experience had proved a tendency in our governments to throw all power into the legislative vortex. The executives of the states are in general little more than ciphers; the legislatures omnipotent. If no effective check be devised for restraining the instability and encroachments of the latter, a revolution of some kind or other would be inevitable.[21]

During the years after the adoption of the federal constitution, a number of states revised their own constitutions but few were yet convinced to copy the new national government's unified and independent executive. Among the states, weak governors continued to be the norm for quite a few decades. Both South Carolina (1778) and New Hampshire (1784) adopted new constitutions soon after the federal constitution's ratification but retained legislatively elected executive councils in place of or in addition to governors. Vermont (1786) gave its governor only a one-year term and created a 12-member council to oversee the governor's actions. Only Massachusetts followed the federal example, providing its governor with the power to veto legislation and eliminating the state's executive council.

During the first half of the 19th century, growing concern over legislative corruption led every state but South Carolina to strengthen its governor vis à vis the state legislature. This effort generally took the form of constitutionally providing for direct popular election rather than legislative selection of the chief executive. At the same time, however, early 19th century constitutions weakened gubernatorial power within the executive branch by providing for direct popular election of a host of other state executive officials as well—"Every public official save the dog catcher," a delegate to the Kentucky constitutional convention of 1850 complained.[22]

The period between the Civil War and World War I was an era of great political ferment and reform in America driven by populism and progressivism. When it came to the powers of state governors, Populists and Progressives had very different ideas. Populists, who spoke for the interests of farmers and workers, saw executive power as an agent of trusts and monopolies and destructive of democracy. According to the Populist platform of 1892, "Executive power and patronage have been used to corrupt our legislatures and defeat the will of the people, and plutocracy has thereby been enthroned upon the ruins of democracy." Accordingly, new constitutions adopted after the Civil War in the Populist strongholds of the South and West tended to weaken governors by reducing their salaries and powers and increasing the number of independently elected executive officials.

Progressives, on the other hand, usually representing the interests of business and the upper middle class, thought the state legislatures were controlled by corrupt political party machines and stood in the way of aggressive state action to deal with economic development and other pressing state concerns. Thus, Progressives generally favored strengthening state governors and consolidating state agencies to bring them under firmer gubernatorial control. While serving as governor of New Jersey, one quite well-known Progressive politician, Woodrow Wilson declared,

> The people of the United States want their governors to be leaders in matters of legislation because they have serious suspicion as to the source of the legislation, and they have a serious distrust of their legislatures ... there is nothing inconsistent between the strengthening of the powers of the executive and the direct power of the people.[23]

In a similar vein, a Progressive delegate to the Ohio constitutional convention of 1912 made the case for strengthening gubernatorial veto powers saying,

> We know a law-making body is far more apt to make blunders and mistakes and be led into corruption than an executive, and I think the more power you give an executive the better he will do. He is sure to do the best if you give him responsibility.[24]

Indeed, governmental leadership became a significant factor in the success of Progressive legislation in a number of states.[25]

States have revised their constitutions many times over the past century. Yet, the politics of the Populist and Progressive eras established patterns that persist to this day. Contemporary governors tend to be strongest in the former Progressive bastions of the Northeast and upper Midwest, while today's governors are generally weakest in the former Populist strongholds of the South and near West. If, for example, we map the United States in terms of the degree to which executive officials are independently elected, we find that the states of the North East and upper Midwest adhere more closely to the model of the unitary executive that tends to concentrate executive power in the governor's hands (see Figure 4.4). In the states of the South and West, by contrast, executive power tends to be dispersed among multiple independently elected officials. Not surprisingly, states in which gubernatorial power is greatest were also best able to attract individuals of greater ability and ambition to run for the office.[26] In this way, institutional and personality factors enhance one another. History matters.

Strengthening State Governors

The idea that states would generally benefit from stronger governors seemed politically fashionable during the 1960s and 1970s when the

74 *State Governors*

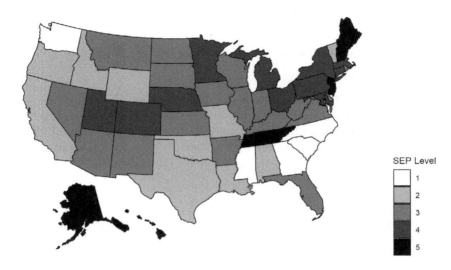

Figure 4.4 Distribution of "Separately Elected" (SEP) Executives across the U.S.
Note: Data on the election of executive branch officials are from Ferguson (2018). States with an SEP level of 5 have the most unified executives. The SEP level definitions appear in Table 4.2.

activism of the federal government appeared to contrast with the passivity of many of the states. Accordingly, during this era, civic activists proposed a number of constitutional and statutory measures that would strengthen state governors. These included extending governors' terms, concentrating political authority in governors' hands by reducing the number of executive branch officials who were independently elected and enhancing governors' budgetary powers.[27] These ideas encountered stiff political opposition from state legislatures and from the supporters of independently elected officials. Eventually, many states extended their gubernatorial terms to four years and many strengthened governors' appointment and budget powers. Few, however, significantly reduced the number of independently elected executive officials. To this day, as we saw, most American states retain the plural executive model.

Allowing voters to choose a variety of executive officials is sometimes defended as a democratic feature of state constitutions, but this is illusory. Though independently elected, few of these officials actually have electoral constituencies and most voters can neither name them nor recall having voted for them. In our survey of 1500 Americans, 27 percent of respondents did not know whether any executive officials other than the governor and lieutenant governor were elected. Most respondents knew the name of their state's governor, but few could name any other executive branch *office*, much less identify the *official* currently holding that office. These findings have implications for the federal level as well. Some have recently suggested rethinking the decision made at the federal constitutional convention and "unbundling" the presidency.[28] The growing problem of unilateral presidential action needs to be addressed, but creating a plural presidency would reduce the potential for effective action and lessen democratic accountability, effectively trading one set of problems for another.

There seems currently to be little political interest in strengthening the power of state governors. America's present-day focus is on the federal level where contemporary political struggles have led to calls for revamping the courts, correcting problems in the electoral system and rethinking the presidency. Some have called for a "Convention of the States," or second federal convention, to revise the entire federal structure. For the moment, at least, institutional reform at the state level seems beneath the nation's political radar. So, while stronger governors would be a good thing, the states seem fated for now to retain the governors bequeathed to them by their populist and progressive forebears. It is, of course, possible that the public health crisis of 2020 will lead some states to reexamine their gubernatorial institutions. States like New York, Ohio and Maryland benefitted from having governors accustomed to exercising strong legal and constitutional powers. Other states might do well to revisit their own institutional structures.

Notes

1 Robert F. Williams, "Comment: On the Importance of a Theory of Legislative Power under State Constitutions," *Quinnipiac Law Review* 15 (Spring, 1996): 57–64.
2 Kendra A. Hovey and Harold A. Hovey, eds., "D-12-Number of Statewide Elected Officials, 2006." *CQ's State Fact Finder, 2007* (Washington, DC: CQ Press, 2007).
3 Margaret Ferguson, "Governors and the Executive Branch," in Virginia Gray, Russell L. Hanson and Thad Kousser, eds., *Politics in the American States*, 11th ed. (Thousand Oaks, CA: CQ Press, 2018), pp. 235–274.
4 Thad Beyle, "Governors and Lieutenant Governors Clash," *North Carolina Center for Public Policy Research*, November, 1982. https://nccppr.org/wp-content/uploads/2017/02/Govenor_and_Lt._Governors_Clash.pdf.
5 Vikram David Amar, "Lessons from California's Recent Experience with Its Non-Unitary (Divided) Executive: Of Mayors, Governors, Controllers and Attorneys General," *Emory Law Journal* 59 (2009): 469–491.
6 Margaret Ferguson, "Governors and the Executive Branch," in Virginia Gray, Russell L. Hanson and Thad Kousser, eds., *Politics in the American States*, 11th ed. (Thousand Oaks, CA: CQ Press, 2018), pp. 235–274.
7 Vikram David Amar, "Lessons from California's Recent Experience with Its Non-Unitary (Divided) Executive: Of Mayors, Governors, Controllers and Attorneys General," *Emory Law Journal* 59 (2009): 469–491.
8 Ballotpedia, "State Government Triplexes," 2017. https://ballotpedia.org/State_government_triplexes:_Conflicts_between_governors_and_secretaries_of_state.

9 Ballotopedia, "State Government Triplexes," 2017.
10 Justin Weinstein-Tull, "State Bureaucratic Undermining," *The University of Chicago Law Review* 85, no. 5 (September, 2018): 1111.
11 The public safety rankings come from Wallet Hub (https://wallethub.com/edu/safest-states-to-live-in/4566/), the healthcare rankings comes from The Commonwealth Fund (https://interactives.commonwealthfund.org/2018/state-scorecard/files/Radley_State_Scorecard_2018.pdf), the education rankings come from U.S. News and World Report (www.usnews.com/news/best-states/rankings/education), the environment ranking come from Wallet Hub (https://wallethub.com/edu/greenest-states/11987/) and U.S. News and World Report (www.usnews.com/news/best-states/rankings/infrastructure/transportation).
12 Each state's democratic advantage is calculated by subtracting the estimated percentage of Republican identifiers from the estimated percentage of Democratic identifiers. These estimates come from a 2017 Gallup survey (https://news.gallup.com/poll/226643/2017-party-affiliation-state.aspx).
13 The state population and density numbers come from World Population Review (http://worldpopulationreview.com/states/state-densities/).
14 The health disparities measure combines 19 indicators of health and compares how well those in a state's low-income population fare relative to those in the state's higher-income population (https://interactives.commonwealthfund.org/2018/state-scorecard/files/Radley_State_Scorecard_2018.pdf).
15 James E. Alt, Ethan Bueno de Mesquita and Shanna Rose, "Disentangling Accountability and Competence in Elections: Evidence from US Term Limits," *The Journal of Politics* 73, no. 1 (2011): 171–186.
16 Marta W. Aldrich, "Here's Why People Are Talking About Tennessee, a 'Bright Green Rectangle' on a New U.S. Map of Student Growth," *Chalkbeat*, Sec. 20, 2017. www.chalkbeat.org/posts/tn/2017/12/20/heres-why-people-are-talking-about-tennessee-a-bright-green-rectangle-on-a-new-u-s-map-of-student-growth/.
17 The turnout data come from www.electproject.org/.
18 Dennis L. Plane and Joseph Gershtenson, "Candidates' Ideological Locations, Abstention, and Turnout in US Midterm Senate Elections," *Political Behavior* 26, no. 1 (2004): 69–93.
19 G. Alan Tarr, "Models and Fashions in State Constitutionalism," *Wisconsin Law Review* 3 (1998): 729.
20 Alexander Hamilton, "The Federalist No. 70" in Clinton Rossiter, ed., *The Federalist Papers* (New York, Mentor, 1961), pp. 423–431.
21 Max Farrand, ed., *Record of the Federal Convention of 1787*, rec. ed., Vol. 2 (New Haven, CT: Yale University Press, 1966), p. 35.
22 G. Alan Tarr, "Models and Fashions in State Constitutionalism," *Wisconsin Law Review* (1998): 729.
23 Saladan M. Ambar, *How Governors Built the Modern American Presidency* (Philadelphia, PA: University of Pennsylvania Press, 2012).
24 John Dinan, *The American State Constitutional Tradition* (Lawrence, KS: The University Press of Kansas, 2006).
25 Larry Sabato, *Goodbye to Good-Time Charlie: The American Governorship Transformed* (Washington, DC: Congressional Quarterly Press, 1983).
26 Larry Sabato, *Goodbye to Good-Time Charlie: The American Governorship Transformed* (Washington, DC: Congressional Quarterly Press, 1983).
27 G. Alan Tarr, "Models and Fashions in State Constitutionalism," *Wisconsin Law Review* (1998): 729.
28 Christopher Berry and Jacob E Gerson, "The Unbundled Executive," *University of Chicago Law Review* 75 (2008): 1385.

Appendix

Table 4.5 Gubernatorial Powers by State

State	Unity	Tenure	Appointment	Budget	Veto
Alabama	0	0	0	1	1
Alaska	1	0	1	1	0
Arizona	0	0	0	1	0
Arkansas	0	0	0	0	0
California	0	0	0	1	0
Colorado	1	0	1	0	0
Connecticut	1	1	1	0	1
Delaware	0	0	1	1	1
Florida	0	0	0	0	0
Georgia	0	0	0	1	0
Hawaii	1	0	0	0	0
Idaho	0	1	0	0	1
Illinois	0	1	0	0	1
Indiana	0	0	0	1	0
Iowa	0	1	1	0	0
Kansas	0	0	0	1	0
Kentucky	0	0	1	1	1
Louisiana	0	0	1	0	0
Maine	1	0	1	0	0
Maryland	1	0	0	1	1
Massachusetts	1	1	1	1	1
Michigan	1	0	0	1	0
Minnesota	1	1	1	0	0
Mississippi	0	0	0	0	0
Missouri	0	0	0	1	0
Montana	0	0	0	1	0
Nebraska	1	0	0	0	0
Nevada	0	0	1	1	0
New Hampshire	1	0	0	1	0
New Jersey	1	0	1	1	0
New Mexico	0	0	1	1	0
New York	1	1	1	0	1

(*Continued*)

Table 4.5 (Cont.)

State	Unity	Tenure	Appointment	Budget	Veto
North Carolina	0	0	0	0	0
North Dakota	0	1	0	1	0
Ohio	1	0	1	1	0
Oklahoma	0	0	0	0	0
Oregon	0	0	0	0	0
Pennsylvania	1	0	1	1	0
Rhode Island	0	0	1	0	0
South Carolina	0	0	0	0	0
South Dakota	0	0	0	1	0
Tennessee	1	0	1	0	0
Texas	0	1	0	0	0
Utah	1	1	0	0	0
Vermont	0	1	0	1	0
Virginia	0	0	1	1	0
Washington	0	1	0	1	1
West Virginia	0	0	1	1	0
Wisconsin	0	0	0	1	0
Wyoming	0	0	1	0	1

Note: 1 indicates that the particular gubernatorial power is strong and 0 indicates that the power is weak.

The coding is derived from Table 8.4 in Ferguson (2018).

Table 4.6 Regression Results (without Political Participation Interaction)

	Health Afford.	Health Prevent.	Hospital Use	Healthy Lives	Disparity	Personal Safety	Road Safety	Financial Safety	Emer. Preparedness	PreK-12	Higher Ed	Climate Change Contrib.	Eco-Friendly	Public Transit
Exec Unity	-12.9***	-11.7**	-6.1	-8.7*	-4.2	-4.1	-6.7	-8.9	-10.0*	-10.0*	-0.9	-9.0*	-5.4	-7.3*
	(3.4)	(4.3)	(4.6)	(3.6)	(3.8)	(4.8)	(4.7)	(4.4)	(4.5)	(4.4)	(5.1)	(3.9)	(4.1)	(3.4)
Appointment	2.7	1.0	7.4	6.4	0.5	-3.4	-0.1	5.4	-1.0	0.9	4.2	5.3	3.8	-0.2
	(3.4)	(4.3)	(4.6)	(3.6)	(3.8)	(4.8)	(4.7)	(4.4)	(4.5)	(4.4)	(5.1)	(3.9)	(4.1)	(3.4)
Tenure	-7.0	-6.6	-10.1	-17.6***	-14.4**	-9.5	-13.7*	-15.8**	-4.6	-8.7	-7.2	1.2	-8.7	-4.3
	(4.1)	(5.1)	(5.5)	(4.4)	(4.6)	(5.8)	(5.6)	(5.3)	(5.4)	(5.3)	(6.1)	(4.7)	(4.9)	(4.1)
Budget	-6.1	-4.8	-3.8	-1.3	-1.1	-2.9	-2.4	-0.9	-7.4	-4.8	0.3	-0.1	-7.0	-3.2
	(3.1)	(4.0)	(4.3)	(3.4)	(3.5)	(4.5)	(4.4)	(4.1)	(4.2)	(4.1)	(4.7)	(3.6)	(3.8)	(3.2)
Veto	-0.1	-0.9	4.2	2.5	-4.3	0.9	-2.3	8.5	0.5	-1.8	3.4	-4.4	4.3	-3.0
	(4.0)	(5.1)	(5.5)	(4.4)	(4.5)	(5.8)	(5.6)	(5.3)	(5.4)	(5.2)	(6.1)	(4.6)	(4.9)	(4.1)
D advantage	-0.4**	-0.2	0.2	-0.2	-0.1	-0.2	0.1	-0.0	-0.1	-0.2	0.2	-0.5**	-0.3*	-0.5***
	(0.1)	(0.2)	(0.2)	(0.1)	(0.1)	(0.2)	(0.2)	(0.2)	(0.2)	(0.2)	(0.2)	(0.1)	(0.1)	(0.1)
Gov party	3.8	4.5	11.2*	8.5*	11.1**	-0.5	3.4	3.2	3.8	2.6	4.3	3.8	8.7*	5.8
	(3.6)	(4.5)	(4.8)	(3.8)	(4.0)	(5.1)	(4.9)	(4.7)	(4.7)	(4.6)	(5.4)	(4.1)	(4.3)	(3.6)
Unemploy.	1.0	-0.4	0.4	0.7	-2.2	0.9	0.7	2.5	2.1	-2.6	3.1	-2.5	-0.4	-1.3
	(2.0)	(2.5)	(2.7)	(2.1)	(2.2)	(2.8)	(2.7)	(2.6)	(2.6)	(2.5)	(3.0)	(2.3)	(2.4)	(2.0)
Pop. Density	0.0	-0.0	-0.0	-0.0	0.0	-0.0	0.0	-0.0	0.0	-0.0	-0.0	0.0	-0.0	0.0

(Continued)

Table 4.6 (Cont.)

	Health Afford.	Health Prevent.	Hospital Use	Healthy Lives	Disparity	Personal Safety	Road Safety	Financial Safety	Emer. Prepared-ness	PreK-12	Higher Ed	Climate Change Contrib.	Eco-Friendly	Public Transit
	(0.0)	(0.0)	(0.0)	(0.0)	(0.0)	(0.0)	(0.0)	(0.0)	(0.0)	(0.0)	(0.0)	(0.0)	(0.0)	(0.0)
Population	-0.0	-0.0	-0.0	-0.0	-0.0	-0.0	-0.0	-0.0	0.0	-0.0	-0.0	0.0	-0.0	-0.0
	(0.0)	(0.0)	(0.0)	(0.0)	(0.0)	(0.0)	(0.0)	(0.0)	(0.0)	(0.0)	(0.0)	(0.0)	(0.0)	(0.0)
Intercept	31.0***	35.8**	22.9*	25.8**	34.8***	31.6**	28.3*	19.7	23.7*	44.2***	12.5	33.8**	31.5**	33.3***
	(8.2)	(10.3)	(11.1)	(8.8)	(9.2)	(11.7)	(11.3)	(10.8)	(10.9)	(10.6)	(12.3)	(9.4)	(9.8)	(8.4)
N	50	50	50	50	50	50	50	50	50	50	50	50	50	50

Standard errors in parentheses;
* $p < 0.05$,
** $p < 0.01$,
*** $p < 0.001$; the first five independent variables are dummies where 1 indicates a strong institutional power in that area (see Table 4.3)

Table 4.7 Regression Results (with Political Participation Interaction)

	Healthy Lives	Financial Safety	Higher Education	Eco-Friendly
Executive unity	−73.3*	−78.4*	−73.1	−52.2
	(32.7)	(34.5)	(40.5)	(33.7)
Appointment	4.0	2.1	1.0	1.8
	(4.0)	(4.3)	(5.0)	(4.2)
Budget	6.1	7.7*	5.6	−2.4
	(3.7)	(3.9)	(4.6)	(3.8)
Veto	−3.8	3.0	1.4	1.4
	(4.3)	(4.5)	(5.3)	(4.4)
D advantage	−0.3	−0.1	0.1	−0.4**
	(0.1)	(0.1)	(0.2)	(0.1)
Gov. party	2.6	−4.3	−0.7	4.7
	(4.3)	(4.5)	(5.3)	(4.4)
Unemploy.	−0.2	2.3	3.2	−0.6
	(2.2)	(2.4)	(2.8)	(2.3)
Pop. density	−0.0	−0.0	−0.0	−0.0
	(0.0)	(0.0)	(0.0)	(0.0)
Population	−0.0	−0.0	−0.0	−0.0
	(0.0)	(0.0)	(0.0)	(0.0)
Turnout	−1.4***	−1.9***	−1.4**	−1.0*
	(0.4)	(0.4)	(0.5)	(0.4)
Turnout x executive unity	1.3*	1.4*	1.5	0.9
	(0.6)	(0.7)	(0.8)	(0.7)
Intercept	96.6***	113.0***	82.9**	83.1***
	(22.3)	(23.6)	(27.7)	(23.1)
N	50	50	50	50

Standard errors in parentheses;
* $p < 0.05$,
** $p < 0.01$,
*** $p < 0.001$.

5 State Legislatures and Representative Government

In recent years, the federal government has often been gridlocked while the states have become legislatively very active in critical areas of policy making including education, healthcare and the environment. Collectively, the states enact some 20,000 pieces of legislation each year. Of course, this regular outpouring of new laws could have more than one explanation. Ideally, perhaps, high levels of legislative activity might reflect state law makers' attention to the public interest. An alternative and perhaps less sanguine possibility, though, is that state legislators are more than moderately responsive to the blandishments of the armies of lobbyists – nearly 50,000 by last count – currently employed by special interests to influence state law making.

Many Americans doubt whether state legislatures are particularly responsive to their needs.[1] There has, indeed, been debate on this point since the time of the nation's founding.[2] The anti-federalists argued that the states, and particularly their citizen legislatures, were close to the people and could be trusted to produce good governance. Prominent New York anti-federalist, Melancton Smith, for example, declared that the states and citizen legislators were best suited to serve as, "the guardians of our domestic rights and interests."[3] The federalists, on the other hand, thought many of the state governments had been proven ineffective – hence the need for a national government – and argued that the legislatures of the individual states would be dominated by powerful local interest groups that would have no regard for the more general good. In *Federalist 10*, James Madison famously argued that citizens' liberties were far safer in the nation as a whole than in the individual states where narrow special interests might more easily dominate the legislature and, "execute their plans of oppression."[4]

In this chapter, let us explore the representative character and effectiveness of contemporary state legislatures through an investigation of the effects of four different influences on state legislative activity, including both policy outputs and outcomes. Specifically, we examine the influence of legislatures' institutional strength and capacity, state interest group activity, the strength of political parties in the state and levels of citizen engagement. The findings demonstrate that state legislative outputs, particularly bill introductions, are highly responsive to interest group activity. Policy outcomes, however, continue to show the strongest correlation with a state's executive structure, as described in Chapter 4; it appears that neither lobbying nor citizen engagement is as important as the influence of a strong state governorship on policy results. As we shall see, there is a need for far more scrutiny and strengthening of state legislatures to ensure that the states' policy priorities align with citizens' interests.

State Legislative Activity

While the federal government has been gridlocked for a number of years, the states have been legislatively very active. In recent years, the states have collectively averaged nearly 20,000 new laws each year, or an average of 400 per state. California and Texas each typically enact more than 1000 new laws per legislative session. Through most of the 20th century, state legislatures were generally in session only every other year. Today, all but four state legislatures are in session every year and the legislatures today enact roughly the same number of bills every year that were once enacted every other year, effectively doubling legislative productivity. For example, during the two-year period, 1968–1969, the California legislature enacted 1474 new laws as compared to the 1289 enacted in 2015, alone. Similarly, during the same two-year period, the Texas legislature passed 905 laws while during 2015, alone, the same legislature enacted 1323 new laws.

The U.S. Congress, by contrast, has in recent years reached historically low levels of legislative productivity, enacting an average of only slightly more than 150 pieces of legislation each year. A substantial percentage of these new federal laws, moreover, have been hortatory in character such as legislation naming federal buildings or national historic sites for worthy individuals. Quite a few new state laws, too, are more symbolic than substantive. In 2018 Illinois, for instance, declared corn to be its official state grain. Yet, growth in state legislative activity has been accompanied by a substantial growth in state spending—attesting to the substantive rather than symbolic character of much state legislation. Figure 5.1 shows state spending over time in constant dollars. Since 2012, state spending has consistently increased and it is projected to continue to increase into the future.

Each year the 50 states enact many pieces of legislation that have major impacts upon the lives of their citizens. In 2018, Iowa and West Virginia enacted controversial voter ID laws requiring prospective voters to show identification at the polls. California enacted laws limiting the ability of employers to demand personal information from job

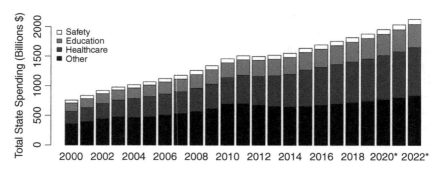

Figure 5.1 Growth in State Spending over Time.
The data come from usgovernmentspending.com.
Note: State spending is measured in billions of dollars. * indicates projected stated spending.

applicants. New York required paid family leave for many employees, while Washington required employers to offer paid sick leave to their employees. Illinois stiffened penalties for cyberstalking. Texas required insurers to provide more comprehensive coverage for breast cancer treatment. Tennessee prohibited colleges from adopting speech codes. Indiana imposed new restrictions on the civil forfeiture rules used by local law enforcement agencies to seize property they deemed connected to criminal activity. Eighteen states raised the minimum wage.

But, despite the fact that the state legislatures are quite busy, most citizens seem unaware of the activities of their state legislatures. As noted earlier, we surveyed a nationally representative sample of 1500 Americans in October 2018 to determine what the public knows about state government institutions, electoral processes and recent policy decisions. The results demonstrate that the public is deeply uninformed about how their state legislatures operate. Approximately 82 percent of respondents cannot so much as name their state representative and 72 percent cannot name their state senator. Eighty percent do not know whether serving in the state legislature is a full-time position of whether legislators can simultaneously hold other compensated positions.

Moreover, as our survey shows, citizens know almost nothing about their state's legislative agenda. Figure 5.2 shows the percentage of survey participants who responded "don't know" to questions about their state legislatures. Almost half say they do not know which issue was most debated in their state legislature, and of those who claim to know, about one-third gave a vague response when asked to actually name that issue (e.g. "don't remember," "auto insurance," "the system"). Further, nearly half of respondents say they don't know the issue on which their state spent the most money in the past year. Taken together, the survey results

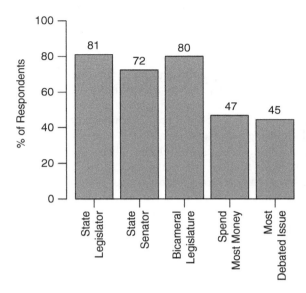

Figure 5.2 Percentage Responding "Don't Know."
Note: This graph displays the percentage of respondents who indicated they "don't know" the name of their state legislator, name of their state senator, whether their state has a bicameral legislature, the policy area(s) in which their state spends the most money and the most debated issue in their state in the previous year. The survey included a nationally representative sample of 1500 respondents.

suggest that citizens simply may not know enough to hold legislators accountable for their actions. We suspect that most professional lobbyists, for their part, would have little difficulty answering these and many other questions about the names and actions of their state legislators.

One reason that citizens know so little about their states is that state government is not given much attention in America's public schools where civic education is focused mainly on the national government and on general civic values such as tolerance and participation. And, even when a state mandates some brief exploration of state government, the focus is on that particular state. Texas, for example, requires all students to learn about Texas history and government. Tens of millions of Americans, though, do not live in the state where they attended school. Tens of millions, indeed, were not born or educated in the United States and received little or no exposure to any civics lessons, much less discussions of state government. The short civics test administered to prospective citizens tests only familiarity with national institutions. We shall return to the matter of civic education in our concluding chapter.

News Coverage of State Legislative Activity

Compounding the effect of a lack of civic education is the decline of news coverage of state politics. Figure 5.3 presents an historical analysis of state news coverage by the *New York Times*. This graph plots the number of *Times* stories about state politics and policy by decade since 1850. Coverage peaks during the 1930s and then continually declines since the 1980s.

Over the past 15 years, according to a recent Pew Research Center study, as newspapers have been forced to implement sharp budget cuts, the number of full-time reporters assigned to state capitals has declined by 35 percent. All told, only about 700 journalists cover the state capitals full time, with several hundred more assigned to the capitals on a part-time basis.[5] The same study revealed that less than one-third of U.S. newspapers assign any reporter, whether full or part time to the state capital. As to the broadcast media, 86 percent of local television news stations assign neither a full- nor a part-time reporter to cover the state capital.

Figure 5.4 visualizes modern coverage of state politics. The graph plots the percentage of state news stories that appeared on publications' front page. In recent years, it is evident that state news stories rarely make the front page. This paucity of news coverage, coupled with a lack of relevant education, helps to explain why citizens know so little about state government.

It is also noteworthy that, for their part, state legislators know very little about the citizens they represent.[6] Since surveys are relatively inexpensive, the problem here might be lack of interest. State legislators could determine what their constituents want but unfortunately do not take the trouble to do so.

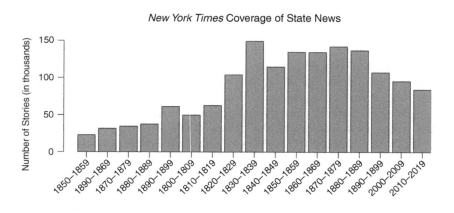

Figure 5.3 Historical Coverage of State Politics.

These counts were computed through searches of keywords in Proquest's New York Times Database.

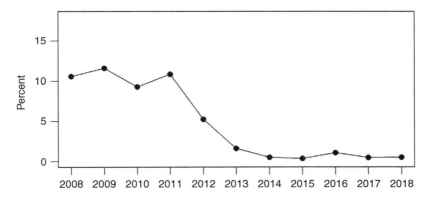

Figure 5.4 Modern Front-Page Coverage of State Politics.
These counts were computed through searches of keywords in ProQuest's New York Times database.
Note: The graph shows the percentage of front-page news stories about state politics in U.S. newspapers from 2008–2018.

Poor media coverage combined with the public's lack of basic knowledge about state law making seems a situation made to order for both corruption and interest group domination of the state legislatures. A century ago, expanded newspaper coverage of state and municipal affairs in the form of "muckraking" journalism helped to reduce the prevalence of corruption in America's states and cities.[7] Possibly, declining newspaper coverage could open the way for a resurgence of corruption. A century ago, however, states and cities policed themselves, which often gave corrupt politicians control over both the law enforcement agencies responsible for investigating corruption and the courts charged with punishing it. Not surprisingly, state and municipal self-policing was not a very effective deterrent to political thievery. Today, however, state and municipal corruption is chiefly investigated by federal law enforcement agencies and prosecuted in the federal courts.[8] This federalization of law enforcement may explain why levels of corruption at the state level have not—at least not yet—risen despite declining media coverage, though one study does suggest that corruption has increased in cities that have lost their local newspapers.[9] The issue of corruption in state government will be discussed further in Chapter 7.

Interest Groups

Levels of overt corruption in America's state capitals may have waned since their 19th century heyday. However, lawful efforts by interest groups to influence state legislators appear to have reached an all-time high. During the 1980s, analysts began to take note of a sharp increase in state-level lobby activity. Writing in 1990, Gray and Lowery reported that the average number of interest groups per state had increased from 195 in 1975 to 342 in 1980, and then to 617 in 1990.[10] Over the ensuing years, both the number of interest groups and their lobbyists working in the 50 state capitals as well as lobby expenditures have continued to grow. By 2017, according to data collected by the public interest group, FollowThe Money.org, nearly 50,000 lobbyists were registered in the 50 states. Roughly 2000 lobbyists were registered in the state of Texas, alone, with similar numbers in California, Arizona and Illinois (see Table 5.1).

Table 5.1 Number of Registered Lobbyists in the U.S. States, 2017

State	Number of Registered Lobbyists	State	Number of Registered Lobbyists
New York	5903	Kentucky	620
Arizona	2461	Wisconsin	617
Illinois	2359	Alabama	615
Florida	2318	Rhode Island	612
California	2171	Oklahoma	611
Texas	1926	Tennessee	604
Ohio	1536	Utah	598
Michigan	1532	Kansas	557
Minnesota	1463	Arkansas	542
Pennsylvania	1239	Colorado	500
Massachusetts	1158	Vermont	496
Missouri	1151	Idaho	426
Nevada	1048	Hawaii	419
Georgia	1032	Mississippi	408
New Jersey	1015	Nebraska	408
Oregon	988	Montana	395
Connecticut	906	New Hampshire	393
Washington	885	South Dakota	369
Virginia	786	West Virginia	365
North Carolina	749	South Carolina	355
Iowa	725	Delaware	329
Maryland	681	Maine	221
Louisiana	678	North Dakota	172
New Mexico	670	Wyoming	135
Indiana	647	Alaska	119

Data source: FollowTheMoney.org

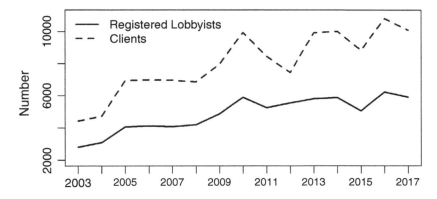

Figure 5.5 Lobbying in New York State.
Data source: FollowTheMoney.org

In 2017, New York boasted nearly 6000 registered lobbyists, or more than 28 lobbyists for every New York state legislator. Figure 5.5 shows the growth of state lobbying in New York from 2003–2017. Over the course of this time period, the state experienced a 111 percent increase in the number of registered lobbyists and a 128 percent increase in the number of clients of these lobbyists.

In 2017, New York lobbyists spent $254 million in efforts to influence the state legislature on behalf of some 10,000 clients. Their California counterparts, though fewer in number, actually spent more money—a whopping $330 million, or more than $27 million to influence each of the state's 120 legislators on behalf of some 6000 clients. From 2002 to 2017, lobbyists increased their spending by 67 percent (see Figure 5.6). All told, according to estimates published by FollowTheMoney.org, in the year 2017, state-level lobbyists spent more than $12 billion dollars to influence law-making activities in the 50 states. This enormous sum is nearly four times the $3.4 billion spent by lobby groups seeking to influence the U.S. Congress in the same year.

According to political scientist Alan Rosenthal, this great upsurge in lobbying activity at the state level is explained by the fact that the states have taken on new responsibilities, some mandated by the federal government, in healthcare, education, consumer affairs, the environment and the workplace, and have continued to impose new regulations in such areas as banking, consumer protection, transportation, hazardous waste disposal, housing, senior care, and automotive emissions as well as healthcare.[11] Growing numbers of lobbyists are hard at work seeking to make certain that their client industries are not adversely affected by

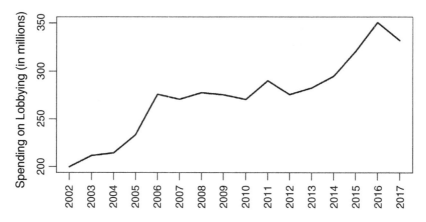

Figure 5.6 Spending on Lobbying in California, 2002–2017.
Data source: FollowTheMoney.org

these regulations and, at the same time, benefit from the more than $2 trillion that the states now spend each year—much of it to purchase goods and services from private contractors.

Regulation of Lobbying

The growth of interest group activity in the 50 states has taken place against the backdrop of generally weak lobbying, campaign finance and conflict of interest rules. Every state, to be sure, has adopted a number of legislative ethics laws governing such matters as conflicts of interest, disclosure of lobby activities, campaign contribution limits, and lobbyists' gifts to law makers. Most states have imposed restrictions, such as one-year waiting periods, on the "revolving door" through which some legislators and members of their staffs hope to walk to lucrative positions as lobbyists when they leave state office. Nearly all states have also established ethics commissions to monitor compliance with these rules.

State ethics laws, however, are generally ineffectual, filled with loopholes and exceptions, and are only sporadically enforced. State ethics commissions have very limited investigative and enforcement capabilities. According to one study, current commissions are ineffective.[12] Absent effective enforcement of existing laws, according to another study, conflicts of interest "run rampant" in state legislatures. In most legislatures, members are part-time "citizen-legislators" who hold private sector positions as well. Often, legislators will vote on or even introduce legislation that affects their private interests. One New Mexico legislator, for example, owns a small oil and gas company active in the state. He saw no conflict of interest when he worked to defeat a bill that would have raised the fees and penalties that New Mexico imposed on energy companies. "I don't think it's a conflict of interest," the legislator said. "I think it's a blessing that a few of us have some understanding of that industry."[13] In an extreme example, Illinois House Speaker Michael Madigan has reportedly steered millions of dollars in state funds to clients of his law firm, Madigan & Getzendammer. These clients included nursing homes, banks and pharmacies that had hired his firm to represent them in dealings with the state. One *Chicago Tribune* columnist called Madigan a "walking conflict of interest," but a spokesperson for Madigan's office said the speaker complied with a "personal code of conduct."[14]

In several states, including Louisiana and Alabama, conflict of interest laws require law makers to recuse themselves from voting only if a bill benefits them but no one else. Thus, under state law, there was no conflict of interest when an Alabama state senator who happened to be president of a company that owned a chain of pharmacies in the state recently proposed legislation exempting pharmacies from business license taxes. The senator stood to benefit, but so would all the other pharmacy owners in Alabama. "I'm just one little person. I'm one little spoke in the wheel," said the senator.[15]

As to prohibiting legislators from accepting gifts from lobbyists, most states' laws on this matter allow major exceptions. For example, many states with seemingly strict gift limits do allow lobbyists to send legislators to international conferences or on trips that will ostensibly enhance their knowledge regarding possible public programs. In one case, a lobbyist spent $17,000 to take Georgia House Speaker David Ralston, along with his family and staff, to Europe to learn about high-speed trains. In Iowa, which prohibits lobby gifts worth more than $3, lobbyists have sponsored expenses-paid trips to conferences in Brazil.[16]

Efforts to strengthen gift bans and other ethics requirements have met stiff legislative resistance in a number of states.[17] The same has been true for efforts to strengthen state campaign finance laws. Currently, 11 states allow unlimited contributions to state-level political candidates. In other states, contribution limits are as high as $44,000 per candidate. Even when groups working to strengthen state ethics rules have bypassed legislatures and taken their case directly to the people, the results have sometimes been disappointing. In North Dakota, for example, a popular referendum limiting lobbyist gifts, prohibiting legislators from joining lobbying firms within two years after leaving office and creating a state ethics commission, was passed by the state's voters in 2016. The state legislature responded by employing an "emergency" clause in the state's statutes to overturn the referendum's results.[18]

92 Legislatures and Representative Government

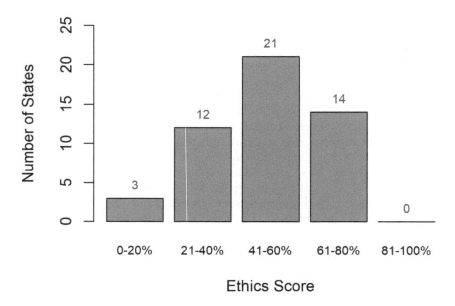

Figure 5.7 Distribution of Scores of State Ethics Laws.
Data source: Coalition for Integrity, "States with Anti-corruption Measures for Public Officials," 2018.

In 2018, the Coalition for Integrity published a study scoring every state on its ethics laws. Each score was based on eight questions about how the state's laws addressed ethics agencies, gifts for public officials, campaign finance issues and client disclosure. A score of 100 indicates that the state has an extremely strong ethics framework in place, while lower scores indicate that there are areas for improvement. Figure 5.7 shows the distribution of scores for all 50 states. Not a single state scored between 80 and 100, 14 states scored between 60 and 80 and three states received a score in the lowest category (0 to 20). Taken together, the results suggest that most states have some ethics laws in place, but all states can do much more to improve transparency and reduce corruption.

Who Governs?

There seems little question that interest group influence is important in state legislatures.[19] But, legislators are ultimately accountable to their constituents and citizen engagement might also be important. Who is more influential? What promotes legislative action, citizen activity or interest group activity?

These questions are especially important because today's legislators have a heightened capacity to govern. At one time, most state legislatures were composed of part-time citizen legislators and were only in session for brief periods every other year.[20] Most legislators had neither staffs nor office space, turnover was frequent and many served without pay. Most state legislators lacked the means to even secure information, much less play an active role in state government. In recent years, following a spate of reforms that started in California in the 1960s, some legislatures have become more professionalized with less turnover, longer and in some cases annual sessions, better salaries and substantial staff support.[21] These changes have given at least some legislatures a greater capacity to participate in their states' governance.

But, what do they do with that capacity? To whom are they most responsive? An examination of the relationship between lobbying expenditures and citizen engagement (operationalized as turnout in a midterm election) reveals that both legislative bill introductions and enactments appear far more responsive to monied interests than to citizens. The left-hand graphs in Figure 5.8 show a strong, positive correlation between lobbying expenditures and both forms of legislative outputs, while the right-hand graphs show a strong, negative correlation between citizen engagement and these outputs.

To make matters worse, not only do interest groups influence the introduction and enactment of legislation, they sometimes actually write the legislation. While there is a long-held belief that much of the actual language of state legislation is directly influenced by interest groups, researchers have recently documented the extent of this practice. Investigators at the Center for Public Integrity, in partnership with USA Today and The Arizona Republic, analyzed state legislation from 2010–2018. They found that over 10,000 state bills that were introduced had been almost entirely copied from model bills (i.e. bills written by corporations and activist groups.)[22] Of these, over 2100 were signed into law. These "copy and paste" bills span all 50 states, with approximately 54 percent coming from corporate entities, 38 percent coming from conservative groups and 7 percent coming from liberal groups.[23] For example, the Center for Security Policy and ACT for America (two conservative groups) have worked together to ensure that bills they have written that target Islamic law have been introduced over 70 times. Opponents of the bills worry that the legislation, and the rhetoric it generates, breeds and sanctions Islamophobia.

Although examples of "copy and paste" bills can be found across the country, there is wide variation in the numbers of these bills that are passed into law. Together, Illinois, Oklahoma, Arizona and Tennessee passed more than 550 "copycat" bills into law in the eight years under analysis.[24]

94 *Legislatures and Representative Government*

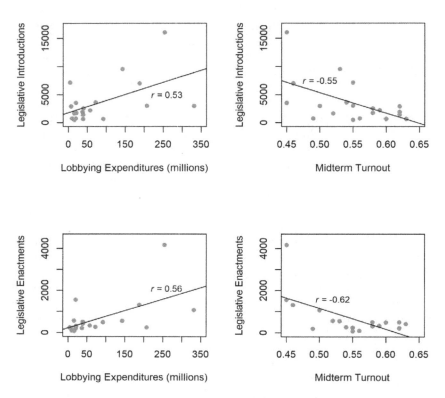

Figure 5.8 Lobbying, Citizen Engagement and Legislative Outputs.
The lobbying expenditure data (from 2017) come from FollowTheMoney.org. Turnout data is from the 2018 midterm election. Legislative output data come from the *Book of States* (2018).

It therefore appears that all of the money pouring into state lobbying has yielded tangible results. Lobbyists, more than citizens, influence the introduction and enactment of state laws. Indeed, lobbyists actually write many state laws. These findings should deeply concern anyone who believes elected officials should instead be most responsive to their constituents.

Political Parties

When evaluating state legislative outputs, it is also important to consider the role of parties. Parties provide ideological order to a legislature, and the majority party exerts near full control over the legislative agenda.[25] Perhaps

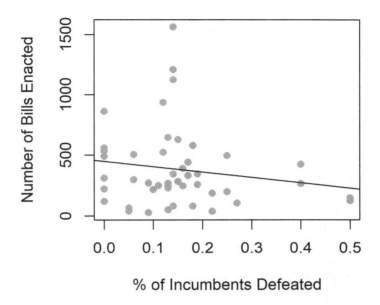

Figure 5.9 Effect of Party Strength on Bills Enacted.
The data on party strength come from ballotpedia.org (2016 election) and the data on bill enactments come from the *Book of States* (2017).

strong parties can enhance citizen influence over legislation. One way to measure party strength in state legislatures is the percentage of incumbent members who are defeated in an election; states with strong parties tend to retain their incumbents.[26] Figure 5.9 displays a scatterplot of the number of bills enacted in state legislatures against this measure of party strength. There is a weak negative correlation (-0.16) indicating that as the number of defeated incumbents increases (meaning party strength weakens), the number of enacted bills declines.

We can examine the relative influence of each of the factors discussed (lobbyists, citizens, party strength and gubernatorial structure) on legislative outputs through a regression analysis (see Table 5.2). The models quantify the relationship between these four factors and legislative outputs, measured as both bills that were introduced and that were enacted into law.

The models reaffirm the relationships evident in the above graphs. In terms of bills introduced in state houses, only lobbying exhibits a strong, positive influence. The results suggest that each additional lobbyist is associated with an additional two bill introductions, which highlights the power of lobbyists to shape legislative narratives and thus political narratives about their topics of interest. With respect to bill enactments, the

Table 5.2 Influences on Legislative Outputs

	Bills Introduced	Bills Enacted
Lobbyists	2.2** (0.3)	0.02 (0.01)
Citizen engagement	-63.9 (43.6)	-15.3* (8.4)
Party strength	1602.0 (2154.5)	-300.2 (413.9)
Gubernatorial unity	789.1 (529.3)	-45.3 (101.7)
(Intercept)	2941.6 (2247.3)	1207.4** (431.7)
N	41	41

** $p < .05$,
* $< .1$; OLS regression estimates with standard errors in parentheses. Lobbying is the number of registered lobbyists in each state in 2017, citizens engagement is measured as turnout in the 2018 election; party strength is measured as the percentage of incumbents defeated; and gubernatorial unity is a dichotomous variable where 1 indicates a unified executive (see Chapter 4 for more details about measuring executive unity).

results are somewhat inconclusive. Citizen engagement appears negatively related to enacted legislation, underscoring the disconnect between state legislators and their constituents.

Effects on Policy Outcomes

It is also valuable to consider the influence of these factors on outcomes rather than activity alone. Enacting a bill is useful only to the extent that it results in some kind of positive outcome. As in our analysis on the effects of state executive structure (see Chapter 4), we examine the effect of legislative determinants on a range of policy outcomes, including those in the areas of healthcare, education, energy and public safety. Policy outcomes are measured using state rankings from multiple reputable sources, including U.S. News and World Report (2018).

The models for this analysis (see Table 5.3) examine the relative influence of lobbying, citizen engagement, party strength and gubernatorial unity on state rankings in four policy areas (while controlling for a state's unemployment rate and population). As we saw in the previous chapter, gubernatorial unity shows a strong, significant relationship with states' rankings in all four policy areas. In healthcare, for example, having a unified executive is associated with an improved ranking of

Table 5.3 Influences on Policy Outcomes

	Healthcare	Education	Energy	Safety
Lobbyists	0.00 (0.00)	0.00 (0.00)	0.00 (0.00)	0.00 (0.00)
Citizen engagement	-1.0** (0.3)	-0.9** (0.3)	-0.8** (0.3)	-0.6* (0.4)
Party strength	-12.3 (16.4)	7.2 (16.6)	5.8 (15.8)	-17.1 (17.4)
Gubernatorial unity	-9.4** (4.0)	-8.5** (4.0)	-11.8** (3.8)	-8.3** (4.2)
(Intercept)	78.8 (18.2)	75.7 (18.5)	80.0 (17.5)	45.8 (19.4)
N	39	39	39	41

** $p < .05$,
* $< .1$; OLS regression estimates with standard errors are in parentheses. The models also controlled for a state's unemployment rate and population.

nine places. In education, this type of executive structure is associated with an improved ranking of eight places. Similar effects emerge with respect to energy and public safety.

The results also consistently show a negative relationship between citizen engagement and policy outcomes. As in the previous models, there is worrying lack of association between how much effort citizens put into their government and what they get out of it.

Whom do State Legislatures Represent?

Our analysis indicates that the state legislatures are generally better at representing organized interests than citizens. Legislative activity seems unrelated to citizens' engagement in state politics. At the same time, state legislatures seem quite responsive to organized interests, even allowing them to write the law.

These findings come as no surprise. Interest groups are highly active and quite knowledgeable. Citizens may be sporadically active but know next to nothing about what actually transpires in state legislative chambers. Most citizens cannot name their legislators and have no real idea of the issues discussed in the legislature. Citizens' lack of state-level civic knowledge also comes as no surprise. Media coverage of the state capitols is thin and few citizens have enough basic knowledge about the operations of state government to evaluate any information they might receive. Let us turn to this problem in the next chapter.

Notes

1. Peverill Squire and Gary Moncrief, *State Legislatures Today: Politics under the Domes* (Lanham, MD: Rowman & Littlefield, 2019).
2. Herbert Storing, *What the Anti-Federalists Were For* (Chicago, IL: University of Chicago Press, 1981), ch.3.
3. Herbert Storing, ed., *The Anti-Federalist* (Chicago, IL: University of Chicago Press, 1981), p. 355.
4. Edward M. Earle, ed., *The Federalist, No. 10* (New York: Modern Library, 1937), p. 61.
5. Jodi Enda, Katerina Eva Matsa and Jan Lauren Boyles, "America's Shifting Statehouse Press," *Pew Research Center*, Jul. 10, 2014. www.journalism.org/2014/07/10/americas-shifting-statehouse-press/.
6. David E. Broockman and Christopher Skovron, "Bias in Perceptions of Public Opinion among Elites," *American Political Science Review* 112, no.3, March 2018. www.cambridge.org/core/journals/american-political-science-review/article/bias-in-perceptions-of-public-opinion-among-political-elites/2EF080E04D3AAE6AC1C894F52642E706.
7. Matthew Gentzkow, Edward L. Glaeser and Claudia Goldin, "How Newspapers Became Informative and Why It Mattered," in Edward Glaeser and Claudia Goldin, eds., *Corruption and Reform: Lessons from America's Economic History* (Chicago, IL: University of Chicago Press, 2006), pp. 220–221.
8. Adriana S. Cordis and Jeffrey Milyo, "Measuring Public Corruption in the United States: Evidence from Administrative Records of Federal Prosecutions," *Public Integrity* 18 (December, 2013): 5.
9. Kriston Capps, "The Hidden Costs of Losing Your City's Newspaper," *CityLab*, May 30, 2018. www.citylab.com/equity/2018/05/study-when-local-newspaper-close-city-bond-finances-suffer/561422/.
10. Virginia Gray and David Lowery, "The World of Contract Lobbying," paper presented at the annual meeting of the Midwest Political Science Association, April 6–8, 1995, Chicago. Cited in Alan Rosenthal, *The Third House: Lobbyists and Lobbying in the States* (Washington, DC: CQ Press, 2001), p. 3.
11. Rosenthal, *The Third House*, p. 3.
12. Kayla Crider and Jeffrey Milyo, "Do State Ethics Commissions Reduce Political Corruption? An Exploratory Investigation," *UC Irvine Law Review* 3 (2013): 717.
13. Nicholas Kusnetz, "Conflicts of Interest Run Rampant in State Legislatures," *Center for Public Integrity*, May 19, 2014. https://publicintegrity.org/state-politics/conflicts-of-interest-run-rampant-in-state-legislatures/.
14. Kusnetz, 2014.
15. Decca Muldowney, "The Malleable Conflicts of Interest in State Legislative Rules," *Pacific Standard*, Jun. 7, 2018. https://psmag.com/news/conflicts-of-interest-in-state-legislatures.
16. Chris Joyner, "Loopholes Abound in Some Lobbyist Gift Bans," *Atlanta Journal-Constitution*, Oct. 14, 2012. www.ajc.com/news/loopholes-abound-some-lobbyist-gift-bans/SWrBHUFQKqVDtkGNVDKnBN/.
17. Scott Rod, "Lobbyist Gift-Giving at Issue in More States," *Stateline*, Jul. 19, 2017. www.pewtrusts.org/en/research-and-analysis/blogs/stateline/2017/07/19/lobbyist-gift-giving-at-issue-in-more-states.
18. Gregory Krieg, "South Dakota Uses Emergency Rules to Repeal Anti-Corruption Law," *CNNPolitics*, Feb. 2, 2017. www.cnn.com/2017/02/02/politics/south-dakota-corruption-bill-republican-repeal/index.html.
19. Nathan Grasse and Brianne Heidbreder, "The Influence of Lobbying Activity in State Legislatures: Evidence from Wisconsin," *Legislative Studies Quarterly* 36,

no. 4 (2011): 567–589; Lewis, Daniel C., "Advocacy and Influence: Lobbying and Legislative Outcomes in Wisconsin," *Interest Groups & Advocacy* 2, no. 2 (2013): 206–226.
20 Peverill Squire and Gary Moncrief, *State Legislatures Today*, 2nd ed. (Lanham, MD: Rowman & Littlefield, 2015), pp. 62–63.
21 Virginia Gray, Russell L. Hanson and Thad Kousser, eds., *Politics in the American States: A Comparative Analysis* (Washington, DC: Cq Press, 2017), p. 189.
22 Mark Olade and Dustin Gardiner, "The Network behind State Bills 'Countering' Sharia Law and Terrorism," Center for Public Integrity, Jul. 18, 2019, https://publicintegrity.org/state-politics/copy-paste-legislate/many-state-bills-one-source-behind-the-push-to-ban-sharia-law/.
23 Mark Olade and Dustin Gardiner, "The Network behind State Bills 'Countering' Sharia Law and Terrorism."
24 www.usatoday.com/pages/interactives/asbestos-sharia-law-model-bills-lobbyists-special-interests-influence-state-laws/
25 Gerald C. Wright and Brian F. Schaffner, "The Influence of Party: Evidence from the State Legislatures," *American Political Science Review* 96, no. 2 (2002): 367–379; Gary W. Cox, Thad Kousser and Mathew D. McCubbins, "Party Power or Preferences? Quasi-experimental Evidence from American State Legislatures," *The Journal of Politics* 72, no. 3 (2010): 799–811.
26 https://ballotpedia.org/Incumbents_defeated_in_2018%27s_state_legislative_elections

6   State Justice Systems

As we noted in the Introduction, justice systems can be another problematic feature of the states' institutional structures. Though the scope of federal law enforcement activity has been expanding in recent years, most citizens who come into contact with the police and courts interact with local and state, not federal, officials. Indeed, protecting the public from crime and disorder is among the chief tasks of state and local governments. For this purpose, such governments collectively employ approximately 700,000 full-time police officers.[1] In addition, state and local governments employ nearly 90,000 attorneys, investigators and support staff to prosecute the cases brought to them by the police.[2] These are joined by about 30,000 judges to hear the cases and as many as 500,000 correctional officers to deal with those found guilty and sentenced to serve time in state and county facilities.

As a result of the work of these police officers and prosecutors, in a typical year, roughly ten million Americans are placed under arrest.[3] Of those charged with serious crimes, about two-thirds are convicted, 95 percent as a consequence of plea bargains. Tens of thousands of these individuals each year join the more than two million Americans already incarcerated in state prisons and county jails. A surprising percentage of the jail population—as much as one-fourth in some jurisdictions—is incarcerated for non-payment of municipal fines and fees arising from traffic offenses and quality of life matters such as noise and littering offenses. A number of local governments have attempted to boost revenues by drastically increasing such fines and pressuring the police to produce more revenue by stepping up enforcement. Such policies often have an especially adverse impact upon poor residents who find themselves in jail when they are unable to pay.[4]

Many Americans who, for whatever reason, are arrested and prosecuted are treated properly and in accord with prescribed rules and procedures. However, each year thousands of Americans are victims of misconduct on the part of the police, prosecutors, judges and prison officials. Some cases of misconduct, including several highlighted by the

Black Lives Matter movement, seem to stem from angry confrontations between the police and citizens that escalate to the point of violence. Other misconduct cases result from efforts by the police or other officials to clear cases and produce guilty verdicts or pleas. In response to pressure from the media and their superiors to identify and arrest criminals, the police sometimes circumvent evidentiary and other rules and then offer false testimony on the witness stand to cover their tracks. Police officers call this practice "testilying" and both former New York City Police Commissioner Benjamin Bratton and former San Francisco Police Commissioner Peter Keane have acknowledged that testilying was commonplace among the officers in their departments.[5]

State and local prosecutors, for their part, are under pressure to secure convictions. They may sometimes cut corners and engage in such forms of misconduct as failing to apprise the defense of exculpatory information as has been required since the Supreme Court's 1963 decision in the case of *Brady v. Maryland*.[6] According to Alex Kozinski, former chief judge of the 9th federal Circuit Court of Appeals such "Brady violations" have become an epidemic in America's court system.[7] And, some judges, to avoid the charge of being soft on crime, may overlook misconduct by both the police and prosecutors in order to hand down guilty verdicts. Prison officials, as we shall see, have their own reasons for engaging in misconduct.

Though instances of misconduct may affect only a relatively small percentage of the millions of Americans who face arrest, trial and punishment in the U.S. each year, the result is still thousands of instances in which citizens are treated inappropriately by the authorities. Its relatively low incidence, moreover, offers little solace to those who are the victims of misconduct. To make matters worse, such individuals are very unlikely to find redress through the courts. In America's state and local criminal justice system, wrongs are seldom righted and official wrongdoers seldom punished. Let us begin with the police.

The Police

Police officers, especially those patrolling urban areas, have dangerous jobs. In 2017, some 57,000 officers were assaulted while on duty and 159 were killed. During the same year, police officers killed more than 1000 individuals and injured many others. Generally, these deaths and injuries involved individuals who attacked police officers, refused to relinquish weapons or resisted arrest. Even though they may not appear to present a threat, those who flee from the police seem to be in particular danger. As they pursue a fleeing suspect, officers often develop an increasing sense of tension and fear that builds to a climax and an emotional rush when the suspect is stopped. Sociologist Randall Collins refers to this moment as one of "forward panic," in which police officers are capable of engaging in violent actions that they would normally abjure.[8]

Despite dramatic headlines, the police only use violence against a small percentage of those whom they confront. Even in high-crime areas, the police use force, mainly grabbing and restraining, in only 5 to 8 percent of their encounters with suspected offenders.[9] A small percentage of officers tend to account for a large percentage of violent interactions. For example, Chicago police officer Jason Van Dyke, found guilty in 2018 of the 2014 murder of an unarmed black teenager, Laquan McDonald, had previously been the target of 20 citizen complaints including ten complaints that he used excessive force, two involving the use of a firearm. One of the complaints resulted in a $350,000 jury award paid by the city to a man who alleged that Van Dyke had employed excessive force during a traffic stop.

Unlike Van Dyke, most officers have never drawn or fired their weapons. The other eight officers at the scene of the McDonald shooting kept their weapons holstered. Of course, the use of violence in even 5 to 8 percent of ten million arrests means tens of thousands of violent confrontations between the police and the public—a number that might make everyone uneasy when dealing with the police. And, again, the fact that its statistical probability is relatively small is little comfort to those who do become victims of police violence. In recent years, indeed, a number of highly publicized cases have shown the dangers facing those—particularly but not exclusively African Americans—who find themselves in confrontations with armed police officers.

Many examples of police violence in the United States, such as the infamous Rodney King beating, have come to light in recent years because of the ubiquity of cell phone and surveillance cameras. Take the well-publicized recent case of New York City police officer Patrick Pogan, who, on July 25, 2008, attacked a cyclist riding through Times Square with a group of "Critical Mass" activists who frequently staged bike rides on behalf of environmental and other causes. Unaware that a tourist was photographing the event, Pogan strode several feet to intercept the passing cyclist, Christopher Long, who swerved away in an effort to avoid a collision. Seemingly without provocation, Pogan shoved Long to the ground and then handcuffed and arrested him, charging the cyclist with assault, disorderly conduct and resisting arrest. Unfortunately for Pogan, a tourist who happened to video the confrontation posted the clip on YouTube where it was viewed several million times. This widespread publicity compelled the district attorney to take action. In 2010, Pogan was found guilty of making false statements when he filed his criminal complaint against Long. Pogan, though, was acquitted of several other charges, and given a conditional discharge.[10]

Or, take the case of a Denver man, John Heaney, who rode his bicycle past three undercover Denver police detectives outside Coors Field on the Colorado Rockies's opening day, April 4, 2008. For reasons that are not entirely clear, the three officers attacked Heaney, knocked him to the ground, slammed his head into the pavement and allegedly broke several of his teeth. The officers then arrested Heaney, charged him with assaulting a police officer and with criminal mischief (for allegedly breaking one officer's sunglasses during the melee). The assault charge potentially carried a three-year prison term. The detectives alleged that Heaney attacked them and hit one in the face and chest as they sought to subdue him. They denied slamming Heaney's face into the ground or breaking his teeth. Unfortunately, for the police, a local television crew was in the vicinity taping the Rockies opening day festivities. The crew turned its camera on the arrest and shot tape clearly contradicting the story told by the detectives.[11] Charges against Heaney were dropped and one of the three detectives was charged with assaulting the cyclist but later acquitted when jurors found that the video showed the officers shaking Heaney's head near the pavement but did not show his head actually striking the pavement.

In April, 2015, North Charleston, South Carolina police officer Michael Slager shot and killed a 50-year-old motorist, Walter Scott, who was fleeing on foot after Slager stopped his car for a broken tail light. Slager said he was acting in self-defense but a bystander's cell phone video shows the police officer firing several shots as Scott runs from him. Subsequently, the same video showed Slager staging the crime scene to bolster his claim of self-defense. In 2017, Slager was sentenced to 20 years in prison in federal court for violating Scott's civil rights.[12]

In 2010, in Maryland, a group of five Prince Georges County police officers confronted a crowd of rambunctious students who were noisily celebrating the Maryland basketball team's victory over arch-rival Duke. The officers arrested one of the students, Jack McKenna, and charged him with assault and resisting arrest, claiming that he attacked them and fought when they sought to detain him. Several students who witnessed the event had cell phone cameras and shot videos which they posted on the Internet. The videos show the officers launching an unprovoked attack against McKenna whom they threw against a wall and beat with their batons. When the videos aired on national television news, charges against the student were dropped and the police officers suspended.[13]

Of course, law enforcement officials assert for the record that these cases are isolated and unusual events. It seems more likely, though, that what makes these cases unusual is that the events in question were filmed so that conduct normally hidden from the public's view came into the open. There are many reasons to believe that police abuse of ordinary citizens is not entirely unusual. One recent study indicates that between April, 2009 and June, 2010, the national news media reported 5986 instances of police misconduct.[14] In a study published in 2008, University of Chicago Law Professor Craig Futterman found that between 2002 and 2004 more than 10,000 complaints of police brutality were filed by the citizens of Chicago, alone. In 85 percent of the cases, the police department cleared the accused officers without bothering to interview them. Only 19 complaints resulted in any disciplinary action.[15] Chicago, remember, is the same city where in 2010 a top police commander was sent to prison on charges stemming from his involvement in the torture of hundreds of suspects held by the police over more than a decade.[16] Between 2004 and 2016, moreover, Chicago spent more than $600 million to resolve claims stemming from police misconduct.[17]

A good deal of police misconduct is never reported. A study conducted by the Justice Department's Bureau of Justice Statistics indicated that only 10 percent of the citizens who believed that they were victims of police brutality bothered to file formal reports. Most were afraid to make complaints or believed that their reports were unlikely to result in any action.[18]

And, as to those pesky videos, several police departments have harassed and, in some cases, arrested individuals spotted photographing problematic police activities. For example, in 2009 in Oakland, California, a police officer, Johannes Mehserle, firing at point-blank range, shot and killed a 21-year-old black man who had been pulled from a BART train. The unarmed man was lying on his stomach and offering no resistance. Dozens of frightened commuters photographed the killing on their cell phones. Police officers fanned through the crowd of onlookers attempting to confiscate the phones and, at one point chased an uncooperative cell phone owner onto a subway car.[19] Despite these police efforts, several photos of the shooting were posted on the Internet, leading to riots in Oakland and forcing the local authorities to take action. The officer was charged with manslaughter and served 11 months in prison.[20]

In several states, such as Maryland, Pennsylvania and Illinois, statutes stipulate that individuals cannot be recorded without their consent. The police maintain that this prohibits citizens from taping or filming their activities, though no court has ever upheld the idea that such a statute can apply to the police or other public officials performing their duties, especially in a public setting where there is no expectation of privacy. Nevertheless, police departments have arrested a number of individuals and charged them with violating anti-taping or wiretapping statutes. Thus, Chicago police arrested a woman who recorded efforts by internal affairs officers to discourage her from filing a complaint against a police officer who she says groped her breast.[21] Maryland and Pennsylvania police have brought charges against a number of persons who sought to make a record of their confrontations with police officers.

By preventing photos and videos, of course, the police hope to prevent incontrovertible evidence of their misconduct from becoming a matter of general knowledge. From their perspective the problem is not misconduct but the public perception that misconduct is widespread. Without the photos, police denials seem plausible, as do claims that inappropriate and violent action on the part of officers is aberrational rather than a routine aspect of police interactions with citizens.

Violence, as was suggested above, is only one element of police misconduct. The police are under pressure from their superiors, from prosecutors and from the media to fix responsibility for the commission of crimes and to make arrests. In 2008, for example, the Chicago *Sun-Times* castigated the police in an editorial for failing to make even one arrest after 71 shootings in the city.[22] This pressure can lead to two forms of misconduct. The first entails breaking legal rules when it comes to the collection of evidence and the arrest and interrogation of suspects whom the police believe to be guilty. Police officers distinguish between actual guilt and legally provable guilt and may see no moral reason to refrain from cutting whatever legal corners might help to prove the guilt of those whom they believe to be guilty. This sort of misconduct is generally applauded in cinematic portrayals of police work where dedicated officers are often shown breaking the rules to ensure that the guilty are punished.

A second form of misconduct entails violating established evidentiary and procedural rules in order to facilitate a conviction even though the officers in question have no reason to believe that the individual they are taking into custody is actually guilty of the crime in question. This form of misconduct is generally viewed as morally repugnant and is certainly not celebrated by the mass media. Unfortunately, though, looking the other way when the police break the rules to catch the guilty may also open the door to practices that ensnare the innocent.

The rules of criminal procedure are complex and offer many opportunities for police errors and misconduct. Misconduct is most likely to manifest itself in the realm of search and seizure, though witness identification and interrogations also offer room for police misconduct. Search and seizure is governed by the Constitution's 4th Amendment which declares,

> The right of the people to be secure in their persons, houses, papers and effects, against unreasonable searches and seizures, shall not be violated, and no Warrants shall issue, but upon probable cause, supported by Oath or affirmation, and particularly describing the place to be searched, and the persons or things to be seized.

This 4th Amendment prohibition was applied to the states by the Supreme Court's 1961 decision in the case of *Mapp v. Ohio*.[23] The case involved the search without a warrant of an apartment where the police believed they could find evidence of illegal gambling and other crimes.

As detailed in the *Mapp* case and subsequent court decisions, the language of the 4th Amendment means that before police officers can search private property, they must obtain a warrant from a judge authorizing them to conduct the search. Generally, this means the police must convince the judge that there is probable cause to believe that the evidence in question is likely to be found at the premises to be searched. When it comes to searches of persons, the police may search individuals, or vehicles in the course of a traffic stop, when they have reasonable grounds to believe the person is engaged in criminal activity or represents a threat to them. They may not stop individuals randomly and conduct searches without a specific reason. The 4th Amendment is enforced by the "exclusionary rule" under which evidence obtained in violation of its strictures is inadmissible in a criminal trial. Moreover, any evidence or information subsequently obtained by the police because of facts they discovered in the original unconstitutional search is also deemed inadmissible. This is sometimes known as the "fruit of the poisonous tree" doctrine. The main purpose of the exclusionary rule is deterring police misconduct and preventing it from adversely affecting individual rights.

According to some authorities, the actual impact of the exclusionary rule is minimal. Evidence is excluded in only a very small percentage of criminal cases where the defense argues during a pre-trial suppression hearing that the evidence in question resulted directly or indirectly from an illegal search.[24] Often, of course, prosecutors will offer defendants favorable plea deals if they determine that the evidence proffered by the police is likely to be suppressed, thus heading off an adverse ruling in a suppression hearing.[25]

In many instances, the police scrupulously follow the rules. Empirical studies suggest, however, that a major reason little evidence is excluded is that the police often shade the truth, "testilying" when describing in depositions and preliminary hearings how they obtained relevant evidence.[26] Indeed, in the *Mapp* case, itself, the lead investigator testified that the police had a warrant for the search, though no such warrant was ever produced in court.

Examples of testilying are endless. After conducting an illegal search, officers will give "dropsy" testimony, claiming that contraband was dropped by the defendant in the officer's plain sight.[27] In a 2012 case, for example, a New York detective testified that a man loitering in the lobby of a Bronx apartment building threw a bottle filled with oxycodone on the ground as the police approached him. A security camera, however, captured the entire incident and showed that the officer's testimony was false.[28] Officers will claim that evidence was found in plain sight, obviating the need for a warrant. In a 2017 New York City case, a police officer testified that he wanted to search an apartment for evidence in the wake of a shooting but was blocked by a woman standing in the way with a laundry bag. When he took the bag and set it on the floor, said the officer, he heard "a clunk, a thud." He opened the bag and found a nine-millimeter hand gun and arrested the woman. A hallway security camera, however, showed that there had been no laundry bag. The laundry bag story had been concocted by officers to hide the fact that without a warrant or any particular cause, they had barged into the apartment where they found the gun in question. Charges against the woman were dismissed.[29] Officers will falsely claim they had consent for a search. In a recent Chicago case, for example, a motorist was charged with felony possession with intent to sell marijuana. Five officers testified that the defendant had consented to a search of his car. A dash cam video of which the police were not aware proved that there had been no consent for the search and charges were dropped.[30]

Witness identification is another realm where testilying is commonplace. Take, for example, a 2015 New York case. Two suspects in a Brooklyn carjacking were arrested by the police. Detectives testified that the suspects had been identified by the victim in a photo lineup. The case seemed quite strong until it became clear that the photo lineups submitted as evidence were fabrications. The photos of the two suspects were real. However, the "filler" photos added to create the lineup had not been taken until after the date of the lineup. The victim could not possibly have compared them to the photos of the suspects.[31]

Studies suggest that these and other cases reported by the media represent the tiniest tip of an enormous iceberg of police deception lurking just beneath the surface. Research undertaken in New York, Chicago, Philadelphia and other cities all found that false police reports are commonplace, particularly in cases of search and seizure. A study conducted in Chicago by Law Professor Myron Orfield concluded that, "police commit perjury between 20 percent and 50 percent of the time they testify on 4th Amendment issues."[32]

Despite the fact that falsehoods by the police seems commonplace, only a handful of officers ever face misconduct charges stemming from the practice. One reason is that the cases that come to the attention of the media and may lead to misconduct charges are the results of cross-examination in criminal trials. Hardly any criminal cases, though, ever go to trial. Almost all criminal cases are resolved through plea bargains, which means that there will probably not be a suppression hearing or cross-examination. One veteran Brooklyn police officer said, "There's no fear of being caught. You're not going to trial and nobody is going to be cross-examined."[33] This officer was correct in his assessment. In 2016, 99.5 percent of all criminal cases resolved in New York City involved negotiated settlements. Suppression hearings were held in only 2.4 percent of felony cases and one-tenth of 1 percent of non-felony cases.

Moreover, even in those rare instances when cases go to trial, suppression hearings are held and witnesses are cross-examined, judges are reluctant to find that a police officer has committed perjury.[34] Many officers are experienced witnesses who have learned to describe investigations in ways that conform to constitutional requirements even when the reality is different. Judges, for their part, dislike suppressing evidence that may allow guilty individuals to walk free. This is particularly so since state and local judges are elected officials who do not relish the idea of future political opponents claiming that they are soft on criminals.

To be sure, no one wishes to see guilty persons go free so, as mentioned above, police officers who lie to make sure the guilty are punished despite "technicalities" are usually seen by the public and the media as heroic figures. Consider, however, that false police testimony can be used against the innocent as well as the guilty. In a recent case, four Florida police officers were caught on camera conspiring to bring a false driving under the influence (DUI) charge against a motorist whose car had been hit by one of the officers at a stop light. While the motorist was handcuffed in the back seat of one of the squad cars, the officers discussed their story. "I don't lie and make things up ever because it's wrong," said one officer whose voice is quite audible on the tape, "but if I need to bend it a little to protect a cop, I'll do it." The officers rehearsed their story before driving the motorist to the city lock up.[35] Similarly, in 2011, seven New York City narcotics detectives were convicted of planting drugs on innocent individuals to meet their arrest quotas. Another officer was accused of making a false arrest as a favor for his cousin.[36] Allowed to take root, testilying can quickly lose its heroic hue.

Though the likelihood of criminal prosecutions for their misdeeds is low, police misconduct might be deterred by the prospect of law suits. Each year a number of suits are filed against the police alleging excessive use of force or evidentiary violations such as illegal searches. Generally, as we saw in Chapter 2, such suits are filed under Title 42, Section 1983 of the U.S. code and allege that the police violated an individual's constitutional rights "under color of state law." For example, a suit might allege that the police carried out an unlawful search in violation of the plaintiff's rights under the 4th Amendment.

Quite a number of 1983 suits are filed against the police each year but few are successful. Since 1982, the Supreme Court has held that police officers have "qualified immunity" from such suits.[37] Qualified immunity means that a plaintiff must prove that under the color of law, the police officer knowingly violated a clearly established constitutional right. As interpreted by the courts, this is a very high bar and in all but a handful of cases where the police claim qualified immunity, this claim is upheld. One recent review of Supreme Court decisions from 1982 through 2017 found that the Court nearly always held that the police conduct in question did *not* clearly violate established law.[38] The Supreme Court, moreover, often reversed lower court decisions that denied immunity to police officers but never reversed decisions that supported such immunity. This case pattern sends a clear signal to lower courts to err on the side of police immunity from suit. The Court has generally viewed qualified immunity as necessary to avoid hindering police work.[39]

In those rare cases when Section 1983 suits prevail, police officers are almost never personally liable for whatever monies are awarded to the plaintiffs. Usually, officers are indemnified by the state or municipal governments that employ them. The end result of indemnification, qualified immunity and lack of much risk of criminal prosecution is that officers may not always have adequate reason to respect the rights, or even concern themselves with the physical wellbeing of those whom they encounter, particularly in hostile confrontations. Perhaps this is part of the explanation for such phenomena as police violence against African Americans.[40]

Prosecutors

The police are under pressure from their superiors to make arrests. Prosecutors, for their part, are pressed to obtain convictions. District attorneys (sometimes called state's attorneys) are usually elected officials who serve as the chief prosecutors in a county or other subdivision of a state. Each district attorney may employ a number of assistant district attorneys (ADAs) who, in larger counties do the actual trial work while the district attorney serves as a manager. District attorneys are anxious to show voters that they are diligent and effective crime fighters. ADAs are usually evaluated on the basis of their success in securing convictions, whether by plea bargain or trial, and sending criminals to prison. ADAs who win cases are likely to receive commendations, are seen as stars and are more likely to be promoted. "The measure of your worth came down to the number of cases you tried and the outcomes," said one former assistant district attorney.[41]

Some ADAs are, themselves, politically ambitious and are anxious to obtain convictions, especially in high-profile cases that may serve as launching pads for political careers. One ambitious ADA in Tennessee reportedly hid evidence, helping her to win a highly publicized murder case and used the publicity to run successfully for district attorney. She is reportedly considering a run for governor on a law-and-order platform. The voters don't seem to care that the great courtroom victory that launched the then-assistant district attorney's career might have come about because of her decision to withhold exculpatory evidence.[42]

The pressures and incentives to obtain convictions can lead some prosecutors to cut legal corners. Among the most common forms of prosecutorial misconduct is failure to provide the defense with potentially exculpatory evidence in the prosecution's possession (a Brady violation). This form of prosecutorial misconduct is commonplace or, as a recent *New York Times* editorial declared, "rampant" in the criminal justice system.[43]

There is, in fact, very little to prevent an unscrupulous prosecutor from hiding exculpatory evidence or engaging in other forms of official misconduct. If sanctions against police officers found to have engaged in misconduct are unusual, punishment for prosecutorial misconduct is exceedingly rare. According to one study, the 1999 trial of the so-called "DuPage Seven," a group of police officers and prosecutors accused of perjury and obstruction of justice for allegedly framing an innocent defendant in a capital murder case, was the first time in American history that a felony prosecution of a prosecutor even reached the verdict stage.[44] All seven were acquitted. Prosecutors almost never face criminal charges and are seldom sanctioned by state bar authorities. And, while police officers enjoy qualified immunity from liability, prosecutors generally possess absolute immunity from civil liability for actions undertaken in relation to their official duties.[45] When a prosecutor commits a violation and the violation comes to light, the only real consequence might be dismissal of the case, but only if the judge concludes that prosecutorial misconduct substantially prejudiced the outcome of the trial. Otherwise, the prosecutor's conduct, however egregious, is likely to be deemed harmless error.

Consider some of the cases that have come to light in recent years. Most readers are familiar with the so-called Duke lacrosse case. In that 2006 case an African American woman, hired by several Duke University students to dance at an off-campus party, charged that she had been raped by several white members of the school's lacrosse team. Though the accuser's story seemed riddled with inconsistencies, the Durham County district attorney, Michael Nifong, brought rape charges against three team members. The story of privileged white students allegedly raping a poor black woman quickly became a media sensation and caused outrage in Durham's black community. Nifong, who was up for reelection that very year, was anxious to maintain good relations with Durham's black leaders and voters as well as with white progressives who quickly championed the woman's cause.

Apparently motivated by these political considerations, Nifong ignored evidence that cast any doubt upon the accuser's story and ultimately sought to hide DNA evidence in his possession that all but proved the innocence of the three lacrosse players. Nifong had sent the accuser's clothing to a private laboratory for testing. The tests revealed genetic material from several men on her clothing, as well as her body, but none from any of the lacrosse players. Nifong, in consultation with the director of the laboratory, withheld this information from defense attorneys while affirming to the court that he had disclosed all relevant evidence and telling the news media that defense efforts to obtain additional DNA evidence was a "witch hunt," aimed at the accuser. However, after a thorough document review and analysis of the DNA evidence that Nifong had given them, defense attorneys were able to surmise that critical information had been withheld and filed a motion describing the tests they knew must have been conducted and demanding to see the results.

After the judge ordered Nifong to produce the missing information and the DNA test results became public, the North Carolina bar charged Nifong with breaking the state's rules of professional conduct by making false statements to the court and the media. He was ultimately disbarred as well as cited by the court for criminal contempt and sentenced to one day in jail. The rape case was taken over by the state's attorney general and the charges dropped. A happy ending—at a cost to the falsely accused mens' families of several million dollars in legal fees (which they sought to recover in a series of civil suits) and enormous anguish.

Nifong's efforts to hide clearly exculpatory evidence and various other forms of prosecutorial misconduct were characterized by state officials as an unfortunate and unusual example of a rogue prosecutor who engaged in, "a tragic rush to accuse."[46] Unfortunately, however, what is unusual about the Duke case is not the prosecutor's misconduct but, rather, that the prosecutor's misconduct actually came to light and led to sanctions.

However reprehensible, Nifong's tactics were not particularly unusual. In 2011, for example, the U.S. Supreme Court heard a case involving a failure by New Orleans prosecutors to turn over potentially exculpatory evidence to the defense in a capital case. This marked what according to some observers was the 28th time in recent years that New Orleans prosecutors had been caught failing to turn over such evidence. Their policy was said to be, "keeping away as much information as possible from the defense attorney." One inmate spent 18 years on death row while prosecutors withheld evidence pointing to his innocence.[47] In the most recent case, the Supreme Court overturned the conviction. Similarly, in a Texas case, a man convicted in 1987 of murdering his wife was released in 2011 when a court finally ordered DNA testing of evidence withheld by the original prosecutor in the case. The evidence proved conclusively that another man had committed the murder but it and other evidence was hidden by the prosecutor—who is now a state judge.[48] And, along the same lines, in a recent New York case, a man named Jabbar Collins spent 16 years in New York prisons for a murder he didn't commit. He was released in 2010, after a federal judge found that the prosecutor, Michael Vecchione, had withheld critical exculpatory evidence during the trial. The judge called the behavior of the district attorney's office "shameful." The ADA who prosecuted Collins retired with benefits in 2013. He never faced any public sanctions for his misconduct in the Collins case, or for his questionable actions in several other cases over the years.[49]

The problem of misconduct seems most common in state court, where the great majority of criminal cases are heard but, to be fair, such misconduct crops up in federal court as well. In a 2010 report, USA TODAY identified more than 200 recent cases in which federal prosecutors engaged in various forms of misconduct to obtain convictions—a number that may, itself represent only the proverbial tip of the iceberg. These instances of misconduct include withholding evidence, misrepresentations to the court, improper efforts to influence witnesses, improper vouching of witnesses and so forth.[50] Take, for example, the case of Orlando, Florida businessman, Antonino Lyons, reported by USA TODAY. In 2001 Lyons, a college graduate and respected formed basketball star with no criminal record, was arrested and convicted of selling large quantities of cocaine. The allegations and evidence against him consisted entirely of the testimony of several convicted felons who hoped to win sentence reductions and other favors from the government in exchange for their assistance. Under the U.S. sentencing guidelines in effect in 2001, Lyons faced a mandatory sentence of life in federal prison for his alleged offenses.

Fortunately, prior to his sentencing, Lyons retained the services of a new and extremely able attorney who, after examining the government's case, concluded that the government had withheld evidence that might have exonerated Lyons and that the prosecutor had failed to correct what was probably false testimony from the witnesses against Lyons. Withholding exculpatory evidence is called a Brady violation after the 1963 case of *Brady v. Maryland*.[51] Failing to correct testimony against the accused when the prosecutor knows the testimony to be false is called a Giglio violation after the 1972 case of *Giglio v. U.S.*[52] In May 2002, a federal district judge found that, indeed, in at least one instance federal prosecutors had failed to provide the defense with exculpatory material in their possession and had, moreover, presented testimony against Lyons they knew to be false. The judge ordered a new trial. The government appealed the district judge's order and a federal appeals court declared that Lyons was not entitled to a new trial because of the weight of other testimony against him. Prior to his sentencing, however, Lyons filed a motion to force the government to disclose additional documents that threatened to impeach all the testimony against Lyons. For more than a year—while Lyons sat in jail without bond—the government failed to accede to the judge's order to produce the documents demanded by Lyons, engaging in what the district court judge characterized as a "concerted campaign of delay and denial ... [as the] ... government brazenly refused to comply with the order."[53]

When prosecutors finally produced the relevant documents, it became clear that the prosecutors had committed not one but numerous Brady and Giglio violations, hiding many pieces of exculpatory evidence and remaining silent as witness after witness presented testimony prosecutors knew to be false. Forced to reveal these facts, prosecutors dropped all their charges against Lyons. Furious, the judge declared the case to have been the result of "a prosecution run amuck."[54] A new federal prosecutor assigned to the case apologized to Lyons and conceded that, "the United State's prosecution of Lyons did not reflect the government at its best." Subsequently, the trial judge certified that Lyons was completely innocent of all the charges brought against him.[55]

Though Lyons was exonerated, his life was ruined. He had spent 1003 days in jail awaiting trial and sentencing, his businesses failed, he lost his house, his wife lost her job as a school principal, and he exhausted all his savings defending himself against false charges. Lyons is a free man but how can his life ever be repaired?

Another individual whose life was turned upside down by federal prosecutors is former U.S. Army Lt. Col. Robert Morris. Morris was a decorated combat veteran and logistics expert who became involved in a dispute with the Defense Logistics Agency. An anonymous tipster to a Defense Department hot line had claimed that Morris had diverted for his own use $7 million of surplus medical equipment from a Marine Corps base near Morris's own base at Fort Benning, Georgia. After an investigation by the Fort Benning commander, Morris was cleared. He had sent the equipment to a charity in Rwanda approved by the Army.[56] Nevertheless, for reasons that never became clear, the Defense Logistics Agency looked for a federal prosecutor willing to take the case. After being turned down by prosecutors in Georgia and elsewhere, the agency found a federal prosecutor in Dallas, Texas willing to file charges against Morris. The federal judge in Texas to whom prosecutors brought the case warned them that it seemed to be a very dubious effort before granting a defense motion to transfer the case back to Georgia for trial. The prosecutor was not deterred and moved the case to Georgia where a jury deliberated for only a few minutes before acquitting Morris. Another happy ending? Not exactly. His legal defense cost Morris hundreds of thousands of dollars. The prosecution, moreover, essentially ended Morris's military career and generally upended his life—for reasons that remain difficult to understand.

Let us consider, also, the tragic case of the Aisenberg family. Early in the morning of November 24, 1997, the Aisenbergs, a young Florida couple, called the police to report that their five-month-old daughter Sabrina was missing from their home. The Hillsborough County Sheriff's office conducted a search and investigation. Lacking other suspects, the sheriff's office focused on the parents and obtained a court order to tap the couple's phone and install listening devices in their home. In this case state officials acted properly. Local and state authorities concluded that there was no evidence against the couple. A federal prosecutor, however, had a federal grand jury indict the Aisenbergs on charges that they lied to investigators and conspired to deceive the authorities.[57] Federal authorities sought unsuccessfully to induce each Aisenberg to testify against the other, promising favorable treatment to the first one to cooperate.

Much of the government's case against the Aisenbergs was based upon statements allegedly captured by the various wiretaps. An assistant U.S. attorney averred in court that the government had recordings in which the Aisenbergs made incriminating statements that would be presented at trial. According to the government these statements indicated that the husband had killed the child and that the wife was conspiring to help him cover up his crime. When the Aisenbergs's defense attorney asked the U.S. District Court judge to review the tapes, the government opposed the idea and it soon became clear why. Judge Steven Mayberry listened to the tapes in his chambers and declared that they were "inaudible" and "insubstantial as evidence." He found that the disparity between the tapes' contents and the government's contentions was "shocking." The judge found that even the initial warrants that had been granted for the phone taps and listening devices were based on false information "that left a trail of reckless disregard for the truth." In 2001, with the tapes discredited, the government moved to dismiss the indictment against the Aisenbergs.

In 2003, the Aisenbergs joined the 13 individuals who have succeeded in winning Hyde Amendment sanctions against the government. The 1997 Hyde Amendment was intended to provide some possibility of redress for victims of federal prosecutorial abuse. Exonerated defendants may bring a civil action against the government in which they endeavor to show that their prosecution was "vexatious, frivolous or in bad faith." With such a showing they may be awarded attorneys fees and other legal expenses they incurred. Generally speaking, the federal courts have indicated that to succeed, a Hyde Amendment case must prove that prosecutors acted maliciously and pursued a case even when they knew or should have known it was utterly without merit. This is a very high threshold, almost never met, but in 2003 a federal judge awarded the Aisenbergs more than $2 million in legal fees (later reduced to $1.5 million). Essentially, the judge found that the prosecution of the Aisenbergs had been malicious and oppressive. The government conceded the point and agreed that it was liable under the Hyde Amendment, contesting only the amount of the award. While the government focused its efforts on incarcerating the parents, the daughter was never found.

As an example of ordinary injustice, let us not fail to mention the politically ambitious Massachusetts prosecutors who destroyed the Amirault family. The case began in 1984 when Gerald, his sister Cheryl and his mother Violet Amirault, operators of a Malden, Massachusetts, day care center, the Fells Acres School, were accused of sexually abusing several children under their supervision.[58] The charges were both sensational and fantastic. Gerald Amirault, for example, was accused of plunging a wide-blade butcher knife into the rectum of a four-year-old boy. Surprisingly, the knife left no mark or injury. Violet was accused of tying a boy to a tree in broad daylight in full view of everyone at the school, and assaulting him anally with a "magic wand," which also produced no injury.[59]

The evidence against the Amiraults consisted entirely of heavily coached testimony by the children, often memories "recovered" by counselors who claimed to specialize in helping individuals retrieve memories of which they, themselves, had not been aware prior to coaching. The absence of conventional evidence did not seem to trouble the prosecutors, led by Middlesex County District Attorney Scott Harshberger, who urged jurors to strike a blow against child abuse by validating the testimony of the children who had bravely come forward.[60] Against the backdrop of a nation-wide panic over what the media called an epidemic of child abuse, all three Amiraults were convicted. Gerald was sent to prison for a term of 30–40 years, and his mother and sister to terms of 8–20 years.

Eight years later, in 1995, a judge ordered Cheryl and Violet be released immediately, declaring that all the testimony against them had been the result of prosecutorial coaching. The new district attorney, Martha Coakley, appealed the judge's order and succeeded in having it reversed by the state's appeals court. Violet Amirault died before she could be returned to prison and Coakley agreed to a revision of Cheryl's sentence to time served after asking the Amiraults' attorney to agree as a condition of Cheryl's release that he would halt his efforts to win Gerald's release.[61] The attorney refused.

In 2001, the Massachusetts Board of Pardons and Paroles voted 5–0 to recommend that the governor commute Gerald's sentence. The Board pointed to the lack of evidence against Gerald and the bizarre character of the charges. Coakley responded with a media campaign bringing the now-adult alleged victims of abuse at the Fells Acres School to interviews where they could once again tell their stories to reporters. The governor turned down the Board's recommendation and Gerald served two more years in prison before being paroled in 2004, having spent nearly 20 years behind bars. As a convicted sex offender who had refused to "take responsibility" for his crimes, Gerald is subject to numerous restrictions and conditions including the requirement to wear an electronic tracking device at all times.

As to the prosecutors who gained political visibility in the Amirault case, Scott Harshberger was elected Massachusetts attorney general and later named president of Common Cause. Martha Coakley was later elected Massachusetts attorney general and in 2010 was the Democratic candidate for the U.S. Senate seat vacated by the death of Edward Kennedy. Coakley lost the election but is not required to wear a tracking device.

Whenever an instance of prosecutorial misconduct comes to light, the relevant government agencies are quick to declare that this is an exceptional instance and not typical of the work of prosecutorial officials. Attorneys and even judges, however, know this is not true. Questionable prosecutorial tactics are the norm, not the exception. Marvin Schechter, a defense attorney who chaired the criminal justice section of the New York State Bar Association, wrote in 2012 that prosecutorial misconduct was "not a trickle but a polluted river." He went on to write that misconduct by prosecutors was "learned and taught" in prosecutorial offices.[62]

Schachter's "polluted river" metaphor is supported by a study of prosecutorial practices in California conducted over a ten-year period by the Northern California Innocence Project.[63] The study found that the issue of prosecutorial misconduct was raised in about 4000 criminal cases during this period. In 707 cases courts explicitly found that prosecutors had committed misconduct and in another 282 cases courts refrained from making a ruling, holding that the conduct in question would not have affected the outcome of the case. These numbers, according to the study's authors, greatly understate the actual incidence of prosecutorial misconduct in criminal cases since they are drawn from the tiny number of criminal cases (3 percent) that actually went to trial. Ninety-seven percent of the felony prosecutions undertaken during this period were resolved by guilty pleas. Only six of the prosecutors in the 707 cases where misconduct was identified were disciplined by the California bar, though several had committed misconduct on multiple occasions—a polluted river, indeed.

Over the past decade, 60 local prosecutors across the United States have established conviction integrity units to review potential cases of wrongful convictions in their jurisdictions.[64] These units have to date cleared some 400 individuals imprisoned for crimes they did not commit. There are approximately 2300 state and local prosecutorial offices in the United States, so 2250 still lack conviction integrity units. If we extrapolate from the results in the 60 jurisdictions that have created such units, there may be 15,000 innocent persons sitting in state penal institutions with no recourse.

Judges

Like prosecutors, judges enjoy absolute immunity from suits relating to their judicial functions. And, like prosecutors most state trial court judges—unlike federal judges who receive life-time appointments—are also elected officials. In most jurisdictions, however, once elected or, in some instances appointed, judges are subject only to unopposed retention elections, sometimes every ten years, where they can be removed from office only if a majority or other designated percentage of votes are cast against their retention.

Traditionally, sitting judges have seldom lost retention elections; they are under less pressure than prosecutors to be stricter in their handling of cases. Perhaps, for this reason, judicial misconduct is less common an issue than improper action by the police or prosecutors.[65] Occasionally, however, judges are compelled to respond to electoral considerations. In recent years, political forces interested in the outcome of a judicial election have raised millions of dollars to influence the result. In 2010 in Illinois, for example, a pro-business group, the Illinois Civil Justice League, raised $3 million in an effort to block the retention of Chief Justice Thomas Kilbride of the Illinois Supreme Court. The group was angered by Kilbride's decisions in a number of civil cases. The judge raised $2 million in support of his retention effort and kept his position.[66]

Another recent case illustrates the dangers involved in judicial campaign spending. In 2004, Brent Benjamin sought to win a seat held by Justice Warren McGraw on the Supreme Court of Appeals in West Virginia. During the campaign, $3 million, or nearly 60 percent of the funds spent on Benjamin's behalf were channeled through an independent expenditure committee controlled by Don Blankenship, CEO of Massey Energy, a major West Virginia coal company. In 2008, Benjamin refused to recuse himself from a case involving Massey Energy and cast the deciding vote in a 3–2 decision overturning a $50 million jury verdict against the company.[67] This case was appealed to the U.S. Supreme Court which ruled that Benjamin's refusal to recuse himself created an appearance of a conflict of interest so extreme as to constitute a violation of the plaintiff's right to due process.[68] The Supreme Court did not look into the question of actual bias on Justice Benjamin's part but observed that the previous campaign contributions created a high probability of such bias.

The Benjamin matter involved a civil case, but electoral concerns may also have an effect on criminal cases. In recent years, there has been a sharp increase in television ads focusing on judges' records, and judges standing for retention have run the risk of being called "soft on crime" by groups opposed to keeping them on the bench.[69] Few judges are defeated by such campaigns but most are conscious of them and eager to avoid being targeted. In one recent study most judges said their own rulings were unaffected by electoral considerations but 83 percent said they believed their colleagues were affected by reelection concerns.[70] Moreover, a Brennan Center review of ten recent empirical studies found that judges facing reelection or retention campaigns, especially in states where television advertising was commonly used during judicial elections, were more likely to rule against criminal defendants and to impose harsher penalties than judges not facing this pressure.[71] Justice is apparently not completely blind.

Prisons

The conduct of the police, prosecutors and even judges pale by comparison to the injustices visited upon inmates in state correctional facilities. Let us focus upon one of the most egregious of these injustices—the problem of sexual assault in prisons.

Male Prison Rape

The general public has little interest in or sympathy for prison inmates, believing that if the conditions of incarceration are harsh, inmates deserve what they get.[72] One thing they get is rape. Precise numbers are not available, but according to some studies, as many as 20 percent of the male prisoners in America's penal institutions are the victims of sexual assault—many are repeatedly assaulted during their incarceration.[73] In a similar vein, a 1993 *New York Times* article estimated that more than 250,000 men are sexually assaulted in prison every year.[74] According to one commentator, prisons promote sexual terrorism.[75] Aggressive and strong inmates commonly exploit weaker inmates without much interference from prison authorities or, in some instances, with their collusion. A new inmate must fight his attackers, seek segregation from the general prison population, or accept a position of subservience to another inmate or group of inmates capable of protecting him. If a man is successfully attacked once, he is like to be seen as an easy target and to suffer additional attacks. Men who are raped in prison are, on average, raped nine times.[76] The 2003 federal Prison Rape Elimination Act (PRE)A, creating national standards, albeit weak ones, for inmate safety was not actually implemented until 2012 and many of its provisions did not take effect until 2017, so its impact on prison rape remains unknown. Indeed, PREA's inmate safety standards are mandatory only within the federal prison system. In the state prisons, which hold the great majority of America's inmates, PREA offers financial incentives but compliance remains voluntary.[77]

Rape can be humiliating and both psychologically and physically devastating for inmates but, beyond this, the effects of widespread prison rape reverberate through the larger society. The most obvious of these effects is related to AIDS. Thousands of prisoners are HIV positive or suffer from full-blown AIDS and, between 1991 and 1995, one in every three deaths in prison resulted from AIDS infection. Accordingly, individuals raped in prison stand a good chance of contracting the AIDS virus. This not only represents a death sentence for the inmate, who can hardly afford the most up-to-date treatments, but means that when that inmate is released he poses a risk to the larger community. Many experts believe that the high rate of new AIDS cases among black women is a result of the large number of black men who leave prison each year carrying the AIDS virus.[78] At the same time, inmates who have been raped may develop a sense of hostility and rage that translates into violent behavior after their release.

State prison authorities are certainly aware of the prevalence of rape in their institutions. Many, however, have either felt powerless to deal with the problem or have been unwilling to treat rape prevention as an institutional priority. The United States currently houses more than two million prisoners mainly in state facilities built to accommodate fewer than one million.[79] This severe overcrowding, coupled with under staffing, has made many prisons difficult to manage and reduces the ability of prison authorities to segregate prisoners who, by virtue of size, race or sexual orientation, may be at special risk for sexual assault from prisoners with a history of or propensity for engaging in such assaults.

Beyond the obvious difficulties faced by authorities in attempting to maintain order within a prison, a number of studies indicate that state prison officials often exhibit a callous disregard for the problem of sexual assault. Not unlike the public at large, guards and other officials sometimes believe that brutal conditions within the prison, including rape, function as a deterrent to crime and a just punishment for its commission.[80] "The guards just turn their backs," one inmate claimed. "Their mentality is the tougher, colder, and more cruel and inhuman a place is, the less chance a person will return."[81] In some instances, according to inmates' allegations, guards and prison officials use the threat of rape as an instrument of control, intimidating inmates by threatening to assign them to bunk with sexual predators, or even allowing violent or predatory individuals access to weaker inmates in exchange for their cooperation in maintaining order in the prison.[82] One inmate wrote, "The main reason why sexual assaults occur is because prison officials and staff promote them. It's their method of sacrificing the weak inmates to achieve and maintain control of the stronger, aggressive or violent inmates."[83] Another inmate said,

> It seems that young men and gays and first timers are used as sacrificial lamb [sic]. The reason is to use these men as a way to keep the gangs and killers from turning on the system which created prison the Hell that it is.[84]

More generally, many guards reportedly view sexual assault prevention as the business of the individual prisoner rather than the responsibility of the institution. This harsh perspective is known colloquially as "f*** or fight" and is the dominant view in the institutional culture of many, if not all, correctional institutions.[85] For the most part, prison rapes are not investigated by the police and their perpetrators are not prosecuted even when victims bring complaints. Prison administrators seldom collect physical evidence or interview witnesses to rapes in their institutions. The local prosecutors who would bear the responsibility for bringing charges typically do not see prison inmates as their constituents, nor do they see any political advantage to championing their cause.[86] To the extent that perpetrators are penalized at all, punishments generally take the form of minor administrative sanctions within the prison. Because their complaints are not taken seriously, many inmate rape victims do not report such assaults. They see little reason to bear public humiliation and possible reprisal when the authorities are unlikely to take any action against perpetrators. The advocacy group, Human Rights Watch recently completed a study of 100 prison rapes and discovered that not a single one resulted in prosecution of the alleged perpetrators.[87]

Cruel but not Unusual

In principle, prison authorities bear a responsibility for protecting prisoners from sexual assault. The courts have held that this responsibility is derived from the 8th Amendment's prohibition of cruel and unusual punishment. Traditionally, the 8th Amendment was conceived to apply to punishments formally prescribed or meted out by the government, not to ills that might befall the inmate during the period of his or her confinement.[88] Beginning in the late 1980s, however, in response to Section 1983 suits, the Supreme Court began to rule that the conditions of a prisoner's confinement, even if not formally mandated by the government as an element of a prisoner's punishment, could be so execrable as to constitute cruel and unusual punishment in violation of the 8th Amendment. The specific question of protection from sexual violence was considered by the Court in the case of *Farmer v. Brennan*.[89] Brennan, a preoperative transsexual with feminine characteristics, alleged that prison authorities had placed him in the general population of a maximum security facility where he was beaten and raped by other inmates. The Court held that prison officials, indeed, had a duty to protect inmates from sexual assault by other prisoners and that failure to carry out this duty could constitute cruel and unusual punishment.

Practically speaking, bringing a suit against state prison officials is not an easy undertaking for the typical inmate. An inmate known to be contemplating or actually undertaking legal action against prison officials may become the target of intimidation and retaliation. Since 1996, moreover, congressionally mandated restrictions on prisoners' suits have placed a number of obstacles in the way of imprisoned victims of sexual assaults who seek redress in the courts. To begin with, Congress prohibited the Legal Services Corporation from providing funding to legal aid organizations that represent prison inmates. This reduced the number of lawyers available to litigate on behalf of prisoners and has meant that the majority of cases filed since 1996 involving the sexual abuse of inmates have been *pro se*. Inevitably, many of these *pro se* filings are dismissed in the early stages of litigation because of procedural errors.[90] In addition, the 1996 Prison Litigation Reform Act limited prisoners' access to the courts by requiring them to first exhaust all administrative remedies within the prison itself. The PLRA also increased filing fees for indigent prisoners and restricted court-awarded attorney's fees for successful suits. These restrictions help to explain why only a handful of sexual assault cases reach the courts, even though many thousands of inmates are the victims of assault every year.

It must also be noted that federal judges are generally not sympathetic to prisoners' claims and do little to protect state prison inmates from sexual violence. Judges are often sensitive to the problems faced by prison administrators and view prison violence as inevitable. Accordingly, when hearing suits brought by state prison inmates, the federal courts are inclined to show considerable deference to prison authorities.[91] Judges believe that prison guards and administrators have extremely difficult jobs and must be given considerable latitude in managing often violent facilities and dangerous inmates. These points are made in case after case. "Federal courts ought to afford appropriate deference and flexibility to state officials trying to manage a volatile environment."[92] "The court should have accorded wide ranging deference in the adoption and execution of policies and practices that in [prison officials'] judgement are needed to preserve internal order and discipline and to maintain institutional security."[93]

In the case of *Farmer v. Brennan*, Justice Clarence Thomas said in his concurring opinion, "Regrettably, some level of brutality and sexual aggression among [prisoners] is inevitable no matter what the guards do ... unless all prisoners are locked in their cells 24 hours a day and sedated."[94] In the *Farmer* case, the Court developed a standard referred to as "deliberate indifference," by which to judge the actions of prison officials. Writing for the *Farmer majority*, Justice Souter said, "deliberate indifference describes a state of mind more blameworthy than negligence."[95] He went on to equate deliberate indifference with the criminal law definition of recklessness and emphasized that the criminal law defined recklessness very differently from the civil law. By equating deliberate indifference with criminal law recklessness, Souter assigned plaintiffs the very high burden of proving subjective intent.

Against the backdrop of judicial deference to prison authorities, it is always extremely difficult for an inmate-plaintiff to meet the burden of the deliberate indifference standard. Since the authorities are presumed to be acting properly, only the most blatant disregard for inmates placed in dangerous situations and only the most egregious failure to act are likely to be seen as deliberate indifference, and even in these extreme situations inmates can most certainly not count on prevailing. The 1996 case of *Langston v. Peters* is all too typical.[96] Eugene Langston, a convicted murderer, was placed in a Joliet Prison cell with Eric Rayfield, another convicted murderer. Several days later, Rayfield raped Langston. Langston told a guard that he had been raped and requested medical attention. Initially, he was denied treatment, but several hours later he was taken to the infirmary where he was treated for rectal bleeding. Langston sued a number of prison officials claiming that his 8th Amendment rights had been violated when the authorities failed to protect him from being raped by another inmate and when he was denied medical attention. The 7th Circuit, however, found that all defendants were entitled to summary judgment. Rayfield had a history of committing sexual assaults which, as Langston was able to show, was known to prison authorities. However, the court ruled that Langston had not proven that the particular official who decided to place Rayfield in his cell knew of Rayfield's past record at the time of the cell assignment.[97] Given the obvious fact that the prison is a huge bureaucracy, requiring the plaintiff to prove that each and every bureaucrat knew a particular fact creates an almost impossible burden for the plaintiff. As for the delay in obtaining medical care, this was held not to have produced any actual harm to the plaintiff. The amount of blood found in Langston's rectum when he was finally examined was deemed by the court to have been "microscopic."[98]

Another typical case is *Lewis v. Richards*, where rather foolish actions by the authorities were held to show that they were not indifferent.[99] In this case, inmate Tommy Lewis was allegedly raped by two members of a prison gang. He reported the rape to prison officials but recanted his account when threatened by a large group of gang members. Several months later, he told officials his story again and was transferred to another prison dormitory. After his transfer, members of the same gang raped Lewis again. He reported the rape and was placed in protective custody. Subsequently, Lewis was raped again by three gang members. Most of Lewis' allegations were accepted by the court, but in dismissing his complaint, the 7th Circuit held that prison authorities had not been deliberately indifferent to his plight. Indeed, authorities had responded to Lewis' original complaint by moving him to another part of the prison. As was generally known in the institution, members of the same gang were housed in that part of the prison as well and Lewis was subsequently sexually assaulted in his new housing unit. Was failure to foresee the obvious an example of deliberate indifference? Not at all. At worst said the court, the prison's authorities had used poor judgement in their handling of the case. And, said the court, "exercising poor judgement falls short of meeting the standard of consciously disregarding a known risk to safety."

Thus, while the federal courts look the other way, the inmates of state correctional facilities are subjected to the constant threat of sexual humiliation and rape. One would be compelled to conclude from this sordid tale that an inmate victimized by sexual predators has little hope of protection from state authorities and minimal recourse in the court system.

Law Enforcement in the States

Each year, thousands of Americans are victims of improper treatment on the part of the police, prosecutors, judges and prison officials. For the most part, they have little recourse. These officials almost never face criminal action and are generally immune from civil action. The American constitutional system is organized around checks and balances and accountability. State law enforcement systems are not.

Notes

1 Shelley Hyland, "Full-Time Employees in Law Enforcement Agencies, 1997–2016," *Bureau of Justice Statistics*, Aug., 2018. www.bjs.gov/content/pub/pdf/ftelea9716.pdf.
2 Steven W. Perry and Duran Banks, "Prosecutors in State Courts," *Bureau of Justice Statistics*, Dec., 2011. www.bjs.gov/content/pub/pdf/ftelea9716.pdf.
3 www.prisonpolicy.org/reports/pie2018.html#dataheaderucr.fbi.gov/crime-in-the-u.s/2016/crime-in-the-u.s.-2016/topic-pages/tables/table-18.
4 Anne Kim, "A Fine Mistake: Are Increases in Fines for Minor Infractions a Revenue Remedy? Don't Bet On It," *Governing*, Sep., 2018, p. 62.
5 Peter Keane, "Why Cops Lie," *SF Gate*, Apr. 14, 2014.
6 373 U.S. 83 (1963).
7 Dissenting opinion in U.S. v. Olsen, No. 10–36063, 9th Cir. 2013.
8 Randall Collins, *Violence* (Princeton, NJ: Princeton University Press, 2008), p. 85.
9 Collins, *Violence*, p. 375.
10 Jennifer Peltz, "Patrick Pogan, Biker Shove Cop, Gets No Jail," *HuffPost*, Jul. 14, 2010. www.huffingtonpost.com/2010/07/15/patrick-pogan-biker-shove_n_646517.html.
11 Jeffrey Wolf, Deborah Sherman and Nicole Vap, "Videotape Shows Man Beaten By Denver Police," *9News.com*, Aug. 12, 2008. www.9news.com/article/news/local/9news-evenings/videotape-shows-man-beaten-by-denver-police/73-342246668.
12 Hannah Granebstein and Joshua Barajas, "5 Police Misconduct Caseshad New Developments Last Week. Here's What Happened," *PBS News Hour*, Dec. 13, 2017. www.pbs.org/newshour/nation/5-police-misconduct-cases-had-new-developments-last-week-heres-what-happened.
13 "Did Cops Intend to Cover Up Videotaped Beating?" *CBS News*, Apr. 14, 2010. www.cbsnews.com/stories/2010/04/14/earlyshow/main6394678.shtml.
14 National Police Statistics Misconduct and Reporting Project, 2010. www.termlifeinsurance.org/police-brutality-information/.

15 Bryan Gallagher, "Study: Police Abuse Goes Unpunished," *Medill Reports*, Apr. 4, 2007. www.thenation.com/article/archive/chicago-has-spent-half-a-billion-dollars-on-police-brutality-cases-and-its-impoverishing-the-victims-communities/.
16 Matthew Walberg and William Lee, "Burge Found Guilty," *The Chicago Tribune*, Jun. 28, 2010. http://articles.chicagotribune.com/2010-06-28/news/ct-met-burge-trial-0629-20100628_1_burge-chicago-police-cmdr-special-cook-county-prosecutors.
17 Carrie Sloan and Johnae' Strong, "Chicago Has Spent Half a Billion Dollars on Police Brutality Cases–And It's Impoverishing the Victims' Communities," *The Nation*, Mar. 11, 2016. www.thenation.com/article/chicago-has-spent-half-a-billion-dollars-on-police-brutality-cases-and-its-impoverishing-the-victims-communities/.
18 Gallagher, "Report."
19 Radley Balko, "The War on Cameras," *Reason*, Jan., 2011. http://reason.com/archives/2010/12/07/the-war-on-cameras.
20 "Oakland Remains Calm as Johannes Mehserle Is Freed," *San Francisco Examiner*, Jun. 13, 2011. www.sfexaminer.com/news/oakland-remains-calm-as-johannes-mehserle-is-freed/.
21 Radley Balko, "Chicago State's Attorney Lets Bad Cops Slide, Prosecutes Citizens Who Record Them," *HuffPost Politics*, Jun. 8, 2011. www.huffingtonpost.com/2011/06/08/chicago-district-attorney-recording-bad-cops_n_872921.html.
22 "Editorial," *Chicago Sun-Times*, 71 Shot and No Arrests? Aug. 7, 2018. https://chicago.suntimes.com/2018/8/7/18390265/editorial-71-shot-and-no-arrests-chicago-pays-high-price-for-police-mistrust.
23 367 U.S. 643 (1961).
24 Jerold Israel, Yale Kamisar, Wayne R. LaFave and Nancy J. King, *Criminal Procedure and the Constitution* (St. Paul, MN: West Publishing, 2007), p. 69.
25 Joseph Goldstein, "Police Testilying Remains a Problem. Here Is How the Criminal Justice System Could Reduce It," *The New York Times*, Mar. 22, 2018. www.nytimes.com/2018/03/22/nyregion/police-lying-new-york.html.
26 Morgan Cloud, "The Dirty Little Secret," *Emory Law Journal* 43 (1994): 1311. See Note 5.
27 Cloud, "The Dirty Little Secret."
28 Robert Lewis and Noah Veltman, "The Hard Truth about Cops Who Lie," *WNYC*, Oct. 13, 2015. www.wnyc.org/story/hard-truth-about-cops-who-lie/.
29 Joseph Goldstein, "Testilying by the Police: A Stubborn Problem," *The New York Times*, Mar. 18, 2018. www.nytimes.com/2018/03/18/nyregion/testilying-police-perjury-new-york.html.
30 Michael Komorn, "5 Cops Busted Lying on the Stand: Just Another Day on the Front Lines," *HuffPost*, Jun. 30, 2014. www.huffingtonpost.com/michael-komorn/5-cops-busted-lying-on-the-stand_b_5229900.html.
31 Goldstein, "Testilying by the Police."
32 Myron Orfield, "Deterrence, Perjury and the Heater Factor: An Exclusionary Rule in the Chicago Criminal Courts," *University of Colorado Law Review* 63 (1992): 75.
33 Goldstein, "Testilying by the Police."
34 Cloud, "The Dirty Little Secret."
35 Todd Wright, "Charges Dropped Against Woman Framed By Cops: Police Seen Plotting to Pin Car Accident On Woman They Hit," *NBC Miami*, Jul. 29, 2009. www.nbcmiami.com/news/local/Cops-Set-Up-Woman-After-Crash.html.

36 William K. Rashbaum, Joseph Goldstein and Al Baker, "Trouble Found in Police Department by the Outside," *The New York Times*, Nov. 3, 2011, p. 1.
37 Harlan v. Fitzgerald, 457 U.S. 800 (1982).
38 William Baude, "Is Qualified Immunity Unlawful?" *California Law Review* 106 (2018): 45.
39 See San Francisco v. Sheehan, 135 S.Ct. 1765 (2015).
40 Dan W. Carbado, "Blue-on-Black Violence: A Provisional Model of Some of the Causes," *Georgetown Law Journal* 104 (2016): 1479, 1519.
41 Emily Bazelon, "She Was Convicted of Killing Her Mother. Prosecutors Withheld Evidence That Would Have Freed Her," *The New York Times Magazine*, Aug. 1, 2017. www.nytimes.com/2017/08/01/magazine/she-was-convicted-of-killing-her-mother-prosecutors-withheld-the-evidence-that-would-have-freed-her.html.
42 Bazelon, "She Was Convicted of Killing Her Mother."..
43 Editorial, "Rampant Prosecutorial Misconduct," *The New York Times*, Jan. 4, 2014. www.nytimes.com/2014/01/05/opinion/sunday/rampant-prosecutorial-misconduct.html?action=click&module=RelatedLinks&pgtype=Article.
44 David Keenan, Deborah Jane Cooper, David Lebowitz and Tamar Lerer, "The Myth of Prosecutorial Accountability," *Yale Law Journal* 121 (2012): 103. https://digitalcommons.law.yale.edu/ylsspps_papers/103/.
45 Imbler v. Pachtman, 492 U.S. 409 (1976).
46 Aaron Beard, "Disbarred Duke Prosecutor's Future Dim," *WashingtonPost.com*, Jun. 18, 2007. www.washingtonpost.com/wp-dyn/content/article/2007/06/17/AR2007061700687.html.
47 Campbell Robertson and Adam Liptak, "Louisians Prosecutors' Methods Raise Scrutiny Again," *The New York Times*, Nov. 3, 2011, p. A19.
48 John Schwartz and Brandi Grissom, "Exonerated of Murder, Texan Seeks Inquiry on Prosecutor," *The New York Times*, Dec. 19, 2011, p. A15.
49 New York Times Editorial Board, "A Bill on Gov. Andrew Cuomo's Desk Would Address a Serious Problem in New York State. He Ought to Sign It," Aug. 14, 2018. www.nytimes.com/2018/08/14/opinion/new-york-prosecutors-cuomo-district-attorneys-watchdog.html.
50 "Justice in the Balance," *USA TODAY*, Sep. 23, 2010. http://projects.usatoday.com/news/2010/justice/cases/.
51 373 U.S. 83 (1963).
52 405 U.S. 150 (1972).
53 U.S. v. Antonio Lyons, U.S. District Court, Middle District of Florida, Orlando Division. Case No. 6:01-cr-134-Orl-31DAB. Filed 7/20/10. http://s3.documentcloud.org/documents/6687/united-states-v-lyons-district-court-granting-motion-for-a-certificate-of-innocence.pdf.
54 U.S. v. Antonio Lyons, 352 F Supp. 2d 1231 (MD Fla. 2004).
55 Samuel W. Wardle, "Extreme Circumstances Call for Extreme Measures," *Florida Historical Quarterly* 92, no. 2 (Fall, 2013): 397–414.
56 Kevin McCoy and Brad Heath, "Not Guilty But Stuck With Big Bills, Damaged Career," *USA TODAY*, Sep. 28, 2010. www.usatoday.com/news/washington/judicial/2010-09-27-hyde-federal-prosecutors_N.htm.
57 "Justice in the Balance."
58 The best account of the Amirault case is Dorothy Rabinowitz, *No Crueler Tyrannies* (New York: The Free Press, 2004).
59 Dorothy Rabinowitz, "Martha Coakley's Convictions," *The Wall Street Journal*, Jan. 14, 2010. http://online.wsj.com/article/SB10001424052748704281204575003341640657862.html.
60 Rabinowitz, "Martha Coakley's Convictions."

126 *State Justice Systems*

61 Rabinowitz, "Martha Coakley's Convictions."
62 Quoted in Michael Powell, "Misconduct by Prosecutors, Once Again," *New York Times*, Aug. 14, 2012.
63 Kathleen M. Ridolfi, Maurice Possley and Northern California Innocence Project, "Preventable Error: A Report on Prosecutorial Misconduct in California 1997–2009," *Northern California Innocence Project Publications*, Book 2 (2010). http://digitalcommons.law.scu.edu/ncippubs/2.
64 Richard Oppel and Farah Stockman, "Prosecutors' New Role: Helping Those Wrongly Convicted," *The New York Times*, Nov. 29, 2019, p. A13.
65 On the topic of judicial selection, see G. Alan Tarr, *Without Fear or Favor: Judicial Independence and Judicial Accountability in the States* (Stanford, CA: Stanford University Press, 2012).
66 John Gramlich, "Judges' Battles Signal a New Era for Retention Elections," *Washington Post*, Dec. 5, 2010. www.washingtonpost.com/wp-dyn/content/article/2010/12/04/AR2010120400180.html?noredirect=on.
67 Keith Swisher, "Pro-Prosecution Judges: 'Tough on Crime,' Soft on Strategy, Ripe for Disqualification," *Arizona Law Review* 52 (2010): 318.
68 Caperton v. A.T. Massey Coal Co. 556 U.S. 868 (2009).
69 Kate Berry, "How Judicial Elections Impact Criminal Cases," *Brennan Center for Justice at New York University School of Law*, 2015. www.brennancenter.org/publication/how-judicial-elections-impact-criminal-cases.
70 Amy K. Brown, "Judges Say Politics are Interfering with Independence," *Florida Bar News* 28 (October 15, 2001): 1.
71 Berry, "Judicial Elections."
72 James E. Robertson, "A Clean Heart and an Empty Head: The Supreme Court and Sexual Terrorism in Prison," *North Carolina Law Review* 81 (January, 2003): 433, 477.
73 Human Rights Watch, *World Report 2000*, Part 1, p. 5.
74 Stephen Donaldson, "The Rape Crisis behind Bars," *New York Times*, Dec. 29, 1993, p. A11.
75 Robertson, p. 441.
76 Robertson, p. 435.
77 David Kaiser and Lovisa Stannow, "Prison Rape: Obama's Program to Stop It," *New York Review*, Oct. 11, 2012, p. 51.
78 Lynette Clemetson, "Links between Prison and AIDS Affecting Blacks Inside and Out," *New York Times*, Aug. 6, 2004, Section A, p. 1.
79 Will A. Smith, "Civil Liability for Sexual Assault in Prison," *Cumberland Law Review* 34 (2003/2004): 289.
80 Robertson, p. 446.
81 Robertson, p. 447.
82 Robertson, p. 447.
83 Robertson, p. 448.
84 Quoted in Robertson, p. 448.
85 Olga Giller, "Deliberate Indifference and Male Prison Rape," *Cardozo Women's Law Journal* 10 (Summer, 2004): 659.
86 Shara Abraham, "Male Rape in U.S. Prisons," *Human Rights Brief* 9 (Fall, 2001): 5.
87 Abraham, p. 7.
88 See *Hudson* v. *McMillan*, 503 U.S. 1 (1992).
89 511 U.S. 825 (1994).
90 Abraham, p. 7.
91 Robertson, pp. 453–454.
92 *Turner v. Sufley*, 482 U.S. 78 (1987).

93 *Redman v. County of San Diego*, 942 F. 2d. 1435 (9th Cir. 1991).
94 *Farmer v. Brennan*, at p. 858.
95 *Farmer*, at p. 835.
96 100 F.3rd 1235 (7th Cir. 1996).
97 *Id.* at p. 1239.
98 *Id.* at p. 1241.
99 107 F.3rd 549 (7th Cir. 1997).

7 Corruption in State and Municipal Government

The term public or official corruption refers to the misuse of public authority for private gain. Such corruption can take many forms. Several of the most common forms of public corruption are described in Table 7.1. Many Americans are convinced that public corruption is widespread.

Each of these forms of corruption is potentially costly to state and municipal governments and, as a result, to the citizens who pay for and depend upon the services performed by those governments. The cost to businesses of paying bribes, for example, can, in turn, drive up the costs charged to consumers. Accepting bribes may lead inspectors to ignore unsafe practices. Bid rigging can mean that state and municipal contracts are awarded to less well qualified and more costly service providers. Bid rigging and kickbacks in municipal bond sales are likely to mean lower prices and higher interest rates for public securities and may encourage unnecessary public borrowing. Nepotism and patronage may result in less well qualified and more expensive public employees. Public service fraud can drive up the costs of the work done by state and municipal governments. Overall, corruption adds to the cost of public services and raises questions about their safety and quality. Estimates of the costs of corruption suggest that the "corruption tax" is hundreds of millions of dollars each year.[1]

According to a recent survey, about a third of Americans think all or most government officials are corrupt, with about a quarter of the same survey's respondents specifically citing all or most local government officials as being prone to corrupt practices.[2] It is certainly no wonder that Americans have a jaundiced view of their office holders. In recent years, well-publicized corruption charges have been brought against a number of important politicians and government officials. In one of the most blatant and notorious cases, former Illinois Governor Rod Blagojevich was convicted of influence peddling and extortion after attempting to sell the Senate seat vacated by President Barack Obama. It was up to the governor to appoint someone to complete Obama's unexpired term. In a wiretapped conversation, Blagojevich is heard to

Table 7.1 Common Forms of Public Corruption

Bribe taking	Acceptance of money or other gifts in return for official favors.
Embezzlement	Theft of public funds.
Extortion	Demanding money in exchange for not using official power against the victim.
Bid rigging	Making certain that government contracts are awarded to a favored firm.
Kickbacks	Payments to a government official from the income realized by individuals or businesses who have received government jobs or contracts with the official's help.
Nepotism	Hiring family members or friends rather than more qualified job applicants.
Patronage	Awarding public positions in exchange for political support.
Influence peddling	Use of an official position to extract bribes or services from those wishing favorable treatment from the government.
Conflict of interest	Having a personal stake in an official decision.
Money laundering	Concealing the sources of illegally obtained funds.
Public service fraud	Failing to perform the tasks required by an official position.

say, "I've got this thing [the senate seat] and it's f****** golden. And I'm just not giving it up for f****** nothing ... you know what I'm saying?"[3]

Often, the Federal Bureau of Investigation, an organization with a long-standing penchant for publicity, assigns its corruption investigations colorful names sure to make national headlines. In the 1980s, for example, the FBI's "ABSCAM" investigation led to the conviction of more than 30 political figures, including six members of the United States House of Representatives and one United States senator along with one member of the New Jersey State Senate, members of the Philadelphia City Council, the mayor of Camden, New Jersey, and an inspector for the United States Immigration and Naturalization Service. All were charged with accepting bribes from an informant posing as a Middle Eastern sheik in exchange for official favors.[4]

Similarly, in "Operation Greylord," named for the wigs worn by British judges, 17 Cook County, Illinois judges were indicted for accepting bribes, mainly in exchange for dismissing traffic tickets.[5] In 2008, the FBI's "Tennessee Waltz" operation, led to the convictions or guilty pleas of a dozen Tennessee state and local public officials—including several state senators, a state representative, two county commissioners and two school board members—all charged with influence peddling.[6]

While these cases received national publicity, quite a few other state and local cases are prosecuted every year without much fanfare outside the affected state or municipality. Such cases have included convictions of state and local officials including governors, state legislators, mayors and virtually every category of municipal official. Events in New Jersey in 2016 are an example.

In that year David Samson, former chairman of the powerful Port Authority of New York and New Jersey, pleaded guilty to charges that he strong-armed an airline to restore service for a commercially unviable flight to his South Carolina summer home. Passaic Mayor Alex Blanco pleaded guilty to a federal bribery charge, admitting he received $110,000 in payments from developers in exchange for directing federal housing funds to their projects.[7] Former Chesterfield Mayor Lawrence Durr was accused of selling development rights on his farm to a real estate company at a profit and then using his official positions to advance the company's interests in Chesterfield. Durr later admitted to filing fraudulent ethics disclosure forms that hid his ties to the firm and was sentenced to four years probation and 364 days in the county jail.[8] In late December 2015 and January 2016, a series of officials from the Newark Conservation and Watershed Development Corp. and co-conspirators pleaded guilty for their roles in an illegal kickback scheme. Donald Bernard Sr., a special projects manager at the organization, and contractor Giacomo "Jack" DeRosa pleaded guilty in January, following former director Linda Watkins-Brashear and contractor James Porter, who pleaded guilty in 2015. Federal authorities said Watershed officials exchanged no-bid contracts for bribes over the course of several years.[9]

While New Jersey has long had a reputation for official corruption, the same story could be told about many other states, as well. In New York, during roughly the same time period, the speaker of the State Assembly was convicted of corruption, along with both the majority and minority leaders of the State Senate. Alabama's governor, Robert Bentley, was convicted of converting campaign contributions to personal use. In California, State Senator Ron Calderon and his brother, State Assemblyman Tom Calderon, were convicted of money laundering. In Kentucky, State Representative Keith Hall was convicted of taking bribes. In Pennsylvania, two successive state treasurers and an attorney general were sentenced for corruption. The list, unfortunately, goes on.

Which States are Most Corrupt?

Though examples of public corruption can be found in every state, the incidence of corruption varies considerably across states and municipalities. Corruption is inherently difficult to measure for the obvious reason that those engaged in corrupt actions have a strong incentive to hide their involvement. Various government agencies regularly report data on arrests and convictions for acts of corruption but it is difficult to know what percentage of corrupt acts lead to arrest and conviction. Do the official data reveal most of the iceberg or only its tip? Are some states particularly corrupt or is official corruption a widely distributed problem? Before we can answer these questions, we must take a bit of an excursion through the several forms of data relevant to public corruption.

To begin with, the difficulty of ascertaining the extent of official corruption in the U.S. is increased by the problematic character of the data most frequently used for this purpose, the annual report filed by the Justice Department's Public Integrity Section, known as the PIN report. Since 1976, PIN reports have, among other things, published the number of convictions for public corruption in each federal judicial district in the U.S. Some states consist of only one judicial district while others include as many as four, but no judicial district overlaps a state's boundaries so that the number of convictions per state can be easily observed. The PIN reports do not include convictions in state courts. However, the overwhelming majority of public corruption investigations are undertaken by federal authorities and prosecuted in federal court. Indeed, Cordis and Milyo estimate that more than 90 percent of public corruption charges are heard in federal court.[10] While state and local officials might be prosecuted under one or more of several federal statutes, such prosecutions are most frequently brought under the 1951 Hobbs Act which prohibits officials from obtaining property or payment to which they are not entitled—a charge that carries a relatively low burden of proof. Other common charges include theft or bribery in programs receiving public funds and frauds and swindles conducted through the mail.[11] More than 80 percent of the officials prosecuted in federal court are convicted.

Table 7.2 reports the number of federal public corruption convictions by state as reported by the Public Integrity Section from 2007 to 2017.

At first glance, these data might seem to suggest the existence of significant levels of public corruption in America's states and localities with, perhaps, with Texas, California, Florida, Virginia, New York, Illinois, Louisiana, Pennsylvania and New Jersey leading the pack. The most honest public officials, on the other hand, would seem to be found in New Hampshire, Wyoming, Hawaii, Vermont, North Dakota, Idaho, Delaware, Utah and Rhode Island. This is certainly the interpretation given these numbers each year by the national media when articles are published pointing to one or another state as the most corrupt in America.[12]

The PIN data, though widely circulated and publicized, can be misleading.[13] To begin with, the PIN data offer only totals; they do not take account of the populations of the states or, even more important, the

Table 7.2 Federal Corruption Convictions by State (PIN), 2007–2017

	2007	2008	2009	2010	2011	2012	2013	2014	2015	2016	2017	Total
AL	52	20	28	15	23	22	23	19	20	10	11	243
AK	15	8	1	9	4	4	2	1	4	4	1	53
AZ	32	20	19	16	18	34	40	29	18	8	18	252
AR	8	5	3	17	8	15	4	5	13	14	16	108
CA	76	58	69	44	52	89	63	95	86	64	60	756
CO	3	4	14	6	6	9	3	2	0	3	1	51
CT	17	5	2	4	0	8	13	9	6	0	0	64
DE	5	7	1	1	2	3	5	0	1	0	2	27
FL	69	66	69	52	40	62	49	64	83	56	59	669
GA	8	24	25	37	45	42	27	47	34	73	35	397
HI	1	2	1	0	3	2	0	4	5	0	2	20
ID	1	1	1	0	3	6	4	1	3	4	1	25
IL	42	56	58	52	41	44	69	32	19	35	34	482
IN	24	14	18	12	6	32	23	17	12	20	9	187
IA	9	9	4	11	3	4	3	4	6	9	4	66
KS	2	5	4	5	9	8	4	2	2	0	2	43
KY	39	28	41	34	38	32	15	19	13	20	21	300
LA	42	39	44	55	51	52	50	21	27	41	32	454
ME	4	8	5	1	4	2	2	3	4	5	0	38
MD	21	39	32	21	58	26	47	38	31	23	80	416

MA	29	19	28	27	19	13	22	18	16	17	19	227
MI	12	33	18	30	24	17	19	19	6	34	27	239
MN	3	7	13	6	8	0	6	5	4	5	3	60
MS	25	17	15	24	17	9	18	18	11	7	9	170
MO	20	31	24	25	14	21	10	19	11	18	14	207
MT	0	8	7	10	5	2	5	27	8	26	19	117
NE	0	8	2	4	2	3	3	4	3	6	8	43
NV	4	0	7	4	6	6	2	6	0	0	1	36
NH	0	4	1	1	0	0	0	0	0	1	1	8
NJ	62	49	44	47	28	27	30	33	23	28	21	392
NM	3	6	9	7	4	4	2	10	12	4	6	67
NY	44	48	38	37	52	57	26	41	68	48	46	505
NC	26	17	9	18	13	4	19	8	17	17	9	157
ND	6	4	0	6	2	2	0	0	1	0	2	23
OH	49	37	56	65	31	25	19	20	30	14	12	358
OK	9	22	22	14	24	26	22	22	20	13	21	215
OR	11	3	5	1	7	2	3	4	3	0	1	40
PA	40	36	41	54	37	47	39	43	49	32	48	466
RI	1	2	1	3	8	2	8	4	3	0	1	33
SC	4	8	7	2	11	2	5	7	3	6	0	55
SD	8	19	15	11	19	11	8	8	9	7	15	130
TN	42	12	21	21	17	31	30	19	34	20	17	264
TX	55	112	99	71	88	101	166	102	91	86	67	1038

(*Continued*)

Table 7.2 (Cont.)

	2007	2008	2009	2010	2011	2012	2013	2014	2015	2016	2017	Total
UT	7	5	3	1	2	1	3	2	0	2	1	27
VT	1	5	0	2	5	3	1	1	1	0	0	19
VA	36	74	62	62	57	41	56	39	48	36	35	546
WA	9	12	3	8	7	7	5	7	5	16	8	87
WV	2	6	4	9	5	7	11	22	5	4	7	82
WI	12	6	9	7	10	14	13	9	7	7	8	102
WY	1	1	2	1	5	3	3	0	0	0	0	16

Data source: Public Integrity Section: www.justice.gov/criminal/file/1096306/download

number of government employees in each state. Presumably ten officials convicted of corruption out of 100 working in a state is a much higher rate of misconduct than the same ten out of 1000. The PIN data, moreover, conflate federal, state and local public corruption convictions. From the PIN reports we cannot judge the actual extent of corruption among state or municipal employees. More than half the convictions reported by the PIN table actually represent convictions of federal employees working in each state and, of these, a large percentage of convictions involve theft or destruction of mail by low-ranking federal postal employees.[14]

To make matters worse, the PIN data are based upon surveys completed retrospectively by employees of each federal judicial district rather than official records of federal prosecutions coded at the time of the prosecution. These official records, as Cordis and Milyo note, are available from the annual statistical reports of the Executive Office of the U.S. District Attorneys (EOUSA). These reports, over the past decade, do not include prosecutions of postal employees and show a level of public corruption substantially lower than reported by the widely cited PIN data (see Figure 7.1).

The EOUSA reports are readily available online as national totals but are not further disaggregated. However, as Cordis and Milyo have observed, the Transactional Records Access (TRAC) Clearinghouse at Syracuse University breaks down the official records of federal prosecutions by state, and distinguishes among convictions of federal, state and local government employees within each state.[15] The TRAC data indicate that over the past decade over half of all federal corruption convictions have involved federal employees; approximately 11 percent of

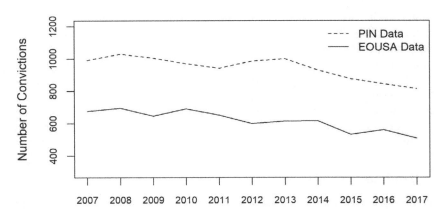

Figure 7.1 Public Corruption Convictions, PIN vs. EOUSA.

Data source: EOUSA Annual Statistical Reports (www.justice.gov/usao/resources/annual-statistical-reports)

Table 7.3 Federal, State and Local Government Corruption (TRAC), 1986–2018.

	Federal	State	Local
Number of Convictions	9624	1812	4479
%	60.5	11.4	28.1

Data source: TRACfed (https://tracfed.syr.edu/).

corruption convictions have involved state officials or employees; and 28 percent have involved local officials and employees (see Table 7.3).

Using the TRAC data also allows us to obtain a reasonably accurate picture of the extent and location of state and local government corruption in the U.S. Table 7.4 reports the state by state distribution of state and local government corruption convictions. These are shown both as total convictions and as convictions per 10,000 employees from 2012–2017.

The TRAC data offer a rather different, and likely more accurate, picture of corruption in the 50 states than is presented by the more widely publicized PIN data. First, the overall level of state and municipal corruption in America is relatively low, at least as measured by convictions. Nationally, the average number of convictions is .08 state convictions per 10,000 state employees and one local conviction per 10,000 employees. In some states, like Idaho and Minnesota, there have been no state or local convictions from 2012–2017. Second, in some states, corruption seems to be a local more than a state-wide problem. In Montana, North Dakota and Michigan, for example, corruption among state officials seems is much lower than among local officials. Third, many of the states that rank at or near the top in levels of corruption, as measured by TRAC, are states traditionally associated with corrupt political practices. These include such states as New Jersey and Louisiana. Thus, the TRAC data raise two important questions. The first is what accounts for the "tradition" of corruption in some states. The second question is why corruption seems to be concentrated in local governments in a number of states. The TRAC data do answer one question, however. Which is America's most corrupt state? At least as measured by convictions in federal court, the answer is Mississippi.

A Tradition of Corruption

By all accounts, public corruption in the United States reached its zenith in the late 19th century and has declined since that time. While there may be no accurate way to measure the actual incidence of corruption in the past, it is possible to measure a possible surrogate, newspaper

Table 7.4 State Corruption Ranking (TRAC), 2012–2017

State Government Corruption				Local Government Corruption		
State	Convictions	Average Number FTE	Convictions per 1000 FTE	State	Convictions	Average Number FTE	Convictions per 1000 FTE
DE	0	23,009	0	CO	0	176,155	0
ID	0	33,966	0	HI	0	15,918	0
ME	0	30,161	0	ID	0	37,024	0
MI	0	113,662	0	MN	0	168,025	0
MN	0	67,951	0	NH	0	24,236	0
ND	0	17,412	0	WY	0	31,706	0
NH	0	34,177	0	SC	2	169,242	0.01
OR	0	59,019	0	UT	1	71,426	0.01
RI	0	16,953	0	WA	1	182,083	0.01
SD	0	12,579	0	AZ	4	186,087	0.02
UT	0	46,989	0	CA	24	1,153,573	0.02
WA	0	102,454	0	CT	2	111,174	0.02
WI	0	53,742	0	WI	4	178,848	0.02
WY	0	12,226	0	IA	4	112,569	0.04
CO	1	58,367	0.02	NC	15	389,062	0.04
NV	1	41,911	0.02	NV	2	53,621	0.04
WV	1	40,151	0.02	OR	4	104,838	0.04

(Continued)

Table 7.4 (Cont.)

	State Government Corruption				Local Government Corruption		
State	Convictions	Average Number FTE	Convictions per 1000 FTE	State	Convictions	Average Number FTE	Convictions per 1000 FTE
IA	1	37,405	0.03	TX	47	1,077,105	0.04
IN	2	68,838	0.03	VA	13	308,470	0.04
NY	6	189,945	0.03	AR	5	98,806	0.05
VT	1	28,841	0.03	AK	1	16,174	0.06
KS	2	45,440	0.04	IL	25	447,674	0.06
MD	3	77,635	0.04	KS	8	130,741	0.06
MO	3	73,098	0.04	MA	13	219,516	0.06
NM	3	70,548	0.04	AL	13	188,215	0.07
PA	7	141,409	0.05	RI	2	27,085	0.07
AK	2	32,993	0.06	TN	16	227,296	0.07
FL	9	160,957	0.06	FL	53	643,910	0.08
HI	3	52,316	0.06	NY	67	890,961	0.08
IL	6	97,836	0.06	ME	3	31,616	0.09
TX	17	270,374	0.06	WV	5	54,363	0.09
OH	8	108,720	0.07	DE	2	20,541	0.10
OK	4	59,425	0.07	MD	19	188,723	0.10
NE	2	24,572	0.08	OK	14	138,097	0.10
SC	6	71,212	0.08	IN	22	209,337	0.11
MA	7	76,299	0.09	KY	16	146,908	0.11

NC	10	110,318	0.09	SD	3	27,973	0.11
AL	7	69,818	0.10	NE	10	79,162	0.13
AR	6	58,907	0.10	OH	52	394,614	0.13
CA	50	337,492	0.15	GA	53	359,166	0.15
CT	8	52,477	0.15	MO	32	212,840	0.15
LA	11	68,292	0.16	NM	7	43,429	0.16
TN	13	70,521	0.18	VT	1	6142	0.16
VA	17	91,201	0.19	NJ	70	317,329	0.22
AZ	13	61,552	0.21	LA	41	171,265	0.24
NJ	25	114,502	0.22	PA	90	358,784	0.25
MT	4	17,010	0.24	MI	69	244,780	0.28
KY	21	74,060	0.28	ND	6	21,501	0.28
MS	16	56,241	0.28	MS	36	121,902	0.30
GA	73	113,206	0.64	MT	24	30,954	0.78

FTS refers to full-time equivalent employees.
Data source: TRACfed (https://tracfed.syr.edu/).

coverage of corruption on the assumption that over long periods of time, changes in the latter likely reflect changes in the former. Making use of a method suggested by Glaeser and Goldin, we have searched the *New York Times* index, available electronically from the newspaper's founding in 1850 to 2019.[16] Like Glaeser and Goldin, we searched for articles containing variations on the words "corruption" and "fraud" as a percentage of the articles containing word "political." This method permits us to calculate the percentage of the paper's politically relevant coverage devoted to corruption over time. Though the *Times* is based in New York City, its coverage is national and other studies have shown that changes in the *Times's* coverage of political corruption parallel changes in coverage of the same topic by papers throughout the U.S. Figure 7.2 presents percentage of *New York Times* political stories dealing with corruption between 1850 and 2019.

If the incidence of newspaper stories about political corruption is at all correlated with the actual incidence of political corruption, the data suggest that corruption was a major factor in American political life from the 1840s through the 1880s. During the 1880s, corruption began to decline and has generally continued to decline into the modern period with a bit of an uptick in the last two decades.

The growth of corruption in the 19th century seems historically coincident with the construction of political "machines" in a number of American states and cities, mainly in the Northeast, urban Midwest and

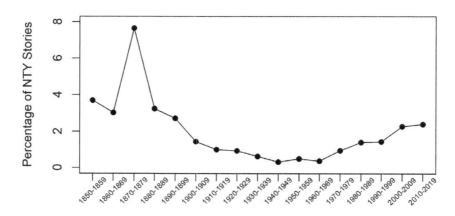

Figure 7.2 New York Times Coverage of Political Corruption, 1850–2019.

This figure shows the percentage of New York Times political coverage (i.e. stories containing the word "political") that focused on corruption. Corruption stories contained the words "corrupt" and "fraud" (and their variants) in accordance with the method outlined in Glaeser and Goldin (2004). The searches were conducted using ProQuest's New York Times Historical Database.

portions of the South. Machines were built by entrepreneurial politicians in the wake of the bureaucratic reforms of the Jacksonian era. The Jacksonians launched a great expansion in the size of federal, state and local bureaucracies and advocated the principle that these positions should be awarded by victorious politicians to their political followers as the "spoils" of political warfare. Hence, this system of political rewards came to be known as the "spoils system." Successful politicians now had the capacity to distribute jobs to the supporters who staffed party organizations as well as funds from the public treasury to saloon keepers, gang leaders, militia leaders and volunteer fire captains who enjoyed local prominence and could bring voters to the polls.[17] These various functionaries understood that success in mobilizing voters was a condition for maintaining a place on the public payroll or at the public trough. Where party functionaries controlled the election machinery, itself, voting fraud was widespread and included ballots cast by non-existent or long-deceased voters.

Over time, what began as informal organizations were often able to rationalize their bureaucratic structures with a military-style chain of command. Machines were led by state or county "bosses," who generally held positions of political power. Below the bosses were district leaders who commanded cadres of sub-leaders, often called precinct "captains." These captains, who generally held patronage jobs, were each responsible for bringing several hundred voters to the polls. Historian Richard Jensen has characterized American political parties of this period as possessing a "militaristic" style.[18]

From their positions of power, machine leaders were able to profit in many ways. They could engage in influence peddling; they might demand kickbacks from business and real estate interests for government contracts and from bankers for handling the sale of government bonds; they might accept bribes and kickbacks for allowing criminal enterprises to flourish; they might profit handsomely from the advance knowledge of pending shifts in the real estate market that came with their ability to award municipal development and construction projects. George Washington Plunkitt, a leader of New York's Tammany Hall political machine, called this last source of profit, "honest graft," to distinguish it from outright theft and embezzlement of government funds which he disparaged as "dishonest graft."[19] Indeed, outright theft was strongly discouraged by machine leaders as bringing the organization into unnecessary disrepute and, perhaps making municipal bonds difficult to market.[20] High levels of fraud, theft and embezzlement tended to reflect weak political machines whose leaders were unable to keep order among their more avaricious members. Huey Long of Louisiana, for example, built a very disciplined political machine in the early decades of the 20th century, but correctly predicted that after his death his associates would all go to the penitentiary because he would no longer be around to keep their greed in check.[21]

In the 19th and early 20th centuries, political machines controlled a number of state and municipal governments. The oldest of these, New York's Tammany Hall machine, was originally built by Aaron Burr to promote his political fortunes. In, 1828, Tammany leaders gave their support to Andrew Jackson in exchange for his promise to give them control over federal patronage in the city. So was born a relationship between Tammany Hall and the Democratic party that would last more than a century. From the 1830s until the 1930s, Tammany leaders controlled New York City and, from that bastion, heavily influenced the politics of the state. Other significant political machines were built in New Jersey, Illinois, Massachusetts, Mississippi, Louisiana, Missouri. Ohio, Pennsylvania and Georgia. For a variety of reasons, strong political machines generally did not develop in the Mountain and Western states.[22] In many cities, machines mobilized immigrant voters though in others, such as Philadelphia and the states of the South, machines drew their support from native-stock working-class voters.

Political Reform

If the growth of political machines helps to explain the high levels of corruption associated with American state and local politics in the 19th century, turn-of-the-century political reforms leading to the collapse of machines can help to explain the decline of corruption in the 20th century. Major efforts to reform political corruption in the U.S. are associated with the "Mugwumps" and the "Progressives." The first group had only limited success while the Progressive movement had considerable success in changing the character of American politics.

The Mugwumps, a term ostensibly derived from an Algonquin word meaning important person, were generally upper middle-class Republican politicians from New York and New England. The construction of strong party machines in those regions had deprived such individuals, who regarded themselves as the nation's natural leaders, of political power and allowed new groups often led by politicians of Irish descent, to replace them. The Mugwumps decried the corruption associated with machine politics but their denunciation of corruption was as much an attack on those who held power as it was an indictment of the purpose for which they used their power.

To break the power of political machines, the Mugwumps called for civil service reform which would end the patronage system that was so important to the machines' ability to recruit and control their armies of political functionaries. Mugwumps pressed their cause by establishing one of the first interest groups in American political history, the National Civil Service Reform League, an organization that worked across the nation to build support for its cause.

The Mugwump's lasting contribution to American politics was the enactment of the Pendleton Civil Service Act of 1883 which mandated the selection of federal government employees by competitive examination rather than patronage, restricted political activity by federal employees and made it illegal to demote or fire employees for political reasons. The Act also established the U.S. Civil Service Commission to monitor compliance with the legislation. The Act initially covered, or "classified," only about 10 percent of federal employees but provided that the president could apply it to additional classes of employees by executive order. Initially, civil service reform had little effect since during the years following the adoption of the Pendleton Act, the number of federal jobs grew more rapidly than the number of positions classified by presidential order.[23] Moreover, most patronage positions were in state and local governments and not covered by the Pendleton Act. Only two states, New York and Massachusetts, adopted civil service acts in the 19th century and both were ineffectual.[24] Nevertheless, the Act turned out to mark the beginning of the end for political machines in America.

The second of the above-mentioned movements, Progressivism, had a more lasting impact on American politics. Progressivism followed in the wake of the 1896 political realignment that replaced two-party competition in the U.S. with a system in which most states, regions and cities were dominated by one or the other party. This worked to the advantage of groups and forces aligned with that party but left many others without much in the way of political influence. Disfranchised groups included business interests whose rivals enjoyed access to the dominant party, politicians like Theodore Roosevelt who were unpopular among their fellow party leaders, and the native middle class in areas where party machines drew their support from the working class. These disparate forces excluded from locally dominant parties banded together under the banner of Progressivism whose intellectual spokespersons articulated an ideology hostile to political parties and calling for reforms that would weaken party strength.

In the Northeast, political machines had often been built on a foundation of Irish, Southern European and Eastern European support. For this reason, Progressive rhetoric could include more than a hint of racism. Some Progressives supported the Immigration Restriction League. The League had been founded in 1894 by a trio of New England bluebloods—Charles Warren, Robert Ward and Prescott Farnsworth Hall—and a group of their Harvard classmates. The League developed affiliates throughout the nation, often making use of the Harvard alumni network. The League's major focus was the threat posed by the newer immigrants to America's institutions and way of life. As distinguished from the older immigrants of Anglo-Saxon or Teutonic stock, the newer immigrants were primarily from Southern and Eastern Europe and were Catholics and Jews. These new "degraded" immigrants were said to be responsible for crime delinquency and drunkenness and, organized by political machines, threatened to debase the political life of the entire nation.

Progressivism also appeared to important segments of America's business community, including some who continued to enjoy cordial relations with political machines. The turn of the century was a period of growth and consolidation in American industry. Major industrial corporations, under the banner of fighting monopolistic practices, were able to secure the enactment of important pieces of legislation that collectively promoted market consolidation and cartelization and created barriers to market entry by new firms. These included the Interstate Commerce Commission Act, the Sherman Anti-Trust Act and the Federal Trade Commission Act.[25]

Expanding national corporations and emergent cartels were now focused on the national or even international level and saw no reason to pay bribes and kickbacks to local political machines. These machines, moreover, provided a vehicle through which local and regional firms that would be uncompetitive in national markets might secure political favors protecting their local markets and then use revenues from municipal and state contracts to compete successfully in regional markets.

Corporate America saw support for Progressivism an opportunity to deal with this problem by weakening political machines. Historian, Samuel P. Hays writes,

> the source of support for reform in municipal government did not come from the lower or middle classes but from the upper class. The leading business groups in each city and professional men closely allied with them initiated and dominated municipal movements.[26]

One vehicle through which business worked to bring about political reform was the Municipal Research Bureau movement. These research bureaus were centers designed to conduct inquiries into and exert influence upon municipal and state affairs. The first of these bureaus, the Bureau of Municipal Research of New York City was financed by Andrew Carnegie and John D. Rockefeller in 1906. Another bureau was established in Ohio in 1912 with funding from John Patterson of the National Cash Register Company. And, George Eastman, the head of Eastman-Kodak, was the founder of Rochester's Municipal Research Bureau.[27] The various bureaus were linked together as a national force in the National Municipal League and by journals such as *The National Municipal Review*.

Progressivism was also championed by the so-called "muckraking" press and its exposes of political scandals. In the mid-19th century readership of newspapers expanded as literacy became more universal and the cost of purchasing a newspaper declined. Improvements in printing technology and delivery systems reduced the costs involved in publishing newspapers and, equally important, the emergent advertising industry subsidized these costs to the reader so that a major metropolitan newspaper might cost as little as a penny and was easily within the reach of most Americans. The result was an explosion in the number of daily newspapers published in America and their daily circulation. Between 1860 and 1900, the number of daily newspapers published in the United States quintupled from about 500 to about 2500, along with a corresponding increase in per capita newspaper circulation to about 20 million newspapers sold each day.[28]

Coincident with increasing circulation was a growth in the number of newspapers representing themselves as "independent" or nonpartisan. Since the early years of the Republic, most newspapers had been linked to political parties and used their pages to launch often vicious partisan attacks. Their impact, however, was blunted because partisans in the electorate tended to read only newspapers that represented their own party's perspective and so avoided exposure to ideas and information that might have affected their outlooks. In the late 19th century, however, the overt partisanship of the press diminished in part because of pressure from the growing advertising industry which saw newspaper partisanship as a barrier to reaching consumers. Advertising agencies encouraged newspapers to avoid partisan diatribes on their front pages and to limit partisan content to a designated space—the "editorial page," where it would be less likely to be seen and to offend potential consumers. To this day, and for similar reasons, editorial pages normally do not contain advertising. In 1870, most of the newspapers read by Americans were tied to political parties but within the next 50 years, most had become at least nominally independent.[29]

The expansion of newspaper circulation and growth of an independent press had important consequences for American politics. Growing numbers of newspapers which, in larger cities, competed with one another for circulation, created an enormous market for stories likely to attract the public's interest. Newspapers appealing to lowbrow readers, like the *New York World* and *New York Morning Journal* specialized in lurid tales of crime and mayhem. Newspapers aimed at a more upscale audience like the *New York Times* and the *New York Sun* took advantage of their political independence by providing their readers with running accounts of political scandal and corruption among municipal, state and national officials of all political stripes.

To satisfy their readers' appetites for this form of news, these papers employed reporters who specialized in identifying and reporting corruption—the so-called "muckrakers." Among the most prominent were Upton Sinclair, Ida M. Tarbell, Ray Stannard Baker and Lincoln Steffens who was, perhaps, the most influential of the muckrakers. Writing for the *New York Evening Post* and *McClure's Magazine*, Steffens wrote hundreds of stories providing detailed accounts of the corrupt practices of America's political machines. A collection of these articles was published in his 1904 book, *The Shame of the Cities*.[30] Steffens's recurring theme is that municipal government belongs in the hands of experienced and honest merchants and financiers who have the city's best interests at heart. Unfortunately, city governments across the United States have been taken over by a class of corrupt politicians. Steffens's description of St. Louis is typical of his writing:

> The corruption of St. Louis came from the top. The best citizens—the merchants and big financiers—used to rule the town, and they ruled it well. They set out to outstrip Chicago. The commercial and industrial war between these two cities was at one time a picturesque and dramatic spectacle such as is witnessed only in our country. Business men were not mere merchants and the politicians were not mere grafters; the two kinds of citizens got together and wielded the power of banks, railroads, factories, the prestige of the city, and the spirit of its citizens to gain business and population ... But a change occurred. Public spirit became private spirit, public enterprise became private greed. Along about 1890, public franchises and privileges were sought, not only for legitimate profit and common convenience, but for loot ... The riffraff, catching the smell of corruption, rushed into the Municipal Assembly, drove out the remaining respectable men, and sold the city—its streets, its wharves, its markets, and all that it had—to the now greedy business men and bribers.[31]

Steffens's theme echoed the arguments of the municipal research bureaus and civic league reports. The machine politicians, the "bribers," needed to be removed from office and power returned to the better class of citizens, the business persons and professionals who would govern for the benefit of all. The muckraking press played a decisive role in bringing down several political machines. For example, in 1871 a series of stories in the *New York Times* suggested that Tammany boss William Magear Tweed and his cronies had stolen millions (now thought to be much as $300 million) from the city. These stories were accompanied by editorial cartoons by Thomas Nast in *Harper's Magazine* that were so effective that Tweed sought to bribe Nast to leave the country, or failing that, to intimidate Harper's by ordering the city school system to refuse to purchase textbooks from the magazine's parent company. The media fusillade led to the indictment and conviction of Tweed and several of his lieutenants and the subsequent decline of the Tammany machine. Tweed, himself, died in jail in 1878. The importance of media exposure as a weapon against corruption is, by the way, one reason that the decline of the local press is a matter of some concern. According to one study, public corruption increased markedly in cities where the local newspaper closed.[32]

The central political goal of Progressivism was to weaken political parties and, so, to pave the way for a restoration of rule by business and the upper classes of society.[33] Progressives, not without reason, equated party government with misrule and corruption. But, as mentioned above, Progressives were concerned with more than just corruption. Generally speaking, strong political party organizations are necessary for politicians who depend upon the support of working- and lower-class voters to compete effectively against rivals who can depend upon the financial resources and access to private institutions enjoyed by their upscale rivals.[34] Organization maximizes the power of numbers and permits those who are individually powerless to become an effective political force. Progressives viewed political parties as a corrupting influence because they allowed the wrong people to acquire political power, as much as they disapproved of the corruption associated with political parties.

With the help of the muckraking press, Progressives were able to bring about a number of political reforms that weakened party machines and allowed the better classes to take power in a number of states and cities. These reforms included a gradual expansion of civil service to include state and municipal officials in much of the country; the introduction of personal registration requirements that sharply diminished voter fraud; the introduction of primary elections that reduced party leaders' control over nominations; and the adoption of secret ballot rules that made it far more difficult for party cadres to control voters at the ballot box. Between 1900 and 1930, machine control of most American municipalities was disrupted if not thoroughly eliminated. Pockets of machine rule remained, Cook County Illinois, for example. But even here, by the 1960s, the Democratic political machine clung to power over some municipal institutions while having to surrender control over others.[35]

The declining power of political machines helps to explain why political corruption in the United States began to decline as well. During the 1930s, the Roosevelt Administration created a national police force, the FBI, and made public corruption one of the new agency's major investigative priorities, a policy which continues to the present time. In addition, the Hobbs Act, enacted in 1934, became and, as we saw earlier, continues to serve as the federal government's most powerful weapon against public corruption at the state and local levels.

Of course, even with the demise of political machines, the creation of the FBI and the enactment of new anti-corruption legislation, public corruption continues to exist, much of it in the old machine states and municipalities. What might be called "legacy corruption" is difficult to eliminate because it is essentially handed down from political generation to political generation. Politicians who rise to power in a corrupt environment are unlikely to become champions of reform and, more likely, corrupt the next generation of politicians. Take the case of Pennsylvania. The foundations of Pennsylvania's state-wide political machine were laid by Lincoln's secretary of war, Simon Cameron in the 1860s. Cameron was succeeded by his son Donald who was, in turn, succeeded by Matthew Quay. All three individuals were noted for soliciting bribes and kickbacks and engaging in influence peddling. Quay was succeeded by Boies Penrose, the last of Pennsylvania's state-wide political bosses. After Penrose's death in 1921, the machine's county leaders gained more autonomy. Foremost among these bosses was Delaware County State Senator John J. McClure, a convicted felon and former lieutenant in the Penrose machine who remained a force in Pennsylvania politics into the 1960s.

The next generation of Pennsylvania politicians included, among others, State Senator Vincent Fumo, convicted of wire fraud and conspiracy, House Majority Whip Brett Feese, convicted of theft and conspiracy, Senate Minority Leader Robert Mellow, convicted of conspiracy, House Minority Whip Mike Veon, convicted of theft and conspiracy, House Speaker John Perzel, convicted of theft and conspiracy, and Senate Majority Whip Jane Orie, convicted of theft of services, obstruction, forgery and tampering with evidence.[36]

Such legacy corruption is difficult to stamp out entirely but seems to be kept in check by contemporary law enforcement efforts. With the decline of political machines, the institutional base for publication has weakened, if not entirely disappeared. What remains in the old machine states amounts to personal venality rather than institutionalized public corruption. Take the case of Illinois, a state whose once-powerful Cook County political machine was a force in national Democratic politics through the 1960s but has since fallen into disarray. A team led by University of Illinois at Chicago Political Science Department chair and former Chicago alderman, Dick Simpson, carefully recorded all the public corruption trials and convictions in Illinois's state and federal courts in 2015, which they called a "banner year in Illinois corruption" (see Table 7.5).[37]

Several things can be learned from this table. To begin with, public corruption certainly exists in Illinois. Some 31 state and municipal officials were indicted, convicted or sentenced for misuse of their official authority—some on more than one count of corruption. In 2015, however, some 227,000 individuals were employed by Illinois's state and municipal governments, for a corruption rate of .01 per thousand public employees. With a number of obvious exceptions, moreover, many of the acts of corruption on this list were relatively minor. A tax and license compliance supervisor stole more than $2000 worth of confiscated cigarettes. A revenue inspector accepted a $500 bribe from a store owner. A police officer was convicted of steering tow truck business to a favored firm and, presumably, accepting kickbacks. An alderman's chief of staff accepted a $7500 bribe and so on. Chicago's old-time

Table 7.5 Public Corruption in Illinois by the Numbers, 2015.

Corruption investigations	11
Corruption convictions	27
Corruption indictments	28
Corruption conviction sentencings	30
% of public that trusts the state government	25

Sources: Simpson et al. 2015: A Banner Year in Illinois Corruption (https://pols.uic.edu/wp-content/uploads/sites/273/2018/10/ac_report9-2015abannercorruptionyear.pdf); https://pols.uic.edu/wp-content/uploads/sites/273/2018/10/ac_report9-2015abannercorruptionyear.pdf

political bosses, like Anton Cermak and Richard J. Daley, would have been embarrassed at the pettiness of their successors. Absent the great political machines, legacy corruption has become a smaller matter, relatively easily kept in check by law enforcement. There is, however, one area of exception—the ongoing proliferation of special districts.

Special Purpose Districts: The New Machines?

In recent years, political corruption appears to have relocated from its traditional bastions in state, county, city and village governments to a new site. This new location is the special purpose district (sometimes called a special authority or just special district), a unit of government that has proliferated over the past decades. There are now nearly 100,000 special districts in the U.S. charged with providing services including education, fire protection, sanitation, parks, maintenance of toll bridges and toll roads, mosquito abatement and real estate development. Most are single-function but in several states, special districts have expanded the scope of their authority to include several functions. These districts are generally supervised by locally elected boards and collectively employ nearly 200,000 local officials.[38] Special districts have fiscal autonomy. They levy taxes, charge fees for their services and issue debt that does not have to be approved by any other unit of government.

Turn-of-the-century Progressives saw in special districts a way of taking public power away from state and municipal governments controlled by political machines and lodging it with smaller units of government that would be close to the people. Borrowing by special district governments, moreover, does not count toward states' constitutional debt limits. Consistent, however, with the general notion that today's solution is tomorrow's problem, as Christopher Berry observes, the proliferation of special districts has added to the number of governmental units seeking to levy taxes and has, as a result, contributed to extremely high tax rates in such states as Illinois where the state legislature has permitted the creation of more than 8000 special districts.[39] From the perspective of state governments, moreover, special purpose districts are useful because their borrowing does not increase the state's nominal indebtedness. It is "off budget" and thus does not count toward the state's constitutionally mandated borrowing limits. This is another way in which state constitutions promote questionable fiscal activities and, as we shall see below, establish a new venue for official corruption.

Special districts represent a heightened danger for official corruption. Most special districts are hidden from public view and their activities, especially their financial practices, lacking in transparency.[40] Many special districts do not make financial information available.[41] Most special district boards are elected but voter turnout is typically less than 10 percent, some scholars say hardly ever more than 5 percent, and boards do as much as they can to avoid publicizing elections.[42] With an overall decline of newspaper coverage of state and municipal affairs, newspaper coverage of special districts is virtually nonexistent. In some states, special districts are required to submit proposed bond issues to the voters, but election announcements are often hidden in small print in the government advertising sections of local newspapers and receive little or no media coverage. The result is that special district boards are self-perpetuating and their decisions seldom exposed to public scrutiny.[43]

The upshot seems to be a significant problem of municipal corruption among special districts. In Texas, where municipal utility districts bear the unfortunate but, perhaps, accurate acronym MUD, the state legislature investigated claims that Dallas area developers gained control of a MUD and received hundreds of millions of dollars in taxing authority from an election in which voter participation was limited to a handful of voters, housed in temporary mobile homes, who received free rent, jobs and other benefits in exchange for their support.[44] In Pennsylvania, the turnpike authority board of directors rigged bids for decades in exchange for kickbacks from contractors.[45] Maine's turnpike authority director recently went to prison for stealing hundreds of thousands of dollars from the agency.[46] Even the special authority that operates the world-famous Golden Gate Bridge is inclined to conduct its procedures in secret and has many times faced charges involving questionable accounting, no-bid contracts and undocumented expenses.[47] Special district corruption goes beyond the venality of some officials. One major problem appears to be procurement. Lack of transparency results in a pattern of purchase from contractors who are friendly with, or will pay kickbacks to, members of district

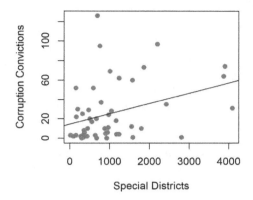

Figure 7.3 Corruption and Special Purpose Districts.
Note: This graph shows the relationship between the number of special purpose districts in the states and the total number of state and local corruption convictions. The line shown is an OLS line of best fit. Data on special districts from Governing (www.governing.com/gov-data/number-of-governments-by-state.html). Data on convictions from TRAC (https://trac.syr.edu/).

boards. In some instances, construction contractors have funded campaigns promoting bond measures for the construction of unnecessary infrastructure in exchange for municipal contracts.[48]

Public corruption thrives in an environment of low visibility, lack of accountability and the absence of media scrutiny.[49] Indeed, many of today's most corrupt states are precisely those with large numbers of special purpose districts (see Figure 7.3).

Possibly, the next generation of muckraking journalists should look into these districts for story ideas. "The Special Shame of the Special Districts" might be a catchy title.

Eradicating Public Corruption

Public corruption is a serious matter, costing Americans tens of millions of dollars every year. However, we should not become so zealous in our efforts to stamp out corruption that we overreach and harm our democratic political process. Take the case of former Virginia governor, Robert F. McDonnell. The former governor was convicted in 2014 under the honest services statute and the Hobbs Act of using his influence as governor to introduce businessman Jonnie R. Williams to potential customers and other business contacts after receiving numerous gifts from Williams. From the government's perspective McDonnell's actions amounted to accepting money and property for taking official actions (Hobbs Act) and depriving Virginians of his "honest services," a vague concept meaning to deprive another of the intangible right of honest services. For the most part, national editorial commentary applauded the verdict as a blow against public corruption.

McDonnell's conviction, however, was appealed and was eventually heard by the U.S. Supreme Court which, in 2016, overturned McDonnell's conviction. Writing for a unanimous Court, Chief Justice Roberts pointed out that McDonnell's actions were those that any politician might be expected to undertake on behalf of a constituent. He arranged meetings and contacts but undertook no official action on William's behalf.

The government's expansive interpretation of "official act" would raise significant constitutional concerns. Conscientious public officials arrange meetings for constituents, contact other officials on their behalf and include them in events all the time. Representative government assumes that public officials will hear from their constituents and act appropriately on their concerns. The government's position could cast a pall of potential prosecution over these relationships.[50]

It is certainly possible, though he denied it, that McDonnell did favors for Williams in expectation of the gifts he received. Yet, McDonnell took no official action on Williams's behalf. Justice Robert's point is that in our zeal to stamp out corruption we should not interfere with democratic politics. The cure would surely be worse than the disease.

Notes

1 Under some circumstances, corruption can also have positive consequences perhaps by giving public officials a direct incentive to undertake useful activities. See, for example, Nathaniel H. Leff, "Economic Development through Bureaucratic Corruption," in Arnold Heidenheimer and Michael Johnson, eds., *Political Corruption*, 3rd ed. (New Brunswick, NJ: Transaction Publishers, 2002), pp. 307–319,
2 Transparency International, "Corruption Perceptions Index, 2017," www.transparency.org/news/feature/corruption_perceptions_index_2017?gclid =EAIaIQobChMIivzegM_83AIVy4KzCh1_zQzpEAAYASAAEgIVJfD_BwE.
3 Eric Zorn, "Blagojevich Trial Tape Transcripts," *Chicago Tribune*, Jul. 8, 2010. http://blogs.chicagotribune.com/news_columnists_ezorn/2010/07/textonly.html.
4 Leslie Maitland, "High Officials Are Termed Subjects Of a Bribery Investigation by F.B.I," *The New York Times*, Feb. 3, 1980, p. 1. Retrieved Dec. 4, 2013.
5 Terrence Hake with Wayne Klatt, *Operation Greylord: The True Story of an Untrained Undercover Agent and America's Biggest Corruption Bust* (Chicago, IL: American Bar Association Press, 2015).
6 John Branston, "U.S. Indicts 4 Tennessee Lawmakers in Corruption Case," *New York Times* (online ed.), May 27, 2005. Retrieved Aug. 7, 2015.
7 www.nj.com/passaic-county/2016/11/passaic_mayor_pleads_guilty_to_federal_bribery_cha.html.
8 www.nj.com/burlington/2016/07/ex-nj_mayor_sentenced_to_probation_on_conspiracy_c.html.

9. NJ.com www.nj.com/politics/index.ssf/2016/12/2016_the_year_in_public_corruption.html.
10. Adriana S. Cordis and Jeffrey Milyo, "Measuring Public Corruption in the United States: Evidence from Administrative Records of Federal Prosecutions," *Public Integrity* 18 (2016): 127–148.
11. Cordis and Milyo, "Measuring Public Corruption," p. 138.
12. For example, Reid Wilson, "The Most Corrupt States in America," *The Washington Post*, Jan. 22, 2014. www.washingtonpost.com/blogs/govbeat/wp/2014/01/22/the-most-corrupt-states-in-america/?noredirect=on&utm_term=.62332160b904.
13. For a full discussion of the problematic character of the PIN data, see Cordis and Milyo, "Measuring Public Corruption."
14. Cordis and Milyo, "Measuring Public Corruption," p. 135.
15. Cordis and Milyo, "Measuring Public Corruption," p. 138.
16. Edward Glaeser and Claudia Goldin, "Corruption and Reform: Introduction," in Edward Glaeser and Claudia Goldin, eds., *Corruption and Reform* (Chicago, IL: University of Chicago Press, 2006), pp. 13–15.
17. Martin Shefter, *Political Parties and the State* (Princeton, NJ: Princeton University Press, 1994), p. 70.
18. Richard Jensen, *The Winning of the Midwest* (Chicago, IL: University of Chicago Press, 1971).
19. William Riordan, *Plunkitt of Tammany Hall* (New York: Signet, 2015).
20. Shefter, *Political Parties*, p. 175.
21. V.O. Key, Jr. *Southern Politics* (New York: Vintage, 1949), p. 163.
22. Shefter, *Political Parties*, p. 177.
23. Shefter, *Political Parties*, p. 74.
24. Ari Hoogenboom, *Outlawing the Spoils: A History of the Civil Service Reform Movement* (Urbana, IL: University of Illinois Press, 1961).
25. Gabriel Kolko, *The Triumph of Conservatism: A Reinterpretation of American History* (New York: Free Press, 1977). Also, Gabriel Kolko, *Railroads and Regulation* (New York: W.W. Norton, 1970).
26. Samuel P. Hays, "The Politics of Reform in Municipal Government in the Progressive Era," *The Pacific Northwest Quarterly* 55, no. 4 (October, 1964), p. vii.
27. Hays, p. 159.
28. Matthew Gentzkow, Edward L. Glaeser and Claudia Goldin, "How Newspapers Became Informative and Why It Mattered," in Glaeser and Goldin, eds., *Corruption and Reform*, p. 196.
29. Gentzkow et al., p. 192.
30. Lincoln Steffens, *The Shame of the Cities*, 2018 Reprint ed. (London: Forgotten Books, 2018).
31. "Tweed Days in St. Louis," in *The Shame of the Cities*, ch.1.
32. Kriston Capps, "The Hidden Costs of Losing Your City's Newspaper," *Citylab*, www.citylab.com/equity/2018/05/study-when-local-newspaper-close-city-bond-finances-suffer/561422/.
33. Shefter, *Political Parties*, p. 77.
34. Maurice Duverger, *Political Parties: Their Organization and Activity in the Modern State* (New York: Science Editions, 1963).
35. Shefter, *Political Parties*, p. 85.
36. Brad Bumsted, *Keystone Corruption* (Philadelphia, PA: Camino Books, 2013).
37. Dick Simpson, Thomas J. Gradel, Leslie Price and Ion Nimerencu, "2015: A Banner Year in Illinois Corruption," Anti-Corruption Report Number 9, Mar. 10, 2016. https://pols.uic.edu/docs/default-source/chicago_politics/anti-

corruption_reports/report-9—2015-a-banner-corruption-year—3-10-16-final-draft.pdf?sfvrsn=4.
38 Christopher Berry, *Imperfect Union: Representation and Taxation in Multi-level Governments* (New York: Cambridge University Press, 2009).
39 Berry, *Imperfect Union*, pp. 2–3.
40 Steven L. Schwarcz, "The Use and Abuse of Special Purpose Entities in Public Finance," *Minnesota Law Review* 97 (2012): 369.
41 Michelle Surka and Rachel Cross, "Governing in the Shadows: Rating the Online Financial Transparency of Special District Governments," U.S. PIRG, Apr. 2017. https://uspirg.org/sites/pirg/files/resources/FtM%202017%20factsheet%20FINAL%20%281%29.pdf.
42 Nancy Burns, *The Formation of American Local Governments: Private Values in Public Institutions* (New York: Oxford University Press, 1994), p. 12.
43 Sara C. Galvan, "Wrestling With MUDs to Pin Down the Truth About Special Districts," *Fordham Law Review* 75 (2007): 3041.
44 Galvan, "Wrestling With MUDs," p. 3055.
45 Brad Bumsted, "Experts: State's Turnpike Corruption the Worst Such Case," *TribLive*, Apr. 11, 2013. https://triblive.com/news/adminpage/3807891-74/turnpike-debt-billion.
46 41. Bumsted, "Experts," p. 2.
47 Louise Nelson Dyble, *Paying the Toll: Local Power, Regional Politics, and the Golden Gate Bridge* (Philadelphia, PA: University of Pennsylvania Press, 2009).
48 Ashly McGlone, "With School Bond Campaigns, Some Things Change and Some Stay the Same," *Voice of San Diego*, www.voiceofsandiego.org/topics/education/school-bond-campaigns-things-change-stay/.
49 Aymo Brunetti and Beatrice Weder, "A Free Press Is Bad News for Corruption," *Journal of Public Economics* 87 (2003): 1801–1824.
50 Syllabus, *McDonnell v. U.S.* No. 15-474 (2016). www.supremecourt.gov/opinions/15pdf/15-474_ljgm.pdf.

8 Conclusion
What is to be Done?

State governments are important and if many Americans were unaware of this fact, the crisis of 2020 should serve as a reminder. Because state governments play important roles, all Americans should take the problems and limitations of these governments very seriously. As we have seen, many state governments suffer from weak constitutional and institutional foundations, legislatures that seem to be more responsive to organized interests than to citizens, histories of public corruption and a general lack of civic knowledge and engagement.

Many of the problems we have identified could be addressed by major institutional reforms. No doubt, states could amend their constitutions to reduce the number of independently elected executives or adopt more effective ethics and conflict of interest rules to reduce the influence of lobby groups in state legislatures. In these and other matters, however, the status quo is generally protected by organized interests.

The popular political will that would have to mobilized for change, however, is generally rendered ineffective by the fact that few citizens are attentive to state politics and most, as our survey indicated, know little or nothing about the political affairs of their states. Overwhelming majorities cannot so much as name their state senator or state representative (see Table 8.1). Large percentages of respondents answer "don't know" to simple questions about their state's government and, among those who offer an answer to at least some of our questions, overwhelming majorities give incorrect answers.

For all that Americans know about them, state governments may as well be covert operations. Citizens are likely to know the name of their governor, and the governor knows that she or he will be held responsible for affairs in the state. Other state officials, whether executive legislative or judicial, are essentially invisible to the citizenry. No wonder that many legislators feel free to engage in actions that involve blatant conflicts of interest and ignore the most basic ethical principles. Their constituents are not looking.

Table 8.1 Percentage Responding "Don't Know" to Survey Questions about Their State

Question	% Responding "Don't Know"
Who is your state representative?	81%
Who is your state senator?	72%
Does your state have special purpose districts?	72%
Who draws the boundaries of legislative districts?	53%
Does your state allow ballot initiatives?	53%
Does your state have a one-house or two-house legislature?	47%
What does your state spend the most money on?	45%
Are members of the state legislature full time or part time?	44%
Does your state have its own constitution?	36%
Can citizens register and vote on the same day?	35%
Who is your state governor?	33%
Is voting absentee an option	27%

Data are from a nationally representative survey of 1500 U.S. residents.

It would be tempting to blame the news media for citizens' lack of knowledge about the operations of their states' governments. Indeed, there is very little media coverage of events in the state capitals, unless of course some hapless official is arrested by the FBI and prosecuted in federal court for wrongdoing. A recent Pew survey showed a 35 percent decline in full-time state house reporters from 2003 to 2014, with the downward trend expected to continue.[1] For the past quarter century, according to Dan Hopkins, the news outlets upon which most Americans have come to rely have offered less and less state and local coverage.[2] Lack of knowledge, as Hopkins shows, also undermines citizen engagement in state and local politics. Citizens are unlikely to take the time to participate in political affairs about which they have no knowledge.

While this evidence seems to lead to the conclusion that more media coverage is needed, this idea does not suggest any realistic way forward. What policies could be developed to compel the media to expand coverage of state and local matters? Would not such policies be inconsistent with the idea of a free press that chooses what to cover and how to cover it?

Increased media coverage, moreover, is problematic in a political environment where citizens do not even have a base of knowledge from which to evaluate the information they might receive. Americans may be woefully ignorant about the national government, but they are even less than woefully ignorant (if such a thing is possible) about their state governments. Our survey showed that, across the country, sizeable percentages of citizens don't know fundamental facts about who represents them at the state level and how their state governments operate. Table 8.1 presented the percentage responding "don't know" to various survey questions. Note that these percentages are almost certainly underestimates, as decades of survey research demonstrate that individuals are much more inclined to guess than respond "don't know."[3] And, as we noted, most of those who claimed to know gave incorrect answers.

It is unreasonable to expect citizens to critically evaluate news accounts from this shaky foundation of knowledge. This is particularly true in an age where disinformation is rampant and highly polarized online news sources have proliferated. It is not possible to be a discerning consumer of state political news without an understanding of the basic facts about how state government works. And a healthy, sustainable democracy requires more than just knowledge of the basic facts. It requires citizens to be actively engaged in learning and thinking about how their government works and whether it is working well for them and their communities. In short, it requires a rich civic education.

Evolution of Civic Education in the United States

The concept of "social studies" as a primary and secondary school subject first emerged in the 1880s as public schools expanded and immigration soared. The National Education Association (NEA), in an effort to standardize the high school curriculum, issued a report titled *Conference on History, Civil Government, and Political Economy* in 1894. The report outlined a social studies curriculum consisting of eight consecutive years or education that covered Greek and Roman history, American history, French history, English history and civil government.

During the first few decades of the 20th century, scholars and practitioners developed ideas for how to teach social studies with a more modern emphasis and in such a way that disentangled American history and government from ancient and European history. These ideas are articulated in the NEA's 1916 report, *The Social Studies in Secondary Education*. The authors of this report believed that the purpose of the social studies curriculum was to provide students with "an appreciation of the nature and laws of social life, a sense of the responsibility of the individual as a member of social groups, and the intelligence and the will to participate effectively in the promotion of the social well-being." To achieve this goal, the report recommended that students complete two years of civic education – one in ninth grade on community life and obligations and one in twelfth grade in which students would apply political, economic and sociological theories to societal challenges. By the mid-1930s, a majority of American high school students graduated having completed formal coursework in civic education.

In the late 1950s, after the Soviet launch of Sputnik in 1957, private foundations and the federal government devoted generous funds to reforming American public education in an effort to keep up with Europe and Russia. By 1967, over 50 national curriculum projects related to social studies were underway.[4] Collectively, the curricula that emerged during this time period emphasized three core areas. First, they returned to a traditional conception of civic education. In the previous two decades, the subject had become a means to glorify American culture and demonize the Soviet system.[5] In the new model of civic education, students were instead taught to think critically when consuming political information and develop their own judgements.

The second and third prongs of the new curricula, minority/ethnic studies and social issues, were developed in response to criticism that social studies education had become detached from society. Current events, such as issues related to urbanization and nuclear proliferation, were incorporated into the curricula, as were historical and cultural issues specific to minority groups. By the end of the 1970s, the new social studies had become an inclusive yet fragmented collection of concepts that had a "kaleidoscopic quality."[6]

In 1983, the National Commission on Excellence in Education issued "A Nation at Risk," a scathing condemnation of education in the U.S. Education policy makers called for a "back to basics" approach with a renewed focus on core academic subjects. For the social studies, this meant a revival of traditional history content and a move away from critical thinking and issues-oriented lessons. The standards movement that followed in the subsequent decades called for a codification of goals for civic education that had been enumerated over the last century. In 2003, the Center for Information and Research on Civic Learning and Engagement released "The Civic Mission of Schools," a report that characterized civic education as the acquisition of skills and knowledge that would empower students to become engaged, participatory citizens. The report emphasized schools as having an indispensable role in the political socialization of young Americans. This perception continues to motivate civic education curricula today, with the goal of civic engagement serving as the overarching framework.

Civic Education in the United States Today

There is wide variation in how civic education is implemented across the country. At the high school level, 40 states require civics coursework to

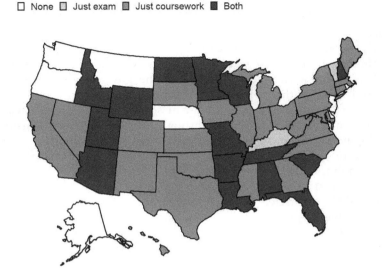

Figure 8.1 High School Civic Education Requirements.
Data compiled by the Center for American Progress. Required coursework includes either a half-year or full-year course in government and civics.

graduate, 17 states require passage of a civics proficiency exam to graduate and 15 require both (see Figure 8.1). Only Vermont and Kentucky require passage of a civics exam without also requiring coursework. Of the states requiring civics coursework, 31 states require a half-year course while nine states require a full-year course on content specifically related to government and/or citizenship. See Table 8.5 in the Appendix for a list of these requirements by state.

In terms of content, the Education Commission of the States reports that only eight states specifically require that units of coursework required for graduation be dedicated to the study of state government.[7] Nonetheless, a deeper analysis of the states' curricula reveals that 30 of the states that require civics coursework have implemented a "full curriculum," meaning the content covers all core pillars of civic education, including "information on state and local voting rules."[8]

In general, high school civic education is focused on three key areas of learning: knowledge, skills and dispositions.[9] Civics curricula therefore tend to cover U.S. government institutions, political processes, participatory skills, and democratic values. In their analysis of the state of civic education in the U.S., for example, the Brookings Institution examined states' attention to ten essential elements of civic education, including instruction in government, discussion of current events, service learning and news media literacy—state government was deemed to be essential. Overall, then, high school civic education is overwhelmingly focused on national political systems and, generally, how citizens can engage with the government. There is minimal attention to state and local government and how young adults can influence and interact with the government officials who live and work in their proximate communities.

When state government is taught in schools, it is almost always at the elementary school level and through the lens of a state's historical development. Elementary-age children frequently take field trips to their state capitals or to visit historical landmarks central to the state's political development. This education is valuable, but it does not fully satisfy the need for students to learn about state government during their formative years. For students to develop a meaningful and durable appreciation for how state governments operate and citizens' role in holding those governments accountable, students must build upon their elementary-school knowledge during their high school years.

While the data show a lack of widespread and consistent standards for the inclusion of state-focused civic education in graduation requirements, specific curricula and resources in this area have been effectively implemented at all levels of K-12 education. Many state capitols, for example, provide learning activities that can be used in the classroom, such as virtual tours, quizzes, videos, worksheets and lesson plans. The Center for Civic Education has developed several curricula with varying emphases. The Center's "We the People: Project Citizen" is a program that "promotes competent and responsible participation in state and local government."[10] Numerous additional resources have been developed by local and national organizations dedicated to furthering student learning about state government.

The Effects of Civic Education on Political Engagement

Civic education is considered one of several key political socializing agents, with others including the family, peer groups, and the media.[11] Each of these agents helps shape an individual's understanding of the political system and his or her role in it. The political socialization process usually begins in the home, with parents discussing current events or political preferences in family conversations. As children grow, their friends, media consumption and schoolwork also help to influence their developing political identities, values and knowledge. Moreover, these factors interact with each other, usually reinforcing each one's influence and, sometimes, conflicting with each other.

Civic Education and Knowledge

Early studies in 1960s and 1970s on the effect of civic education on knowledge generally found no evidence of a relationship, with scholars concluding, "Our findings certainly do not support the thinking of those who look to the civics curriculum as even a minor source of political socialization."[12] More recent research, however, has firmly put to the bed the "no effects" model. The National Center for Education Statistics' 1990 Civics Report Card demonstrated that students who reported studying American government and civics in schools earned a 16-point higher civics proficiency score on the National Assessment of Educational Progress (NAEP). Research on the 1998 civics portion of the NAEP likewise found a positive relationship between government-related coursework and test scores.[13]

Subsequent analyses confirm this effect. A 2003 examination of survey data from a sample of 3050 high school students from the Baltimore-Washington metropolitan region showed civics coursework to be associated with a 3 percent increase in level of political knowledge (along with increases in other forms of engagement, including political discussion and efficacy).[14] The 2010 Civics Report Card demonstrated that fourth graders whose teachers reported covering four specific civics content areas scored achieved higher average tests scores in those areas.[15] The civics portion of the 2014 NAEP continues to show improvements in civic knowledge that align with the slow but steady improvement of civic education across the U.S.

Evaluations of specific civics curricula, such as Kids Voting U.S.A. and We the People: Project Citizen, find that their use significantly increases student's politically relevant skills, such as the ability to discuss politics with friends, describe public policies to others and formulate opinions about political issues.[16] Taken together, the prior research overwhelmingly supports a meaningful link between what is taught in the civics classroom and how much students understand about politics and policy.

Our recent survey results likewise show that more civic education is associated with improved levels of civic knowledge. Table 8.2 shows the relationship between the amount of civic education our survey respondents reported completing and their ability to respond to five basic questions about their state government (name of their governor, name of their state senator, name of their state representative, whether their state has a constitution and the number of houses in their state's legislature). The second column reports the average "knowledge score" (range of 0–5) among respondents who reported studying civics and government generally at various levels of education, while the third column reports these average scores among respondents who reported studying state government specifically. In both cases, more civic education is associated with improved knowledge scores, and there appears to

Table 8.2 Civic Education and Knowledge: Survey Results

	Studied civics & government	Studied state government
	Knowledge score	Knowledge score
Never	1.41	1.61
Elementary school (ES)	1.73	1.77
High school (HS)	1.87	1.98
College	2.07	1.92
ES and HS	2.45	2.35
HS and college	2.79	2.65
ES, HS and college	3.04	2.84

The knowledge score (0–5) is based on whether survey respondents answered five questions about state government (name of their governor, name of their state representative, name of their state senator, whether their state has a constitution, number of houses in their state's legislature). The data are from a nationally representative sample of 1500 respondents.

be a cumulative effect. Studying government at all three levels of education (elementary school, high school and college) is associated with the highest scores.

Civic Education and Participation

There is a scholarly consensus that more educational attainment leads to higher levels of political participation, including discussing politics, contacting elected officials and voting.[17] Education provides students with skills that facilitate participation, such as the ability to communicate effectively, analyze complex issues and develop policy opinions.[18] Moreover, higher levels of education are associated with an increased confidence in one's ability to influence the political process and to overcome the logistical barriers to participation, such as locating one's polling place, determining how to contact one's representative and learning about key political issues. And education is highly correlated with income and other resources that lower the costs of participatory activities such as donating to and volunteering for a political campaign.

The link between *civic* education specifically and political participation has been less widely studied. One important reason for this lack of systematic analysis is the difficulty in measuring students' exposure to civic education. Civic education is often measured using survey questions in which respondents are asked to recall how much coursework related to civics and government they completed in school (e.g., none, half-year course, full-year course). This measure is subject to both memory and consistency problems.[19] First, respondents may simply not remember,

Table 8.3 The Effect of Coursework in American Government/Civics on Voting

Elections	Probability of Voting with No Coursework	Probability of Voting with One Year	Change in Probability of Voting
1992	54.2%	58.5%	4.3*
1993/ 1994	35.8%	40.8%	5.0*
1996	62.7%	66.1%	3.4
1998/ 2000	44.8%	50.0%	5.2*
2004	56.9%	60.7%	3.8*
2005/ 2006	53.5%	56.5%	3.0

The estimates for 1992, 1993/94, 1996 and 1998/00 are based on the NELS:1988 data. The estimates for 2004 and 2004–2006 are based on the NELS:2002 data.
* p <:05. For more details about the regression models used to generate these effects, see Jennifer Bachner. *Learning to Act: The effect of high school civic education on political participation.* Harvard University, 2011.

accurately, exactly how much civic education they completed. Second, respondents may interpret "civic education" differently—some, for example, may include courses in economics while others may not.

Despite these challenges, there is evidence that civic education makes a real difference in youth participation. A study that used transcript data from the National Education Longitudinal Studies (NELS) to measure civic education found that a year of American government and/or civics course work is associated with a 3–5 percentage point increase in youth voter turnout after graduation from high school (see Table 8.3).[20]

The study also examined the effect of civics coursework on other forms of participation. While voting is the most common way for citizens to express their political preferences, it is one of myriad means by which citizens can exert influence. This study uncovered some notable effects. A year of civic education, for example, increased both news viewership and the likelihood that young people would volunteer on political campaigns.

Similar studies provide additional evidence of a direct link between civic education and engagement. One analysis of the effects of student achievement in civic education found that students with higher grades in social studies courses were more likely to both register to vote and cast a ballot on Election Day.[21] An evaluation of the We the People: The Citizen and Constitution program determined that alumni were more likely than non-participating students to volunteer for a political candidate, make a political contribution and contact an elected official.[22]

The Moderating Effects of Civic Education

The key agents of political socialization mentioned above, including parents, schools and peers, do not operate in a vacuum. They influence each other and affect the extent to which each matters. This is particularly the case with parents and schools. The home is generally the first and most enduring influence on an individual's political identity interest and attitudes. Parents (or other primary caretakers) frame their children's perceptions of current events and political figures as they enter into their children's consciousness. Children might also observe their parents participating in the political system. They may accompany them to the voting booth or see them speaking with a canvasser. Through conversations with their parents about politics and observations of their parents' political behavior, children an initial understanding of how the political world works.

We know, however, that political interest and activity vary widely. Many parents have priorities other than politics, and others lack a sufficient knowledge base. Immigrant parents, for example, may not know very much about the American political system or how they can participate in it. For children who receive a scant political education in the home, the school civics curriculum can serve an even more important role as a socializing agent than it does among students whose parents are politically active.

To test this interactive effect, one study compared the effect of civic education for students who reported "never" discussing current events with their parents to students who reported that they "often" had these discussions. The results show that students not exposed to home discussions about politics obtained a larger benefit from civics coursework than their peers.[23] Table 8.4 presents the estimated increases in the probability of voting associated with an additional year of civics course among students who reported *not* discussing current events. The effects range from an increase of 6.7 to 11.4 percentage points (more than double the effect among all students combined).

Subsequent studies have confirmed a compensatory effect of civic education for students from non-political families. One examination of survey data from both the U.S. and Belgium found that civic education increases political engagement in the forms of news viewership, interest in political issues and discussion of political issues with peers, and that this increase is most pronounced among those from homes with low levels of parental politicization. The authors explain, "This substantially reduces the empowerment gap caused by family background."[24] It therefore appears that schools are well situated to fulfill the critical mission of preparing students to participate in American democracy, and especially so for students who are not politically socialized in the home.

Table 8.4 The Interactive Effect of Coursework and Parental Politicization on Voting

Elections	Probability of Voting w/No Coursework and No Discussion	Probability of Voting w/ One Year and No Discussion	Change in Probability of Voting
1992	46.2%	57.6%	11.4*
1993/1994	29.7%	37.7%	8.0*
1996	53.4%	62.6%	9.2*
1998/2000	36.5%	46.1%	9.6*
2004	46.4%	53.9%	7.5*
2005/2006	42.6%	49.3%	6.7*

The estimates for 1992, 1993/94, 1996 and 1998/00 are based on the NELS:1988 data. The estimates for 2004 and 2004–2006 are based on the NELS:2002 data.
* p <:05. For more details about the regression models used to generate these effects, see Jennifer Bachner. *Learning to Act: The effect of high school civic education on political participation.* Harvard University, 2011.

Ongoing Efforts to Enrich Civic Education

In an era of "fake news" and a proliferation of niche news outlets, it is more important than ever to ensure young people develop a citizenship skill set that empowers them to be educated consumers of political information. And while the scholarship on civic education affirms its potential to increase youth political engagement in a variety of forms, only nine states currently require a year of coursework in this area.

There are notable efforts to bolster civic education. Former Supreme Court justice Sandra Day O'Connor founded iCivics to develop engaging lessons and resources that can be incorporated in curricula across the country. The organization is currently leading a massive effort funded by the National Endowment for the Humanities to evaluate and develop best practices in civic education grades K-12. Coordinating with university researchers and expert practitioners, the project, "Educating for American Democracy" will culminate in a report outlining contributors' assessments and recommendations.

While this and similar efforts are valuable, they are overwhelmingly focused on national political systems and democratic values. There continues to be a lack of attention to state government. State political institutions, processes and issues are seldom given much weight in the classroom, nor is increasing attention to these topics emphasized in anyone's plan. Schools are inclined to teach to standardized tests, and several states now require that students take the national citizenship exam as a graduation requirement. This exam, however, includes no questions that address state or local government. When students do learn about state government, it is usually at the elementary level and highly specific to their own state. Today, approximately 40 percent of Americans live in a state other than the one in which they were born and possibly educated. Millions more were born outside the U.S. In many states, more than half of residents were born elsewhere.[25] Students should learn what the states do, not just what their own state does.

Past research in conjunction with our own survey results provide indisputable evidence that the status quo has led to a citizenry that is deeply ignorant about the states that play such an enormous role in their governance. We believe that this can feasibly be addressed through expanding civic education. Specifically, we think that reimagined civics curricula should include the following four areas of emphasis and student learning goals. Note that these topics can be woven into a civics curriculum that spans K-12 education and that the goals are what we think is appropriate to expect of students by the time of their high school graduation.

1. *The institutional and procedural features of state government.* Students should be able to evaluate how the structure of a state government contributes or hinders that government's ability to serve its citizens.
2. *The electoral features of state government.* Students should be able to identify the different electoral features of state governments across the country.
3. *The policy jurisdictions of state government.* Students should understand the areas of public policy in which states exert substantial power and be able to analyze whether state governments are delivering positive policy outcomes.
4. *The means of engaging with state government.* Students should be able to communicate with their state government officials through a variety of means, including voting for elected officials, volunteering on campaigns, donating to candidates, contacting elected officials with concerns and organizing around issues of interest.

Armed with these four bodies of knowledge and skill sets, young citizens will begin to understand how their state governments should work, why their states' constitutions are problematic, why ethics laws are important, how executive institutions should be designed and so forth. Such knowledge is not a cure all but is a beginning to solving the problem of disconnected democracies.

Notes

1 Katerina Eva Matsa and Jan Lauren Boyles, "America's Shifting Statehouse Press," *Pew Charitable Trusts*, Jul. 10, 2014, Accessed Nov. 6, 2019. www.journalism.org/2014/07/10/americas-shifting-statehouse-press/.
2 Daniel J. Hopkins, *The Increasingly United States: How and Why American Political Behavior Nationalized* (Chicago, IL: University of Chicago Press, 2018).
3 George F. Bishop, Alfred J. Tuchfarber and Robert W. Oldendick, "Opinions on Fictitious Issues: The Pressure to Answer Survey Questions," *Public Opinion Quarterly* 50, no. 2 (1986): 240–250.
4 Hazel Whitman Hertzberg, *Social Studies Reform: 1880–1980* (Boulder, CO: Social Science Education Consortium, 1981).
5 Howard D. Mehlinger, "When I See Mr. Jefferson, I'm Going to Tell Him …," *Social Education* 42 (1978): 55–59.
6 Hazel Whitman Hertzberg, *Social Studies Reform: 1880–1980* (Boulder, CO: Social Science Education Consortium, 1981).
7 High School Graduation Requirements, Education Commission of the States, February 2019, https://c0arw235.caspio.com/dp/b7f930000e16e10a822c47b3baa2.
8 Sarah Shapiro and Catherine Brown, "The State of Civics Education," Center for American Progress, Feb. 21, 2018. www.americanprogress.org/issues/education-k-12/reports/2018/02/21/446857/state-civics-education/.
9 Michael Hansen, Elizabeth Mann Levesque, Jon Valant and Diana Quintero, "2018 Brown Center Report on American Education: An Inventory of State Civics Requirements," *Brookings Institution*, Jun. 27, 2018.
10 Project Citizen, The Center for Civic Education, Accessed Nov. 19, 2019. www.civiced.org/pc-program.
11 Herbert H. Hyman, *Political Socialization* (New York: Free Press, 1959).
12 Kenneth P. Langton and M. Kent Jennings, "Political Socialization and the High School Civics Curriculum in the United States," *American Political Science Review* 62, no. 3 (1968): 852–867.
13 Richard G. Niemi and Jane Junn, *Civic Education: What Makes Students Learn* (New Haven, CT: Yale University Press, 1998).
14 James G. Gimpel, J. Celeste Lay and Jason E. Schuknecht, *Cultivating Democracy: Civic Environments and Political Socialization in America* (Washington, DC: Brookings Institution Press, 2003).
15 Jack Buckley, "National Assessment of Educational Progress: The Nation's Report Card, Civic 2010," National Center for Education Statistics, 2011.
16 Michael McDevitt and Spiro Kiousis, *Education for Deliberative Democracy: The Long-term Influence of Kids Voting USA* (Medford, MA: Center for Information and Research on Civic Learning and Engagement, 2004); Thomas S. Vontz, Kim K. Metcalf and John J. Patrick, *'Project Citizen' and the Civic Development of Adolescent Students in Indiana, Latvia and Lithuania* (Washington, DC: Office of Educational Research and Improvement, 2000).
17 Mikael Persson, "Education and Political Participation," *British Journal of Political Science* 45, no. 3 (2015): 689–703.
18 Sidney Verba, Kay Lehman Schlozman and Henry E. Brady, *Voice and Equality: Civic Voluntarism in American Politics* (Cambridge, MA: Harvard University Press, 1995).
19 Richard G. Niemi and Julia Smith, "The Accuracy of Students' Reports of Course Taking in the 1994 National Assessment of Educational Progress," *Educational Measurement: Issues and Practice* 1 (2003): 15–21.

168 *Conclusion*

20 Jennifer Melissa Bachner, *Learning to Act: The Effect of High School Civic Education on Political Participation* (Cambridge, MA: Harvard University, 2011).
21 Rebecca M. Callahan, Chandra Muller and Kathryn S. Schiller, "Preparing the Next Generation for Electoral Engagement: Social Studies and the School Context," *American Journal of Education* 116, no. 4 (2010): 525–556.
22 Center for Civic Education, "Voting and Political Participation of We the People: The Citizen and the Constitution Alumni in the 2004 Election," 2005. Accessed Nov. 21, 2019. https://eric.ed.gov/?id=ED491053.
23 Jennifer Melissa Bachner, *Learning to Act: The Effect of High School Civic Education on Political Participation* (Cambridge, MA: Harvard University, 2011).
24 Anja Neundorf, Richard G. Niemi and Kaat Smets, "The Compensation Effect of Civic Education on Political Engagement: How Civics Classes Make Up for Missing Parental Socialization," *Political Behavior* 38, no. 4 (2016): 921–949.
25 Richard Florida, "The Geography of America's Mobile and 'Stuck,' Mapped," *City Lab*, Mar. 5, 2019, Accessed Nov. 26, 2019. www.citylab.com/life/2019/03/mobile-stuck-us-geography-map-where-americans-moving/584083/?utm_source=feed.

Appendix

Table 8.5 Civic Education Requirements in the U.S.

State	Exam Required to Graduate	Coursework Required to Graduate	Amount of Coursework Required	Full Curriculum	Unit on State Gov. Required to Graduate
Alabama	Yes	Yes	0.5	Yes	No
Alaska	No	No	0	No	No
Arizona	Yes	Yes	0.5	Yes	Yes
Arkansas	Yes	Yes	0.5	Yes	No
California	No	Yes	0.5	Yes	No
Colorado	No	Yes	1	Yes	Yes
Connecticut	No	Yes	0.5	Yes	No
Delaware	No	No	0	No	No
Florida	Yes	Yes	0.5	No	No
Georgia	No	Yes	0.5	Yes	No
Hawaii	No	Yes	1	Yes	No
Idaho	Yes	Yes	1	Yes	No
Illinois	No	Yes	0.5	Yes	No
Indiana	No	Yes	0.5	Yes	No
Iowa	No	Yes	0.5	No	No
Kansas	No	Yes	1	Yes	No
Kentucky	Yes	No	0	No	No
Louisiana	Yes	Yes	0.5	Yes	No
Maine	No	Yes	0.5	No	No
Maryland	No	Yes	1	Yes	Yes
Massachusetts	No	Yes	0.5	No	No
Michigan	No	Yes	0.5	Yes	No
Minnesota	Yes	Yes	0.5	No	No
Mississippi	No	Yes	0.5	Yes	Yes
Missouri	Yes	Yes	0.5	No	No

(*Continued*)

Table 8.5 (Cont.)

State	Exam Required to Graduate	Coursework Required to Graduate	Amount of Coursework Required	Full Curriculum	Unit on State Gov. Required to Graduate
Montana	No	No	0	No	No
Nebraska	No	No	0	No	No
Nevada	No	Yes	1	Yes	No
New Hampshire	Yes	Yes	0.5	Yes	Yes
New Jersey	No	No	0	No	No
New Mexico	No	Yes	0.5	No	No
New York	No	Yes	0.5	No	No
North Carolina	No	Yes	1	No	No
North Dakota	Yes	Yes	0.5	Yes	No
Ohio	No	Yes	0.5	Yes	No
Oklahoma	No	Yes	0.5	Yes	No
Oregon	No	No	0	No	No
Pennsylvania	No	Yes	0.5	Yes	No
Rhode Island	No	No	0	No	No
South Carolina	Yes	Yes	0.5	Yes	No
South Dakota	No	Yes	0.5	Yes	No
Tennessee	Yes	Yes	0.5	Yes	No
Texas	No	Yes	0.5	Yes	No
Utah	Yes	Yes	0.5	Yes	No
Vermont	Yes	No	0	No	No
Virginia	No	Yes	1	No	Yes
Washington	No	No	0	Yes	Yes
West Virginia	No	Yes	1	Yes	No
Wyoming	Yes	Yes	0.5	No	Yes

Columns 2–5 rely on data from The Center for American Progress's "The State of Civic Education." According to the report, a "Full Curriculum" includes course material that include coverage of "state and local voting rules." The amount of coursework requires refers to course length in years. Column 6 is based on the Education Commission of the States's 50-state comparison of units of social studies required for high school graduation.

Index

Note: References in *italics* are to figures, those in **bold** to tables.:

9-11 terror attacks 35, 47

Abbot v. Burke (1997) 25
ACT for America 93
Adams, John 39
Adams, John Quincy 40
ADAs *see* assistant district attorneys
Affordable Care Act (ACA: 2010) 51
African Americans 102, 109, 110, 119
Agricultural Adjustment Administration 46
AIDS 118–119
Aisenberg family 113–114
Alabama: civic education **169**; constitutional amendments 15, **16**, 19; coronavirus crisis xii; corruption 130, **132**, **138**, **139**; gubernatorial powers 77; lobbyists **88**, 91; state constitution 3, 17, 19, 26
Alaska: civic education **169**; corruption **132**, **138**; gubernatorial powers 77; lobbyists **88**; pride of residents 3; state constitution 26
Alexander, Lamar 67, 68–69
Alien and Sedition Acts (1798) 40
American Recovery and Investment Act (ARRA: 2009) 31
Amirault family 115–116
animal rights 20–21
anti-federalism 36, 82
Arizona: civic education **169**; constitutional amendments 13; corruption **132**, **137**, **139**; gubernatorial powers 77; legislative activity 93; lobbyists **88**
The Arizona Republic 93

Arkansas: civic education **169**; corruption **132**, **138**, **139**; gubernatorial powers 77; lobbyists **88**
armed agents 52–53
Armed Forces Reserve Act (1952) 54–55
ARRA (American Recovery and Investment Act: 2009) 31
Articles of Confederation 10, 35, 37, 39, 44, 71
assistant district attorneys (ADAs) 109, 112

Baker, Ray Stannard 145
Benjamin, Brent 117
Bentley, Robert 130
Bernard, Donald, Sr. 130
Berry, Christopher 149
Beshear, Andy 63
Bevin, Matt 63
Beyle, Thad 64
bid rigging 128, **129**
Bill of Rights 10, 21, 22, 46, 53
Black Lives Matter 101
Black, Nancy 52–53
Blagojevich, Rod 7, 8, 128, 129
Blanco, Alex 130
Blankenship, Don 117
Brady v. Maryland (1963) 101
Brady violations 101, 110, 112–113
Bratton, Benjamin 101
Brennan Center 117–118
bribe taking 128, **129**, **129**, 130, 131
Brookings Institution 159–160
Brown, Kate xii

Brown v. Board of Education (1954) 22
Buchanan, James 30
Bureau of Land Management 52
Bureau of the Budget 45
Burr, Aaron 142

Calderon, Ron 130
Calderon, Tom 130
Calhoun, John C. 40
California: Bakersfield 34; civic education **169**; constitutional amendments 18; corruption 130, 131, **132, 137, 139**; employment law 83, 84; Golden Gate Bridge 150; gubernatorial powers 77; and immigration 34, 56; legislative activity 83; lobbyists 88, 89, *90*; plural executive 61, 62; Proposition 13 13; prosecutors 116; state constitution 17, 20, 27; state expenditure 31; state legislature 93; Supreme Court 18
Cameron, Donald 148
Cameron, Simon 148
Canada 34, 39
Cannon, Joe 45
Carnegie, Andrew 144
Center for Civic Education 160
Center for Information and Research on Civic Learning and Engagement 158
Center for Public Integrity 93
Center for Security Policy 93
Cernak, Anton 149
Chase, Salmon 42–43
checks and balances 37, 55–56
Chiang, John 62
Chicago: anti-taping statutes 104; city council corruption 7–8; police misconduct 103–104; *Sunday Times* 105
Chicago Tribune 91
child labor 44
cities 2
civic education: effects on political engagement 160, 161, 163; evolution of 157–158; Kids Voting U.S.A. 161; and knowledge 85, 97, 161–162, **162**; moderating effects of 164–165, **165**; ongoing efforts 165–166; and participation 162–163, **163**; and state government 165–166; in U.S. today 158–160, *159*, **169–170**

civic engagement 3–6, *5*, 69–71, *70*, *71*, 74, 84–85, *85*, 155–157, **156**, 160, 163
civil rights 46, 50, 53, 55
Civil Rights Act (1871) 53
Civil Rights Attorney Fees Awards Act (1983) 53
civil service 44, 142–143, 147
Civil War 41–43, 54
Civilian Conservation Corps 46
Clay, Henry 39
Clinton, George 36
Coakley, Martha 115, 116
Coalition for Integrity 92
coercive federalism 50, 51–55
Cohens v. Virginia (1821) 39
Collins, Jabbar 111–112
Collins, Randall 101
Colorado: civic education **169**; corruption **132, 137**; gubernatorial powers 77; lobbyists 88; state constitution 26
commerce clause 39, 47
Common Cause 116
Commonwealth Fund 65
conflict of interest **129**
Connecticut: civic education **169**; coronavirus crisis xii; corruption **132, 137, 139**; education 23–24; gubernatorial powers 77; lobbyists 88; state constitution (1818) 22; Supreme Court 23, 24
Constitutional Amendments 11; 4th Amendment 105–106, 107, 108; 8th Amendment 120, 122; 10th Amendment 39, 47; 11th Amendment 53; 13th Amendment 43; 14th Amendment 43, 46; 15th Amendment 43; 16th Amendment 45, 48; 17th Amendment 10, 31, 45; 19th Amendment 10; 22nd Amendment 38
constitutional commissions 14
"constitutional legislation" 20
constitutional rights and restrictions 21, 22, 31
Continental Army 54
Continental Congress 39
convention of the states 14
Cooke, Jay 43
cooperative federalism 50
Cordis, Adriana S. 131, 135

coronavirus crisis (2020): federal response to xii, xiii; interstate travel 35; states' response to xi–xiii, 1–2, 56, 75
Corporation for Public Broadcasting 48
corruption 5, 7–8, 128–130, **129**; EOUSA data 135; eradicating public corruption 151–152; federal corruption convictions by state (PIN) 130–135, **132–134**, 136; in House of Representatives 129; in local government **137–138**; newspaper coverage of 136, 140, *140*, 145–146; PIN *vs.* EOUSA *135*; political "machines" 140–144, 146, 147–149; political reform 142–149; special purpose districts 149–151, *151*; "spoils system" 141; in state governments **137–138**; TRAC data 135–136, **136**, **137–139**
Council of State Governments 64
counties 2
crime 51–52; *see also* corruption
Cuomo, Andrew xii–xiii

Daley, Richard J. 149
debt 29–30
Defense Logistics Agency 112
Delaware: civic education **169**; constitutional amendments 12, 13; corruption 131, **132**, **137**, **138**; gubernatorial powers 77; independence of 36; lobbyists **88**
Democratic Party 34, 41, 42, 43, 46, 142, 147, 148
Department of Commerce and Labor 45
Department of Defense (DoD) 47–48
Department of Education 48, 52
Department of Homeland Security 47, 52
Department of State 47
DeRosa, Giacomo "Jack" 130
DeWine, Mike xi–xii
Dick Act (1903) 54
DiNapoli, Thomas 30
disabled persons 51
"disconnected democracies" 2
district attorneys (DAs) 109
Drug Enforcement Administration 52
"dual federalism" 41
"DuPage Seven" 110
Durr, Lawrence 130

Eastman, George 144
Eastman-Kodak 144
Economic Opportunity Act (1964) 51
Educating for American Democracy 165
education 22–25; effects of executive unity on 66, 67; effects of governors' tenure potential on 66, 67–69, *68*; social studies 157–158; *see also* civic education
Education Commission of the States 159
Elkins, Stanley 38
embezzlement **129**
eminent domain 1
employment law 83, 84
enumerated powers 60
environment: effects of executive unity 66, 67; effects of governors' tenure potential 66, 67–69, *68*
Environmental Protection Agency 52
environmental rights 15, 17, 27–28
equal protection clause 23
European Union (EU) 36–37
exclusionary rule 106
executive branch of government 35, 47, 59
Executive Office of the U.S. District Attorneys (EOUSA) 135, *135*
executive privilege 38
extortion 128–129, **129**

Farmer v. Brennan (1994) 120, 121
federal agents 52
Federal Bureau of Investigation (FBI) 51, 52, 129, 147; "ABSCAM" investigation 129; "Tennessee Waltz" operation 129
federal bureaucracy 48
federal courts 53
Federal Deposit Insurance Corporation 46
federal income tax 42, 45, 48–50
federal judges 3, 117
federal law 51–53
Federal Reserve 45
Federal Trade Commission 45, 144
federalism 1, 34–35, 82; checks and balances 55–56; coercive federalism 50, 51–55; cooperative federalism 50; enforcement 43; growth of federal power 34, 35–38, 47; regulated federalism 50; rise and fall of power 38–40; states' rights

coalition 40–41, 44, 45, 55; uncooperative federalism 34–35
Federalist 10 82
Federalist 51 37
Federalist 62 12
Federalist 70 59
Federally Funded Research and Development Center (FFRDC) 48
Feese, Brett 148
Fells Acres School 115
Ferguson, Margaret 61, **62**, 64
finance 42–43
fiscal evasions and restraints 29–30
fiscal illusions 30–31
Fish and Wildlife Service 52
Florida: civic education **169**; constitutional amendments 20–21, 23; Constitutional Revision Commission 14–15; corruption 131, **138**; education 23; gubernatorial powers 77; lobbyists 88; police 108; Taxation and Budget Reform Commission 15
FollowTheMoney.org 89
"Force Bill" 40–41
Fugitive Slave Law (1850s) 56
Fumo, Vincent 148
Futterman, Craig 103–104

geographic mobility 4
Georgia: civic education **169**; coronavirus crisis xii; corruption **132**, **139**; gubernatorial powers 77; lobbyists **88**, 91; political machine 142; state constitution (1777) 22
Gibbons v. Ogden (1824) 1–2, 39
Giglio v. U.S. (1972) 112
Giglio violations 112–113
Glaser, Edward 140
Goldin, Claudia 140
government bonds 43
government departments 47–48
government sponsored enterprises (GSE) 48
grants-in-aid 50, 51
Gray, Virginia 88

Hall, Keith 130
Hall, Prescott Farnsworth 143
Hamilton, Alexander 36, 59, 65, 71
Hammer v. Dagenhart (1918) 44, 47
Harding, Warren 45
Harper's Magazine 146

Harshberger, Scott 115, 116
Hawaii: civic education **169**; corruption 131, **132**, **137**, 138; gubernatorial powers 77; lobbyists 88; state constitution 26
Hays, Samuel P. 144
health and healthcare: effects of executive unity on 66, 67; effects of governors' tenure potential on 66, 67–69, **68**; HIV and AIDS 118–119; insurance 84; laws 1–2; in state constitutions 26–27; *see also* coronavirus crisis
Heaney, John 102–103
High Court 39
HIV 118
Hobbs Act (1951) 131, 147, 151
Hogan, Larry xii–xiii
Homeland Security agency 35
Hopkins, Dan 156
Horton v. Meskill (1977) 23
House of Representatives: during Civil War and Reconstruction 42, 43; corruption 129; and executive privilege 38; party discipline 45; revenue bills 28
Human Rights Watch 120
Hyde Amendment (1997) 114

iCivics 165
Idaho: civic education **169**; constitutional amendments 16; corruption 131, **132**, 136, 137; gubernatorial powers 77; lobbyists 88
Illinois: anti-taping statutes 104; civic education **169**; Civil Justice League 117; Cook County 147, 148; coronavirus crisis xii; corruption 7–8, 131, **132**, **138**, 147, 148–149, **149**; "Granger Constitution" (1870) 15; gubernatorial powers 77; and immigration 34; Joliet Prison 122; legislative activity 83, 93; lobbyists **88**, 91; "Operation Greylord" 129; political machine 142, 147, 148; pride of residents 4; special districts 64, 150; state constitution 26; state expenditure 30, 31; Supreme Court 117
immigration 34, 56, 166
Immigration Restriction League (1894) 143–144

implied powers 60
income tax 42, 45, 48–50
Indiana: civic education **169**;
  corruption **132**, **138**; gubernatorial powers **77**; law enforcement 84; lobbyists **88**
industry 144
influence peddling 128–129, **129**
Inslee, Jay xii
interest groups 3, 6, 17–20, 36, 87–94; and legislation 93; lobbying **88**, 88–92, *89*, *90*
Internal Revenue Service (IRS) 49
Interstate Commerce Commission 45
Interstate Commerce Commission Act 144
Iowa: civic education **169**; corruption **132**, **137**, **138**; gubernatorial powers **77**; ID laws 83; lobbyists **88**, 91

Jackson, Andrew ("Old Hickory") 39–41, 141, 142
"Jay's treaty" (1794) 38
Jefferson, Thomas 15, 40
Jensen, Richard 141
Johnson, Lyndon B. 51
judges 100; federal judges 3, 117; misconduct 117; state judges 3, 25–26, 116–118
Justice Department 104; Public Integrity Section (PIN reports) 131–135, **132–134**

Kansas: civic education **169**; corruption **132**, **138**; gubernatorial powers **77**; lobbyists **88**; Supreme Court 10
Keane, Peter 101
Kennedy, John F. 50–51
Kentucky: civic education 159, **169**; constitution 72; coronavirus crisis xii; corruption 130, **132**, **138**, **139**; gubernatorial powers **77**; lobbyists **88**; plural executive 63; state constitution 22
Kentucky and Virginia Resolutions (1798; 1799) 40
Kerner, Otto 7
kickbacks 128, **129**
Kids Voting U.S.A. 161
Kilbride, Thomas 117
King, Rodney 102
Kozinski, Alex 101

Labor Department 52
Langston, Eugene 122
Langston v. Peters (1996) 122
law enforcement 51–54, 56, 84, 123
Legal Services Corporation 48, 121
Legal Tender Act (1862) 42
legislators 25–26
LePage, Paul 63
Lewis v. Richards (1997) 122–123
lieutenant governors 60
Lincoln, Abraham 41–43
lobbying 7, 87–90, **88**, *89*, *90*; and legislation 92–94, **94**; regulation of 90–92
local government corruption **137–138**
Long, Christopher 102
Long, Huey 141
Louisiana: Battle of New Orleans (1815) 39–40; civic education **169**; constitutional amendments 15, **16**, 20; coronavirus crisis xii, 35; corruption 7, 131, **132**, 136, **139**; gubernatorial powers **77**; lobbyists **88**, 91; political machine 141, 142; pride of residents 4
Lowery, David 88
Lutz, Donald 18
Lyons, Antonino 112–113

McClure, John J. 148
McClure's Magazine 145–146
McConnell, Robert F. 151–152
McCulloch v. Maryland (1819) 17–18, 39
McDonald, Laquan 102
McGraw, Warren 117
McKenna, Jack 103
McKitrick, Eric 38, 43
Madigan, Michael 91, 115
Madison, James 12, 36, 39, 40, 51, 71–72, 82
Maine 150; civic education **169**; corruption **132**, **137**, **138**; gubernatorial powers **77**; lobbyists **88**; plural executive 63
Mapp v. Ohio (1961) 105–106
March, Peyton 54
Marine Mammal Protection Act (1972) 53
Marshall, John 18, 39
Maryland: anti-taping statutes 104; civic education **169**; coronavirus

crisis xii–xiii; corruption **132**, **138**; gubernatorial powers **77**; lobbyists **88**
Mason, George 15, 115
Massachusetts: Board of Pardons and Paroles 115; civic education **169**; civil service act 143; constitution 72; constitutional amendments 13, 18; corruption **133**, **138**; gubernatorial powers **77**; lobbyists **88**; political machine 142; state constitution 10
Massey Energy 117
Mateson, Joel 7
Mayberry, Steven 114
media: coverage of corruption 136, 140, *140*, 145–146; coverage of state politics 4–5, 86, 86–87, *87*, 156–157
Medicaid 31, 50, 51, 63
Mehserle, Johannes 104
Mellow, Robert 148
Michigan: civic education **169**; coronavirus crisis xii; corruption **133**, 136, **137**, **139**; gubernatorial powers **77**; lobbyists **88**; state constitution 26
military force 54
Militia Acts (1792; 1795) 54
Mills, Janet 63
Milyo, Jeffrey 131, 135
Minnesota: civic education **169**; corruption **133**, 136, **137**; gubernatorial powers **77**; legislature 6; lobbyists **88**
Mississippi: civic education **169**; constitutional amendments 13; corruption **133**, 136, **139**; lobbyists **88**; political machine 142
Missouri: civic education **169**; corruption **133**, **138**, **139**, 146; gubernatorial powers **77**; lobbyists **88**; plural executive 61; political machine 142; state constitution 20
money laundering 129
Montana: civic education **170**; corruption **133**, 136, **139**; "environmental" constitution (1972) 15, 17; gubernatorial powers **77**; lobbyists **88**; plural executive 61; state constitution 27; Supreme Court 28
Montana Environmental Information Center (MEIC) v. Department of Environmental Quality (1999) 28
Morgan, J.P. 45

Morgenthau, Henry 49
Morris, Robert 113
"muckraking" journalism 87, 144, 145–146, 147
Mugwumps 142–143
Municipal Research Bureaus 144

Nast, Thomas 146
nation and states 55–56
National Assessment of Educational Progress (NAEP) 161
National Cash Register Company 144
National Center for Education Statistics: Civics Report Cards 161
national citizenship exam 166
National Civil Service Reform League 142
National Commission on Excellence in Education 158
national constitutional conventions 14
National Education Association (NEA) 157
National Education Longitudinal Studies (NELS) 163, **163**
National Endowment for the Humanities 165
national government *see* federalism
National Governors Association xii
National Guard 48, 54–55
National Labor Relations Act 46
National Municipal League 144
The National Municipal Review 144
National Oceanic and Atmospheric Administration (NOAA): Fisheries Office of Law Enforcement 52–53
National Passenger Railroad Corporation 48
National Prohibition Act (1919) 51
national service 54
nationalism 40
Native Americans 54
NEA (National Education Association) 157
Nebraska: civic education **170**; corruption **138**, **139**; gubernatorial powers **77**; legislature 2, 6; lobbyists **88**; plural executive 61
NELS *see* National Education Longitudinal Studies
nepotism 128, **129**
Nevada: corruption **133**, **137**; gubernatorial powers **77**; lobbyists **88**

New Deal 46–50
New Hampshire: civic education **170**; Constitution (1784) 72; constitutional amendments 13; corruption 131, **133**, **137**; gubernatorial powers 77; lobbyists **88**; state budget 30
New Jersey: civic education **170**; coronavirus crisis xii, 35; corruption 130, 131, **133**, 136, **139**; education 24; gubernatorial powers 73, 77; independence of 36; lobbyists **88**; political machine 142; pride of residents 4; Senate corruption 129; Supreme Court 24
New Mexico: civic education **170**; corruption **133**, **138**, **139**; gubernatorial powers 77; lobbying 7; lobbyists **88**, 91; state constitution 27
New Orleans: Battle of New Orleans 39–40; prosecutors 111
New York City: Bureau of Municipal Research 144; criminal cases 107; education 24; police 101, 102, 106–107, 108; prosecutors 111–112; Tammany Hall 141, 142, 146
New York Evening Post 145–146
New York Morning Journal 145
New York State: Bar Association 116; civic education **170**; civil service act 143; Comptroller 30; constitutional conventions 14; coronavirus crisis xi, xii, xiii, 35; corruption 7, 130, 131, **133**, **138**; Court of Appeals 24; education 24; employment law 84; gubernatorial powers 77; independence of 36; lobbyists **88**, 89, *89*; state constitution 3, 26
New York Sun 145
New York Times xiii, 86, *86*, 110, 118, 145, 146; coverage of political corruption (1850–2019) 140, *140*
New York World 145
Newark Conservation and Watershed Development Corp. 130
newspapers: advertising 145; circulation 144–145; coverage of corruption 136, 140, *140*, 145–146; coverage of state politics 4, *86*, 86–87, *87*; "independent"/nonpartisan 145; "muckraking" 87, 144, 145–146, 147

Nifong, Michael 110–111
NLRB v. Jones & Laughlin Steel Corp (1937) 47
NOAA *see* National Oceanic and Atmospheric Administration
Norcross, Eileen 29, 30
North Carolina: civic education **170**; constitutional amendments 15; corruption **133**, **137**, **139**; Duke lacrosse case 110–111; gubernatorial powers 78; lobbyists **88**; state constitution 26
North Dakota: civic education **170**; corruption 131, **133**, 136, **137**, **139**; gubernatorial powers 78; lobbyists **88**, 91
Northern California Innocence Project 116
Nullification Crisis 40–41

Obama, Barack 7, 8, 128
O'Connor, Sandra Day 53, 165
off-budget entities (OBEs) 29–30
Ohio: Bureau of Municipal Research 144; civic education **170**; coronavirus crisis xi–xiii; corruption **133**, **138**, **139**; gubernatorial powers 73, 78; lobbyists **88**; political machine 142
Oklahoma: civic education **170**; corruption **133**, **138**; gubernatorial powers 78; legislative activity 93; lobbyists **88**
"Operation Greylord" 129
Oregon: civic education **170**; coronavirus crisis xii; corruption **133**, **137**; gubernatorial powers 78; lobbyists **88**
Orfield, Myron 107
Orie, Jane 148
"ownership" 1

Pataki, George xi
patronage 128, **129**
Patterson, John 144
Paul v. Virginia (1869) 35
Pendleton Act (1887) 44
Pendleton Civil Service Act (1883) 143
Pennsylvania: anti-taping statutes 104; civic education **170**; corruption 130, 131, **133**, **138**, **139**, 150; gubernatorial powers 78; lobbyists

88; political machine 142, 148; state constitution (1776) 22
Penrose, Boies 148
Perzel, John 148
Pew Research Center 4, 70, 86, 156
Philadelphia City Council 129
PIN reports 130–135, **132–134**, *135*, 136
plea bargains 100, 107
plenary powers 60
Plunkitt, George Washington 141
Pogan, Patrick 102
police 51, 100; deaths and injuries 101; exclusionary rule 106; law suits against 108; misconduct 101–107; power xi, 2; qualified immunity 108–109; search and seizure 105; suppression hearings 106, 107–108; "testilying" 101, 106–108; violence 101–104, 105
political "machines" 140–144, 146, 147–149
political participation: effects of civic education on 160, 161, 163; and executive power 69–71, *70*, *71*, 79–80, 81
political parties 44–45; party discipline 45; and state legislation 94–96, *95*, **96**
political reform 142–149; Mugwumps 142–143; Progressivism 13, 44–46, 72–73, 142, 143–144, 147, 149
political socialization 158, 160, 161, 164, **165**
Populism 13, 72, 73
Porter, James 130
presidency 3, 6, 35–36, 45–46, 59
presidential primaries 44–45
Prison Litigation Reform Act (1996) 121
Prison Rape Elimination Act (PREA: 2003) 118
prisons 100, 118; legal aid 121; male prison rape 118–120, 122–123; sexual assault 120–123
Pritzker, Jay xii
Progressivism 13, 44–46, 72–73, 142, 143–144, 147, 149
Prohibition Enforcement Agency (1919) 51
property rights 1, 44, 45
prosecutors: conviction integrity units 116; convictions 109–110; federal 3, 112–114; immunity from civil liability 110; misconduct 109–116; state 3, 109–112, 115–115
public assistance for the poor 26
public employees: rights 26
public health *see* health and healthcare
Public Integrity Section 131, **132–134**
public service fraud 128, **129**

quasis 48
Quay, Matthew 148

race and racism 22, 36, 41, 43–44, 143
Ralston, David 91
Rand Corporatiion 48
Rayfield, Eric 122
Reconstruction 43–44
Reed, Douglas 21
regulated federalism 50
Rehabilitation Act (1973) 51
Rehnquist, William 53
Republican Party 34, 43, 50, 142
Revenue Acts 42, 49
Revolutionary War 38–39
Rhode Island: civic education 170; constitutional convention 14; coronavirus crisis 35; corruption 131, **133**, **137**, **138**; gubernatorial powers 78; lobbyists 88; pride of residents 3–4
Roberts, John 152
Robinson v. Cahill 25
Rochester Municipal Research Bureau 144
Rockefeller, John D. 45, 144
Roosevelt, Franklin D. 38, 46–47, 48–49, 147
Roosevelt, Theodore 45, 51, 143
Rosenthal, Alan 89
Ryan, George 7

Samson, David 130
San Antonio Independent School District v. Rodriguez (1973) 23
"sanctuary states" 34, 56
Scalia, Antonin 11
Schechter, Marvin 116
Schlesinger, Joseph 64
Schwarzenegger, Arnold 62
Scott, Walter 103
secretaries of agriculture 3, 61
secretaries of state 3, 39, 60, 61
Section 1983 53, 108, 109, 120
Securities and Exchange Commission 46

Senate: appointments 37, 40, 41; during Civil War and Reconstruction 42, 43; corruption 129; elections 45; party discipline 45; terms 12
Sherman Anti-Trust Act 144
Simpson, Dick 148
Sinclair, Upton 145
Slager, Michael 103
slavery 36, 41, 43
Small, Lennington 7
Smith, Melancton 82
social distancing xi–xii
Social Security Act 46
Social Security Administration 48, 49
social studies 157–158; *see also* civic education
Souter, Justice 121
South Carolina: civic education **170**; constitution (1778) 72; corruption **133, 137, 138**; gubernatorial powers 78; lobbyists 88; *Nullification Crisis* 40–41
South Dakota: civic education **170**; corruption **133, 137, 139**; gubernatorial powers 78; lobbyists 88
Southern conservative coalition 50
Spanish American war (1898) 54
special purpose districts 4, 64, 149–151, *151*
speech codes 84
state attorney generals 3, 36, 60, 61, **61**, 63, 111, 116, 130
state auditors 3, 60, **61**
state constitutions 2, 3, 10–11; amendments and revisions 3, 11–19, **16–17**, 72; constitutional conventions 11, 14; constitutional rights 21–28, 31; constitutionalizing policy 19–21; and gubernatorial powers 60; healthcare 26; indirect ratification 13; legislative proposals 12; malleability 11–19; paths to change 12, *12*; popular initiative for change 13; popular ratification 12, 13; restrictions on state legislative power 28–31; structure 11; substantive rights 11, 21, 38; voting rights 43
state elections: voter turnout 5–6, 150; voting rights 10
state governments xi, 2; checks and balances 55–56; and civic education 165–166; coercion 1, 2, 51–55; executive unity effects 66, 67; independent executive agencies 63–64; independently elected officials 60, **61**; lieutenant governors 60; pitfalls of plural executive 60–64; powers of 1, 10–11; "separately elected" executives 61–62, **62**, 73, 74; special districts 4, 64, 149–151, *151*; spending 83, *84*; structure 2, 60; *see also* civic engagement; corruption
state governors 3, 59–60, 155; executive powers 3, 60, 64–66, **65**, 77–78; history of gubernatorial power 71–73; political participation and executive power 69–71, *70*, **71**, 79–80, **81**; stengthening of 73, 74–75; tenure potential effects 66, 67–69, *68*
state justice systems 100–101; arrests and convictions 100; "deliberate indifference" 121–122; fines and fees 100; judges 3, 25–26, 116–118; law enforcement 123; misconduct 100–107; police 2, 101–109; prisons 100, 118–123; *pro se* 121; prosecutors 3, 109–112, 115–116
state law 2, 51–52
state legislatures 2, 6, 60, 82–83; bills 18; campaign finance 91; citizen engagement 92–93, *94*, 97; corruption 87; ethics 91–92, *92*; influences on policy outcomes 96–97, **97**; interest groups 87–94; legislative activity 83–85, *94*; lobbying 87–94, **88**, *89*, *90*, *94*; media coverage of activity 4–5, *86*, 86–87, *87*, 156–157; political parties 94–96, *95*, **96**; popular legislative initiative 13; representation of 97; restrictions on power 28–31; who governs? 92–94
state militias 54
states: founding states 36; independence of 36; and nation 55–56; powers 38, 60; reconnecting with citizens 8; subordination of 50–51
states' rights coalition 40–41, 44, 45, 55
Steffens, Lincoln 145–146

Index

substantive rights: state constitutions 11, 21, 28; U.S. Constitution 21

Taft, William Howard 45
Talleyrand 39
Tarbell, Ida M. 145
tax and expenditure limits (TELs) 29
taxation 13, 18, 23, 25, 27, 28–29, 150; income tax 42, 45, 48–50
Tennessee: civic education 170; corruption 133, 138, 139; district attorney 109; education 68–69; gubernatorial powers 67, 68, 78; legislative activity 93; lobbyists 88; speech codes 84; "Tennessee Waltz" operation 129
terrorism 35
Texas: civic education 85, 170; corruption 131, 133, 138, 150; education 23; gubernatorial powers 78; health insurance 84; legislative activity 83; lobbyists 88; municipal utility districts (MUD) 150; pride of residents 3; prosecutors 111; "self-directed semi-independent" (SDSI) entities 64; Supreme Court 23
Thomas, Clarence 121
trade relations 38
Transactional Records Access (TRAC) Clearinghouse 135–136, 136, 137–139
Trump, Donald xii, 34
Tweed, William Magear 146

Union army 54
unitary executive 59
United Kingdom 36–37
United Van Lines 4
University of Alabama 55
U.S. Civil Service Commission 143
U.S. Congress: legal aid 121; legislative activity 83; lobby group spending 89; power of 6; statutes 1; subordination of 35
U.S. Constitution xi, 1, 2–3, 19; Articles of Confederation 10, 35, 37, 39, 44, 71; Bill of Rights 10, 21, 22, 46, 53; commerce clause 39, 47; constitutional rights 21, 22, 31; judicial interpretation 11; "necessary and proper" clause 39; powers of 10; Preamble 37; "privileges and immunities" 35; procedural rights 21; substantive rights 21; supremacy clause 37; *see also* Constitutional Amendments
U.S. Immigration and Naturalization Service 129
U.S. News and World Report 65
U.S. Supreme Court 117, 152; and Brady violations 101; on campaign spending 117; on corruption 152; on education 22, 23; and executive privilege 38; on interstate travel 35; on police 108–109; and police immunity 108–109; on prisons 120; and prosecutor misconduct 111; on public health 1–2, 51, 63, 111; on punishment 120; and search and seizure 105; on states' rights 44, 46, 50, 53–54
U.S. v. Darby (1941) 47
U.S. v. Nixon (1974) 38
USA TODAY 93, 112
Utah: civic education 170; corruption 131, 134, 137; gubernatorial powers 78; lobbyists 88; pride of residents 3

VanDyke, Jason 102
Vecchione, Michael 112
Veon, Mike 148
Vermont: civic education 159, 170; constitution (1786) 72; corruption 131, 134, 138, 139; gubernatorial powers 78; and immigration 34; lobbyists 88; state constitution (1786) 22
Victory Tax (1942) 49
Virginia: civic education 170; corruption 131, 134, 138, 139; Crime Victims Compensation Program 64; gubernatorial powers 78; independent executive agencies 64; lobbyists 88; plural executive 63; Workers' Compensation Act 64; *see also* Kentucky and Virginia Resolutions
Virginia Convention (1788) 39
Virginia Declaration (1776) 15
Virginia Office for Protection and Advocacy (VOPA) 63
Volunteer Act (1898) 54
voting: and civic education 151, 162–163, 163; regulations 83, 147; rights 10, 43; turnout 5–6, 150

Walker, Dan 7
Wallace, George 55
War of 1812 39, 54
War on Poverty 51
Ward, Robert 143
Warren, Charles 143
Washington, D.C. 39
Washington, George 38, 39, 54
Washington State: civic education **170**; coronavirus crisis xii; corruption **134**, **137**; education 25; employment law 84; gubernatorial powers **78**; and immigration 34; lobbyists **88**; Supreme Court 25
Watkins-Brashear, Linda 130
We the People: The Citizen and Constitution 163; Project Citizen 161
Weinstein-Tull, Justin 63
West Virginia: civic education **170**; corruption **134**, **137**, **138**; gubernatorial powers **78**; ID laws 83; lobbyists **88**; Supreme Court of Appeals 117
Whig party 41
Whitmer, Gretchen xii
Wickard v. Filburn (1942) 47
Williams, Jonnie R. 151
Wilson, Woodrow 45, 73
Wisconsin: corruption **134**, **137**; gubernatorial powers **78**; lobbyists **88**
workers' rights 26
World War I 54
World War II 35, 47
Wyoming: civic education **170**; corruption 131, **134**, **137**; education 24; gubernatorial powers **78**; lobbyists **88**; state constitution 26–27; Supreme Court 24

XYZ Affair 39

Zackin, Emily 27